JASON JONES

Nomad

LETTERS FROM A WESTWARD LAP OF THE WORLD

For Ken & Vera,

Owners of the best coffee
shop in Atlanta, where much
of this book was edited and
written. I hope you enjoy
the trip!

Jason

JASON JONES

Nomad

LETTERS FROM A WESTWARD LAP OF THE WORLD

Palm Island Press

Published by;
Palm Island Press, Inc., 411 Truman Avenue, Key West, FL 33040 U.S.A.
pipress@earthlink.net

Printed in the United States of America

Library of Congress Cataloging-in-Publication Data
Jones, Jason K.
Nomad: letters from a westward lap of the world/Jason K.Jones.—1st ed.
1.Jones, Jason K.—Journeys.   2. Voyages and travels.   I. Title.
G465.J69   2004

910.4—dc21   2003113361

ISBN 0-9643434-2-8

ACKNOWLEDGMENTS

Among many others, four individuals made this book possible. To them I am especially grateful. The first two are my parents who shaped my character and supported my dreams. They continue to do so to this day. Michael Keith in Key West is the publisher and facilitator who believed in my cause and expects big things from me. Thanks Uncle Mike. And to God above, without whom the first keystroke would not have been struck. May this book serve His will.

TABLE OF CONTENTS

Author's Note

This is a collection of essays written over 15 months as I backpacked around the world. They are anecdotes as well as personal reflections of what I did and learned.

I wrote these pieces as e-mails to family and friends whenever I could stop into a cyber-café during my travels in 25 countries from September 18, 2000 to December 18, 2001. They have been edited for clarity, timeliness and length, but for the most part, they remain true to their original.

Since completing my trip I have read one of the classic American travelogues, *Travels With Charley: In Search of America*, by John Steinbeck. In it, Steinbeck describes his country with humor and insight as it appeared in 1960. But Steinbeck disclaims his perspective as simply that of one man, on a single trip, at a single point in time. He writes, "What I set down here is true until someone passes that way and rearranges the world in his own style."

I agree. My essays aren't the right view or the wrong view of the world and its inhabitants. They are simply my view and my experiences at a single point in time. Use them as a resource or a reference point, and perhaps as inspiration for your own voyage of discovery into this great world.

And if you decide that world travel isn't to your liking, then I hope you'll acknowledge a different dream—and dare to make it come true.

Don't wait. Act!

1

A Regular Guy Decides to Do an Irregular Thing

"You know what you should do, man? You should travel. Travel for at least a year…with the possibility to extend."

Whoa.

That was the advice of my friend and fellow erstwhile naval aviator as we sat over a dinner of Mexican food in Scottsdale, Arizona.

"Travel, huh?" I responded. "Now *there's* an idea."

I had been wondering what to do with my life. What turn would it take in the near future? I was on the verge of turning 31 and completing an M.B.A. I was uncommitted to my job as a headhunter and was emerging from the end of a long-term relationship. And to top it all off, I was a transplant to the Phoenix area. No family roots claimed my allegiance to the Valley of the Sun. In other words, I was free of obligation and considering my options.

So I had invited my trustworthy friend to dinner at one of our favorite Mexican joints in south Scottsdale. I value his opinion and wanted to share some thoughts. His travel idea intrigued me, of that there is no doubt.

But a year?!? That sounded like such a long time. Maybe I could go for a few months, six tops. But how would *that* look on my resume? That's a long time to be out of the workforce.

And what would I do when I returned?

I don't have any business experience to speak of. Well, one year as a headhunter in a large search firm. But the other eight years of my post-college experience was all Navy blue: six years as a naval aviator (A-6 Intruders) and two years as a Navy medical recruiter. Great experience, but not specific preparation for a civilian job. (There's not much need for bombardiers in the private sector.)

So I knew that my best shot at a job would be to leverage my recent M.B.A. and immediately plow forward into corporate America—with perhaps a three-month break to travel.

But a year?!? How could I afford it? I'm just a simple Navy man with Navy pay. I'm not independently wealthy and come from a middle-class family. There's no house in the Hamptons or Vail, and certainly no family treasure chest to fund such a project.

I *had* been steadfast in my saving habits, however, from my first day after college. The Navy had forced young ensigns to sit through financial counseling sessions in which we were admonished to "pay yourself first." That meant saving money as a first order of business before paying the bills or buying new toys.

It was this philosophy of providence combined with an innate frugality that made world travel a possibility.

But a year?!? There were doubters, of course. For instance, upon telling a client who was the CEO of his company about my travel plans, he reacted with disapproving astonishment, "How's *that* going to look on a resume?!?"

My heart sank. But it hit a steel stomach that rejected his condemnation and incited me to press on with my plans.

But I had to admit it sounded extravagant. A full *year* of travel? With the possibility to extend?!? Am I *nuts*?

Well, maybe a little. But as a famous admiral once said, "Fortune favors the bold."

I quickly decided that if I were going to travel, I would travel big. A world trip was in order. And if I were going to see the world, I could not do it justice in three to six months. I might as well go whole hog and see as much as possible in one grand, overachieving burst of discovery and exploration. I would do a full lap of the globe. So a year with the possibility to extend began to sound like the only reasonable proposition. How else would I give the world its proper due?

Now the juices were really going. I realized this was a once-in-a-lifetime opportunity that I needed to take advantage of. To hell with the doubters and naysayers. General Patton would be proud.

A million practical questions came to mind:

If I actually do this, where will I go and what will I see?
Where will I sleep and eat?
What transportation is available?
What should I pack?
What visas do I need?
What shots do I need?
What about health insurance?
How will I access money while I travel?
And:

What do I do with my house and worldly possessions? Do I sell or rent it, store my belongings, or what?

I didn't know. I had no idea.

But I knew some people who did. And I knew such trips had been done before. This was not the first ascent of Everest. Nor was I taking the first rocket to the moon. There was a blueprint for success, and all I had to do was find it.

So I began my research. I called old fraternity brothers who had world travel experience and asked my questions. Each encouraged and supported my decision. I also began to formulate a skeleton plan for where I would go. I picked some must-see attractions and began to connect the dots as logically as possible. The Great Wall of China, Hong Kong, Vietnam, Angkor Wat, etc., were on the list.

I knew I would travel primarily in developing countries for my budget's sake, and since I had not visited the majority of them, my biggest problem was to pare the list of possibilities. The jungles of Southeast Asia, palaces in India, a safari in Africa, great cities such as Tokyo, Istanbul and Buenos Aires—there was such a rich and wonderful palette from which to choose the colors of my journey.

How exciting to plan a world trip! But how scary at the same time. This was quite a commitment. Very big. HUGE. I needed some good reasons to carry this out. Something to cling to during the hard times and in the face of that nemesis—discouragement.

DECISION TO GO

So why did I do it? Why did I go through with this adventure? What precipitated my dropping everything—putting life on hold and taking a yearlong vacation to see the world?

I want to make one thing clear: I didn't then and I don't now view this trip as one big vacation. Enviable—yes. Enjoyable—of course. But a vacation it was not. This wasn't an insouciant lark to see how tan I could get on the beaches of the world or how many traveler cafes I could visit in every time zone on the planet. My goal was enrichment and preparation -- *the enrichment of experience unique to world travel that would prepare me to be a better citizen of the world.*

Maybe that sounds too grandiose. I don't mean for it to. But if you want to understand why I risked such a mammoth undertaking—and subsequently my mindset as I approached each day, you must be aware of that overarching philosophy.

But what circumstances would allow a 31-year-old man to leave his home for a year and go tromping around the globe? Most people have responsibilities. Most people don't have the MONEY.

As I hinted at earlier, certain circumstances played a large part in creating a window of opportunity. This was my situation:

- No wife, kids or significant other.
- Just finished an M.B.A. (no longer committed to school).
- Low investment in my current job (only 1.5 years in that line of work—no book of clients and considering a change).
- Healthy parents.
- Good health.
- 10 years of investing during an economic boom (and I was never a big spender).

So through a miraculous confluence of factors and alignment of the planets, I found myself staring through a unique window of opportunity.

There's one more thing that I should add to the previous list:

- Innate curiosity and an unquenchable desire to learn.

That's important. It gives the reason I chose to travel, as opposed to any other activity. Travel satisfies both of those qualities. And besides, I've always loved to travel, to meet new people from places near and far, and see new sights and learn the history. All that fascinates me.

And I have a long history of travel. I grew up as an inquisitive youth traveling with my family around the United States and abroad. In fact, most of my second and third years of life were spent in Singapore as my father covered the Vietnam War for NBC News. During my preteen years, we drove twice from Georgia to California and took a trip to the United Kingdom.

During college I traveled in the summers with the Navy as part of my NROTC (Navy Reserve Officer Training Corps) training. At different times, the Navy took me to the Caribbean island of St. Maarten, Sicily, and all around the southeastern United States. After one of these trips, I continued my travels in Europe, doing everything from drinking beer in Austrian bier gartens to running with the bulls in Pamplona, Spain.

But it wasn't only overseas travel that I enjoyed. After graduating from Duke University in 1991, I delayed my enrollment in naval flight school to travel the United States for two months. I pounded the pavement of 25 states from the driver's seat of my old '84 Mustang GT.

I continued U.S. travel as a naval aviator. Because jets are meant to fly, I saw large tracts of U.S. real estate from both the cockpit and the ground as we took our A-6 Intruders around the country on training missions. As a student learning to operate the A-6, I spent three months flying out of Whidbey Island, Washington, and exploring the Pacific Northwest.

And finally, I was able to visit several ports and see even more global surface area through deployment to the Mediterranean Sea and Persian Gulf on the aircraft carrier USS Enterprise.

So travel isn't a newfound interest. It's been a part of my life since near birth. I've always been fascinated by maps, too—not for the cartography, but because they represent new places to explore. Places to meet people, taste food, hear new music, and learn about other cultures and the history that precedes.

From the time that world travel first crossed my mind, it took only a short while to pass the 50 percent tipping point. I considered all the circumstantial factors and felt that I just couldn't pass this up. If I did, I would be eternally regretful.

And although there were risks and unknowns associated with the endeavor, I didn't feel *brave* for leaving the security of my life in Arizona. In fact, I felt chicken *NOT* to go.

That doesn't mean there weren't moments of doubt—especially when I saw the look on people's faces when I told them of my plans. Or heard the resounding pause of silence when they learned I would be gone for a year. I can tell you, more than one jaw dropped.

But here's something that stiffened my resolve—an image I would replay whenever a doubt crept into my mind. One Saturday afternoon while channel-surfing, I came across a TV documentary about children born with ghastly bone deformities. I don't know what disease did this to the bodies of those poor children, but the sight of them struggling under the burden of that affliction made me tearful. I watched as they enjoyed a few moments of laughter and fun in a pool. The buoyancy of the water allowed a fleeting moment of freedom from the weight of their limbs.

I thought to myself, "Here I sit, with all the faculties that a man could be blessed with. I am limited by neither physical nor mental impediment, yet this good fortune could vanish in an instant. If I were one of those children sentenced to a life of pain and restriction, I would scream at that man on the couch: "*GO!* Get up and *GO!! NOW!!!*

"Do all of the things that I can never do. Travel to the farthest corner of the globe. Squeeze the essence from life, and savor its ruddy flavor. Then tell me all that you've seen so that I may taste life, too."

I'd be damned if I weren't going.

First night of my trip, September 19, 2000.
Norita, Japan.

So I bought what I needed for the trip and subjected myself to a cocktail of inoculations. I put my house in Scottsdale up for rent and stored my household goods. I purchased a travel book for Korea and Japan, along with a Japanese phrasebook, and then hopped a plane for Tokyo. It was just me and a 50-pound backpack, jetting across the Pacific with a head of steam on to get out there and see the world—and not miss this opportunity.

Boy, was I excited. Nervous excitement, I suppose. I touched down in Tokyo with the name of a hotel scribbled on a scrap of paper and nothing else but my wits.

But I had done it. I had crossed the Rubicon, and there was no going back. I loved the feeling. All the world lay in front of me with no restrictions, no boundaries. I was free to choose whichever path my heart desired and to take as much or as little time as my budget would allow. It was joy. Sheer joy.

2

Leave Your Shoes
—and Ethnocentricity—
at the Door

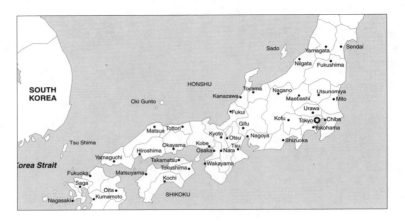

Things are great in the land of the rising sun. After a few days of getting my bearings and realizing the importance of finding a place to sleep, I've finally gotten a bit settled and actually know how to say, "Do you speak English?" and "I don't understand." (my two most common phrases).

I spent four days in Tokyo and am now in Kyoto (about 300 or 400 miles west, I suppose). Tokyo is amazingly crowded and expensive. Part of the city felt like Times Square, and very little looks like "old" Japan. To my pleasant surprise, the people have been friendly. Already I've been helped a number of times with directions and which train to catch.

Unfortunately, I can see signs of the weak economy. One

Top:
Entryway to shopping
arcade near Senjo-ji
temple.
(Tokyo, Japan)

Bottom:
Temman-gu Shrine.
(Dazaifu, Japan)

woman told me that there are now homeless people in the parks of Osaka. That's something many Japanese people have never seen.

Here's a quick story that you may get a kick out of. I stayed in a ryokan the first time two nights ago. (I mispronounced this least 10 times before someone finally filled me in.) A ryokan is lodging that observes Japanese home traditions: Take your shoes off before going inside, for instance, and sleep on straw mats.

When I arrived, the proprietor met me with a quick speech about taking my shoes off and gave me a demonstration on how to do it properly. I watched him take his shoes off and step on the tiled floor with his socks. He then stepped up on the carpeted stair that is considered "inside" the house. Thinking I had it down, I took off my sandals and slowly stepped on the tile just as he had done.

Bad move.

For the next 10 minutes I stood on the receiving end of a venomous lecture about how he couldn't understand why people didn't listen to him?!?, ninety percent of tenants mess up his simple instructions, when he goes abroad he respects foreign cultures, blah, blah, blah, blah.

It turns out that the Japanese custom is not a matter of shoes on or shoes off; it's inside versus outside. As a condition of stepping inside, my bare feet were not supposed to touch the outside world and had to be wiped off before I could step on the carpet or inside the ryokan. He also wiped off my backpack, which I had placed on the tile when I first stepped inside the building.

Now, remember that this was my third day in Japan and my third place to stay in as many days. I had just humped a 50-pound bag on my back halfway across Tokyo to stay at cheap place ($60 a night), and it was 6 in the evening. I really didn't want to lash out at this guy and have him send me out the door to find another cheap hotel in a city where I didn't speak the language.

But after 10 minutes of listening to his lecture and smiling my best and telling him how sorry I was, I had had enough. I finally said to him, "Hey look, have you ever made a mistake in your entire life?"

He didn't say too much after that. He just babbled a little while longer about other tenants who didn't understand his instructions

That's some of the fun you can have while traveling.

I'm now at a ryokan in Kyoto for $20 a night. The 70-year-old woman who runs the place and doesn't speak a word of English (other than numbers when collecting the rent) gave me cup of dried soup last night and an apple this morning as I walked out the door.

Extremes.

3

Mama-San Pitches a Fit

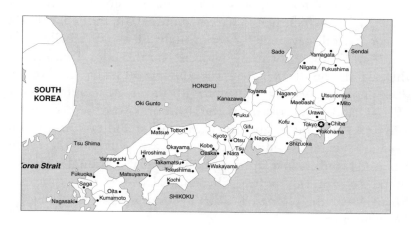

A quick story for you: When I last wrote, I was in Kyoto, Japan, staying at a cheap but clean and quiet ryokan with the nice elderly woman who runs the place—"Mama-san." (No kidding, that's what she and everyone else there called her.) This was the woman who gave me an apple and Styrofoam cup of soup.

Now, everyone knows that the Japanese people are supposed to be quiet and reserved. They go to great lengths to avoid conflict and open expressions of emotion. They never say "No" directly.

Boy, did she break the mold.

I came back from a karaoke party in Osaka one night (a whole other story) to find Mama-san waiting up for me. She wanted money for my room. I had ALREADY PAID for five nights and was currently on my fourth, but had unfortunately thrown away my receipt.

I tried to convey that to her, but she wouldn't listen. She absolutely refused to back down and you can believe that my resolve was just as strong. There was no way in the world that I was going to fork over another $100. Finally, she yelled for the bilingual guy upstairs who had been screaming at the world in drunken English and Japanese the night before. He translated for us, and somehow she allowed me to go upstairs thinking that everything was copacetic.

Two days later, I approached Mama-san about staying one more night – which would have been my sixth. Immediately, she demanded full payment for seven nights. I couldn't believe my ears. As I sat there squatting with her on the floor, I pointed to the calendar on the wall. She was convinced I had arrived on the 20th and kept waving a receipt with the name "Jeremy" on it. Well, I landed in Tokyo on the 19th and was there until the 22nd. No amount of attempted translation and pointing would persuade her of my innocence. She began yelling at the top of her lungs and picked up the phone to dial. I thought she was going to call the police. She misdialed the first time and SLAMMED the phone back down, continuing to yell (I assume Japanese profanity).

At that point, I debated making a break for it.

I quickly trashed that idea, because it was best not to be a fugitive in a land where I couldn't read simple street signs. She spoke for a minute into the receiver and handed the phone to me. Fortunately, she had only dialed a translator. I explained my plight, asked to stay one more night (what the heck, right? It's cheap here.), and handed the phone back to boiling-mad Mama-san. She gave me the phone one more time so the man could tell me no rooms were available. (Shock.)

I packed my bag and walked out in search of another cheap hotel. I wondered if I was destined to upset every hotel manager in Japan.

Lesson learned: Keep your receipt.

4

A Warm Welcome,
With a Taste of Kudzu

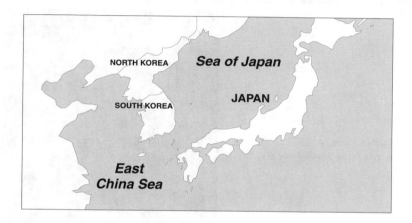

My bag is too heavy, mosquito bites cover my legs, and my lower back hurts. Other than that, I'm having an incredible time. (I mailed some items back to Arizona to lighten my load by about five pounds, so things are looking better.)

Here's an update to cover my short stay in Japan. I visited Tokyo, Kyoto, Nara, Osaka, Hiroshima, Fukuoka and Dazaifu. I spent six days in Kyoto visiting temples and tasting the local cuisine—excellent quality and flavor. In Osaka, I connected with some English students of a family friend. It was great to have a translator and guide, as you can imagine.

By the way, I confirmed with one of the students that the guy who gave me such a hard time at the ryokan in Tokyo about stepping on the "outside" with my bare feet was anal. She said he's right, but a little overzealous about enforcement. (I was very good

Top: The Golden Pavillion. Kyoto, Japan

Center: Osaka jo Castle. Osaka, Japan

Bottom: Ninna-ji. Kyoto, Japan.
  The most famous Buddhist rock garden.

with the shoes on/shoes off process at all of the temples that I visited afterward, so I guess I have to give the guy some credit.)

I made my way west to Hiroshima to check out the peace museum and to simply be in the presence of such a historic site. I was impressed with one monument in particular. The Japanese people left standing a City Hall building that was only a hundred yards or so from the hypocenter of the explosion. It is called the A-bomb dome, and I can't imagine a more visible reminder of what happened there. It is truly a powerful sight.

I also took a day trip to Miya-jima Island, which is near Hiroshima. You would recognize the "floating gate" to the main temple since every Japanese tourist brochure ever made features its photo. There I met two young beautiful Japanese women who were on a short vacation from Osaka. Although they didn't speak a word of English, I wound up touring the island for several hours with them. Let me tell you, the experience was just miserable. Separating at the end of the day, they said, "World travel, look out!" and "Enjoy." Just keeping up international relations, you know?

Fukuoka is a port town where ferries commonly make the run to Korea and back. I rendezvoused with a distant family member there who has spent the past 25 years in Japan. He provided some interesting insights to Japanese culture and what it's like to be an American there. He confirmed that homelessness has gone up noticeably since the Japanese economy's downturn.

I'll finish with some impressions of Japan. Remember that I base these impressions on only two weeks' experience in a land where I don't speak the language and am on a tight budget. Nevertheless, this is what I saw:

Japan is a green, tree-covered and mountainous group of islands. In populated areas, people are packed in the valleys, but no one has built on the hillsides.

The trains are plentiful and on time.

There are vending machines everywhere (at least in the cities and train stations). Beer-vending machines are commonplace.

The beer is excellent: Crisp, cold and delicious.

The food is also high quality and mostly mild. I never had a spicy dish in Japan.

Here's some of the different stuff that I ate:

- Chicken and beef hearts
- Eel
- Chicken cartilage (I think I had some pig ear, too)
- Octopus
- Intestine (I never found out what kind.)

I liked it all. (Some more than others, particularly the hearts)

One Japanese girl told me jokingly that I ate too much wasabi. (Hey, I like it hot.)

I also ate at a Japanese confectionary or tea room, which is like eating in a dollhouse. I couldn't fit my knees under the table and downed the shot of water in one sip. I ordered two pancakes with sweet bean paste and a dish of jelly-type balls coated in soybean powder. My tour guide told me the jelly stuff was made of lotus root, which is a type of kudzu. We have kudzu all over the southern United States, I just never thought I'd be eating it. I liked the pancake better.

In a very general sense, the people are reserved, polite and meticulous. They work long hours and respect authority. Although reserved, they will smile back at you on the street and will go out of their way to help you - unasked. On numerous occasions, as I stood before a wall-mounted subway map with a befuddled look on my face, a Japanese person walked up and offered to help.

There is a strong emphasis on group in the Japanese culture that you can see in the students and their uniforms. A friend told me this affects the way business is conducted. When I asked about the long hours and hard work, one expat told me that although the hours are long, the amount of work completed is not entirely proportional. For instance, given the same eight-hour period, more paper will move in an American company versus a Japanese company. I don't know how true this is, but it's something to keep in mind.

Suits and ties appear to be the standard. I doubt that casual Friday has made it to Japan.

Two final things about Japan:

There is a strong rivalry among Japan, Korea and China. A Japanese student told me that many people in Japan look down on their neighbors, particularly Koreans. I, of course, can't verify this, but my gut tells me it's not far off the mark. I also get the sense that the Japanese people are very proud to be Japanese. External influence is unwelcome.

And, minus the Sumo wrestlers, I was the biggest guy in Japan.

I'm now in Pusan, Korea, and have met a Canadian couple who teach English at a private school. They're very hospitable and are allowing me to stay at their apartment for as long as I like rent-free. I'll probably spend a few more days here and then make my way up to Seoul.

I can already see obvious differences between the Korean and Japanese cultures, although I want to see more of the country than just Pusan before I draw conclusions. Let's put it this way: My 45-pound bag came in pretty handy as I swung it around and into pushy people as I disembarked the ferry. (Koreans have a reputation for being more expressive and forward than the Japanese—so far this is holding true.)

5

Three Monks' Promise: 'We Will Pray for You'

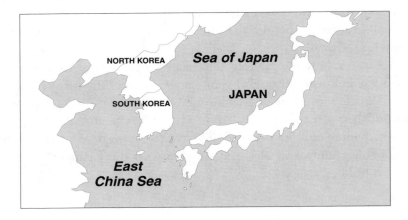

The last two stories I sent involved how I was able to upset the managers of motels in Japan. I thought I'd send a story in which I actually make someone happy.

This incident happened in Pusan, Korea. Pusan, on the southeast tip of Korea, is the landing spot for travelers coming from Japan, and from just about anywhere else in the world. I stayed with a Canadian couple who teach English at a private school. Jock, the husband, mentioned it might be neat to visit the local South Korean army base. I agreed, and we concocted a simple plan to get me on base.

The base is at the foot of a mountain upon which sits a Buddhist temple and the large symbol that commonly indicates such a facility (it looks like a reverse swastika). We asked one of the Koreans with whom Jock works to write a note that said, "I

Top:
Haeundae Beach. Pusan,
Korea. Where I stayed for a
week with Edith and Jock
Simpson.

Bottom:
Edith and Jock Simpson
from Ottawa, Canada. My
hosts in Pusan.

am a prior U.S. Navy officer on a world trip and have an interest in temples. I saw the symbol on the hill and would like to visit. Is this possible?"

I took the note and carefully approached to the heavily armed guards at the base front gate. I started with an unsuccessful attempt to communicate in English. But upon presenting my note, the guard smiled, shrugged his shoulders, and spoke briefly to his partner. I don't think they knew quite what to do with me. The first one summoned me to follow him to the guard shack, where he introduced me to another non–English-speaking soldier. They motioned for me to wait one moment (I think), which I happily did.

A phone call was made, and the guard behind the counter

asked for identification. I hadn't thought to bring any with me. (What was I thinking?) Fortunately, I had my international student ID card that I take everywhere for the discounts at museums and other sights. Unbelievably, my student ID and the handwritten note were enough to get me on base with a personal tour of the temple.

The next thing I knew, a car pulled up with a Buddhist monk dressed in gray robes behind the wheel who motioned for me to get in.

You know, some people just radiate goodness. This guy was one of them.

In silence, we drove up the hill to the temple. I did a good job of taking off my sandals properly and approached the large golden Buddha at the far end of the empty main hall. The monk lit a stick of incense and handed it to me, and I placed it upright in the sand-filled urn before the Buddha. He then demonstrated that I should put my hands together and give a short bow of respect, which I did.

Next, he led me to a nearby room and motioned for me to sit on the floor beside a beautiful wooden table with three-inch legs. Quietly, two more monks floated into the room and sat beside us on the floor. For the next 45 minutes, I sat sipping Korean green tea and trying to communicate with these three men. There was a lot of hand gesturing and drawing on the newspapers that lay beside us on the floor. All three had graduated in the same class from T'ongdosa, the largest and one of the most famous Buddhist temples in Korea. They had been in the army for ten years. The first monk drew all of the rank insignia of the South Korean army and pointed to the rank that he and his colleagues held. I did the same.

They knew very little English but enough to get us by. Baseball was some common ground for our dialogue. Like many Koreans I have met, they love baseball and admire the players who are successful in the America. When we first sat down and I told them that I used to fly planes for the Navy, they were very impressed and said, "U.S. Navy, excellent!" This reaction was a welcome departure from the cold shoulder I have occasionally received elsewhere in the world for merely being an American.

When I told them that I needed to leave soon, the first monk went quickly to a closet and came back with several items. I had mentioned that I liked hot tea so he gave me a package of Japanese green tea. Then he handed me a beaded necklace that many Buddhists commonly wear. Next he held out a beaded wood bracelet for me to put my hand through.

"For good luck," he said.

I smiled and replied, "Sure, I could use it."

Then he gave me a box of two beautiful silk handkerchiefs. I felt like a foreign dignitary on an important State visit. But the goodwill didn't stop there. While looking me directly in the eye, one of the monks said sincerely, "We will pray for you."

As he drove me back to the front gate, my new friend handed a cassette tape of Chinese instrumental music to me. He asked what my primary concern was as I traveled. My answer to him was simple, "Safety." I had the feeling that he wanted to know what specifically he and his friends should pray for.

The experience was heartwarming, to say the least. I couldn't believe I had just spent an hour with three Buddhist chaplains of the South Korean army in one of their temples. I felt as if I had been given a rare chance on a trip like mine to interact with, however briefly, leaders of the temples that I was visiting. Their generosity and goodwill made a strong impression.

I'll be wearing the bracelet for a while now.

6

Despite the Juicy Girls and the DMZ, This Land Is Rough Around the Edges

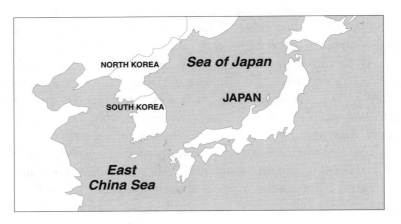

My last update had me landing in Pusan, Korea. I originally intended to spend only two weeks in Korea, but thanks to some kind folks who agreed to house me for undetermined periods, I wound up spending about a month here. Although I have yet to experience the rest of Asia, I sense Korea has a unique culture that I wouldn't have wanted to miss.

Please remember that these are the experiences of just one man as he traveled on a low budget with almost no understanding of the Korean language. (I didn't spend much time rubbing elbows with the upper crust.) I know that my impressions are imperfect and my observations incomplete because I didn't have the time to fully immerse myself in the culture and, just as important, have my own cultural biases. But I can't help what I saw and experienced.

Hiking Mt. Namsan in Central South Korea with my new friends.

Giant Buddha in Soraksan National Park. (NE South Korea)

Temple embellishment. (Soraksan National Park)

Top:
Fountain at temple near Soraksan National Park.

Bottom:
Standing on the border of North and South Korea at Panmunjon. (Where negotiations between the countries have taken place in the DMZ.)

WHERE I WENT AND WHAT I DID

I started in Pusan (on the southeast coast of the Korean peninsula), where I met two friendly Canadians on the ferry from Japan. Jock and Edith Simpson teach English in one of the private schools and offered to let me stay in their apartment for as long as I liked.

I really enjoyed the time that I spent with them. I had access to a TV so I watched some of the baseball playoffs and CNN. Just as important, I was able to put the pack down for a week and sightsee at a leisurely pace. They even let me teach a couple of classes one night. I got more out of it than the kids actually. In addition to learning how to ask where the bathroom is, I saw for myself how parents push their children at an early age to learn the international language—English. The aptitude of these young students was impressive.

Pusan is an enormous city. About 7 million people live in the surrounding area. Construction is taking place all over the city, which secured a share of World Cup soccer for 2002 and the 2002 Asian Games. A new subway line is going in. Bottom line, it was a bear to make my way around. Jock and Edith hooked me up with one of the Korean art teachers from their school. There's nothing better than a local guide.

Hee-Young Yun accompanied me to temples and parks and made certain that I tried traditional Korean dishes. She was a great help for navigating through the city and was a wellspring of information about the culture.

Single at 29 years old by the Korean counting system (Koreans count you as one year old on the day you are born), Hee-Young lives with her mother. It seems that women live with their parents until they are married. Very few people break from this norm. I took advantage of her considerable artistic talents and commissioned a sketch of me as we sat on the beach.

Pusan had a pungent odor. It either smelled like salt air, dead fish, sewage or a glorious mixture of all three. Other than the people I came to know, the city felt unfriendly. Just walking around downtown Pusan, I got either blank stares, or people refused to meet my eyes. Very few people returned my smile. This was the case with most cities I visited in Korea. On the flip side, while hiking in the countryside, I experienced quite a different feeling. People smiled and actually initiated greetings or offered me food and drink. The change in atmosphere was palpable.

From Pusan, I traveled north to Kyongju, about 90 miles away. Kyongju is one of the most important historic regions in Asia. The city and surrounding area are a giant outdoor museum of tombs, stone Buddhas, and other religious and historic sites. I spent a day hiking with about hundred 10-year-olds on a school field trip. They loved exercising their English and, like the students in Pusan, were fascinated by the hair on my forearms. I never thought about it, but I guess if you've never seen hair on someone's body it would look pretty weird. Nothing pleased these kids more than when I could remember their names (they asked me repeatedly, "What is my name???"). I could go on and on about this hike. It's really a story unto itself.

From Kyongju, I headed west, across the peninsula to Kunsan Air Base to meet up with some guys I know through a Navy friend of mine. I wanted to see what it was like for my aviator brethren to be stationed in Korea and was warmly welcomed by Michael "Bolt" Barten and his wife, Kindra, as well as Glen "Juice" Bradly. They fly with the 35th fighter squadron, the Pantons (panthers).

I was impressed with the quality of the squadron and its strong camaraderie. We went out on the town one night for a squadron function that involved a Korean meal and few cold beverages, along with various ceremonies. They made me privy to several squadron traditions that strengthen fraternal bonds and engender *esprit de corps*. Everyone made me feel welcome and included. For that, I thank them.

Back on the base, we spent the night at the squadron bar called Delta House (of *Animal House* fame), where a squadron band played and spirits flowed freely. All in all, it was as good as any party I've been to in Scottsdale, Arizona. The only difference I would note is that when you wake up in the morning here, you're still stationed in Korea. (BIG difference.)

Driving around Kunsan Air Base, I saw concertina wire surrounding the requisite Air Force golf course and occasional machine-gun nests dotting the landscape. Across the way, Patriot missile batteries are positioned, and guards stand at the ready beside checkpoints. F-16s fly overhead while airmen and their families go about their daily tasks. The whole experience was a good reminder that we have some really great people who prepare for the worst and do one hell of a job in faraway places.

En route to Osan Air Base to visit another Air Force friend, I stopped in Kongju city and at Kyeryongsan National Park. Both are roughly 100 miles south of Seoul. I did some good hiking there and enjoyed being in the country. Leaves are turning now. Once again, the people are friendlier to me on the trail than in the city.

After two days, I was on the train/bus/taxi to Osan base, where I was to stay with Donne "Buda" Kang. Donne is from Korea and moved to the United States when he was 2 years old. He is fluent in Korean and has many relatives who live here. Like Bolt and Juice, Donne flies the F-16 and is a graduate of the Air Force Academy. Another great American (even if he is an Air Force guy).

Osan is much closer to its surrounding city than Kunsan and is much larger, to boot. This translates to more creature comforts and better living conditions than the Spartan existence folks stationed at Kunsan must endure. On Friday night, Buda and I went out to sample the nightlife of Songt'an (the city Osan Air Base is located in—not nearby Osan city, as one would logically think).

I debated how much of the following story that I would include for fear of misinterpretation or imaginations running wild. I assure you that nothing salacious occurred. It's just that the story of the "Juicy Girls" is a classic overseas military tale and should be told.

THE JUICY GIRLS

When I spoke with Bolt before arriving in Kunsan, I wondered what he meant by, "When we go out at night, you'll get to see a lot of weird stuff, one of which is the Juicy Girls." I thought, "What the heck is a Juicy Girl?"

It turns out that many Russian women have come to Korea to work in the bars as topless dancers. Remember, I'm trying to be objective, but I think by anyone's standards you would have to classify these women as beautiful. I had to wonder, "Where are these women imported from, and how are they recruited?" I assumed when I went inside the Juicy Bars of Kunsan that prostitution must be part of the operation, but after further investigation, I honestly don't think that prostitution is an official function of these facilities. (Although, of course, it may be an individual decision of the dancers, I'm pretty sure the Juicy Bar owners forbid the practice.)

So why are they called Juicy Girls? When I got to Osan, I decided to get to the bottom of this, since none of my friends in Kunsan knew the answer. Here's how it all works:

Although the women rotate on the main stage dancing for tips, it is during their off time that they and the bar make the majority of their money. After completing a dance rotation, they dress and go out to work the crowd. Often, the madams of the house sternly direct them to sit with specific patrons.

As I sat watching the events around me at one of the bars, a Juicy Girl who spoke very good English joined me. She was Korean. I began asking a few questions about her experience in the "industry," and before I knew it, she had been served a champagne glass of pineapple juice. The elderly cocktail waitress demanded 10,000 won ($10) for the beverage. What?!? I didn't know what else to do but pay up. Not five minutes later, another glass of pineapple juice showed up, and the same elderly cocktail waitress demanded an additional 10,000 won.

I'm on a $40-a-day budget. Half of it just went out the window in less than 10 minutes. Cursing under my breath, I paid the fee and complained. Little good that did. Thus ended any chatting with the Juicy Girls.

Later that night we met some friends in another Juicy Bar. I was careful not to chat with anyone. In fact, I forcefully refused to talk to the women who had been directed to stand beside me as I sat on a barstool. (It didn't take much savvy to know that the booths and tables were for paying customers.) Buda was as annoyed by all of this as I was and decided to investigate in Korean. He wound up talking to the head madam who we noticed bossing the Juicy Girls around.

It turns out the dancers are paid a base salary of about $300 a month which includes housing. They must meet a curfew each night. Out of the $10 paid for each glass of juice, the dancer gets $2, and the house gets $8. The girls are allowed to have drinks bought for them, but not shots of liquor. I'm sure management keeps a close eye on how tipsy the women get. The madam told us that the "industry" is highly regulated by the city. It all felt like slave labor to me.

I never saw a Juicy Bar except those near Osan and Kunsan Air

Bases. (I'm sure they can be found near other U.S. military installations.) Supposedly, these types of bars have been around since at least the Vietnam War era; however, the influx of Russian Juicies has occurred only in the last few years. In addition, the Russian women are supposedly well educated but have difficulty finding well-paying jobs in their homeland. That's about all I could discover about the Juicy Bar business. I'm too poor to spend time asking any more questions.

SEOUL

I took a two-day trip to Seoul: 12 million people, fantastic subway system, and fantastic traffic jams. It's a cosmopolitan city that has grown to the point where planned cities in the suburbs have been built to ease the human crunch.

Interesting point: Buda tells me that the bridges spanning the Han River in central Seoul are wired with explosives in the event of an attack by North Korea. How wild is that?

My original plan was to spend the weekend with Donne and then take a trip to the DMZ on the following Tuesday. On Monday night, I discovered that the tour had been cancelled and there wouldn't be another one until Saturday. I quickly decided to spend four extra days in Korea so that I could see such a historic site. To fill the following week, I headed for the most spectacular park in all of South Korea, Soraksan National Park in the northeast part of the country.

Wow! Fantastic views and beautiful autumn foliage. I went on some strenuous hikes to view waterfalls and sheer granite cliffs. The closest comparison to a U.S. area would be either the Smoky Mountains or West Virginia.

Gorgeous. Absolutely gorgeous.

DMZ—Panmunjom

I found the trip to the DMZ (demilitarized zone) amazing. Before traveling to the border of North and South Korea, the tour bus stopped at one of the four underground tunnels that the North Koreans built for the obvious purpose of attack preparations. At 225 feet below the ground, we walked through a tunnel six feet tall and roughly six feet wide. The tunnel is large enough for vehicles and mounted guns.

Lesson: No matter what the treaty says, one must verify compliance. "Trust with verification" is what I believe Ronald Reagan said to the Soviets about nuclear arms. These North Korean tunnels are ample proof of the truth in that admonition.

Next stop was Camp Bonifas, which was named for an Army captain who was axed to death in the summer of 1976 by North Korean troops as he carried out a routine tree-trimming operation in the neutral area called Panmunjom. There are very clear pictures on display of the four-minute battle that took place. It was here that we received our briefing prior to visiting Panmunjom and the negotiation table that is bisected by the border of the two countries. We had to sign a form that mentioned the possibility of military attack and death, etc.

At Panmunjom, our guides allowed us to take pictures standing beside South Korean soldiers as they stood in a modified taekwondo position. They had very stern and imposing looks on their faces. It was a little bit of propaganda but not overboard given the situation, I think. Later the group drove to the location of the ax murders and the site of a 1985 Soviet defection that resulted in a firefight.

We stood outside and viewed the North Korean countryside, which includes Propaganda Village, an uninhabited city that blares propaganda music on large loudspeakers from the north into South Korea. Ridiculous. Large white letters reminiscent of the Hollywood sign proclaim deceased President Kim Il Sung as the "great leader" and the only one who can reunite the peninsula.

This was an amazing experience, right up there with Hiroshima as a tangible and striking reminder of history. I'm sure the tension on this border has been greater in the past, but a feeling of distrust and danger still hangs in the air. In addition, I could see a bond between the U.S. and South Korean soldiers. There were lots of smiles, salutes and handshakes among them: brothers in arms, I suppose.

OBSERVATIONS/IMPRESSIONS

Right away I could see a difference between Korean and the Japanese people. Even on the ferry ride over, I could sense a difference. Koreans are much more forward in their communication. They bumped and squeezed me in every time I stood in a line. Invariably, as I got to the ticket counter, either an elderly woman or man would butt in front of me to make a purchase. At first, this annoyed me, but I came to realize that the person was not being rude by his or her standards. This is just normal and expected behavior. (I quickly adjusted to this behavior, and although I don't butt in front of others, I fend for myself quite well and am no longer upset at having to do so.)

Later I sat beside two elderly Korean women as we waited for a bus. They were loud and laughing together and asked me where I was going. They opened a box of crackers and offered me the first one. They gave me six or seven crackers as we sat there together and made sure I got off the bus at the right stop.

Now I know that these are the same two women who have butted in front of me all across Korea. My interaction with them on this night reinforced the idea that what appears to be rude behavior is oftentimes the normal action of really nice people.

By Western standards and compared with Japan, the Korean culture comes across as rough around the edges. I'm not saying it's good or bad or otherwise—I'm merely describing what it felt like to me. Remember, I'm on a low-budget trip. I'm not hanging out at five-star resorts and mixing with the social elite. Many people chewed with their mouths half-open, and attractive, well-dressed middle-aged women smacked their gum loudly. Men would often clear their throats loudly and spit. On the other hand, behavior that I would consider normal is deemed rude here. For instance, it is uncouth to blow one's nose in public.

The food in Korea is much spicier than in Japan. I love the kim-chi (pickled vegetables) and pulgogi (spicy meat, beef usually). The most exotic foods I tasted were snails and raw beef. (I know you're not supposed to eat the raw stuff, but I was treating myself to a nice meal in an upscale restaurant and decided what the heck. It turned out to be one of my favorite dishes in Korea, with a sweet honey glaze and delicious Korean pears mixed in.)

People drive like maniacs. Car horns blare frequently. The highways and streets are jammed with vehicles manufactured by either Daewoo or Hyundai. I noticed very few imports.

I'm no Calvin Klein, but I think the fashions speak to a strong Western influence that was more apparent in Korea than Japan.

Blue jeans are prolific, and so are baseball hats. I don't remember seeing a single baseball hat and very few blue jeans in Japan. In Korea, they're everywhere. Baseball caps are quite common, even on women of all ages.

Logo wear is abundant. DKNY, Polo Sport, Hilfiger, the list goes on. But most popular of all is the New York Yankees' "NY." I would bet that the second-most popular place for Yankees hats outside of N.Y.C. is Korea. "NY" hats of every color and style. Pink, red, orange, white, yellow, blue, powder blue, you name it. The UCLA logo follows "NY" as a close second.

Like the Japanese, it seems the majority of women and many of the younger men have colored or highlighted their hair.

Unlike in Japan, I'm not the biggest guy in the country. Although most people are still well below the U.S. average height and weight, I definitely noticed more heavy people than in Japan. I don't know for sure, but I think Koreans eat more beef and pork than the Japanese. I certainly have since I've been here.

Overall, I really enjoyed Korea and am thankful to the folks who either put me up for a while or helped me out when I needed a hand. I'm still enjoying good karma in the sense that I've stayed out of danger and continue to have great experiences.

7

Hello, Mr. Moneybags
Have I Got a Taxi, and Hotel, For You

I'd like to describe what it's like to be a backpacker going through China.

The one English word known by every person throughout the whole of China, it seems, is *hello*. Every type of person from every walk of life can say this word and likes to do so. Young children, old women, hikers on the trail, beggars on the street, bus drivers, men passing on bikes, you name it, they've all said, "Hello" to me.

The meaning of this word is two-fold. The first is what I normally associate with the greeting. It's the how-are-you-doing, It's-so-nice-to-have-you-in-my-country, I-hope-you-enjoy-your-stay meaning.

The second definition of "Hello" is much closer to: "Hey you! Mr. Moneybags. Come on over here so I can overcharge

Mother lion and cub. Inside the Forbidden City.

you for something."

It is the second meaning that greets the traveler after disembarking a train in any city in China or near any sightseeing spot.

Here's what it's like to be a backpacker landing in a different city after an 18-hour train ride:

1) Get off train.
2) Be attacked by touts.

There is no in-between. The pack on my back might as well be a giant BULL'S EYE. Touts are the people hired by hotels to swarm over foreigners at the train or bus stations to persuade them to stay at a certain hotel.

Rivaling touts in their ability to annoy are the bloodthirsty hawkers. These are the people who yell at you to examine and purchase their wares as you quietly try to tour the city. They'd sell you a gust of wind if they thought they could get away with it.

I've come up with a way to fight back, however. The way I look at it, one has a few choices when faced with these unpleasant encounters. First, one can respond in English by either trying to negotiate or simply saying no. But saying no never works. If there's one common quality among professional touts and hawkers, it is that they are amazingly persistent and will go to great lengths for your business, whether you like it or not.

Another choice is just to ignore them. This actually works, but you have to listen to them for a long time.

The choice I've made is my own invention, and if nothing else, it entertains me. I talk to them in Spanish, but not just any old Spanish. I make it funny for myself.

> Hawker: "Hello! You need taxi to hotel? You have hotel to stay?"
> Me (with quizzical look): "Tacos y Enchiladas?"
> Hawker (sometimes puzzled, other times unfazed): "Hello?"
> Me: "TACOS y ENCHILADAS?"
> Hawker: "You speak English? Yes?"
> Me (confidently): "Los pantalones son negros y amarillos."
> (The pants are black and yellow.)
> Confused hawker: "I'm sorry. Goodbye"
> Unfazed hawker: "Hotel? You need taxi?"

With the confused hawker, I shrug my shoulders and move along. With the unfazed hawker, I use the one last phrase I can remember from my meager knowledge of Spanish. It's something that I shouldn't repeat here, but it's quite memorable and rolls off my tongue as if I were a native speaker. This last bit usually gets them.

I don't know if I've gone crazy, or I'm just doing what I learned in the Navy -- creating my own fun.

Afterword: The hawkers can actually be helpful if used properly. I try to find out how much a taxi should cost before exiting the train. I then use the intel quite successfully in negotiations. Because touts pounce upon me so quickly, I rarely have to look around for taxis.

8

Stepping Into a Majestic Capital and Its Crazy Quilt of Traffic

China: Wow! I think that's the best way to start. What a grand, magnificent, dirty, polluted, friendly, rude, cultured and unrefined place. This country is a study in contrasts. The maintaining of the old ways amid blossoming capitalist change could be seen and felt as I spent one month touring the People's Republic. Because I had so many adventures, I'll have to record a truncated version of events. I hope y'all find it half as interesting on paper as it was to experience first-hand. First, I'll race through where I went and what I did and then follow up with highlights and impressions.

Tiananmen Square. Photo of Mao Tse Dong in background.

At the summit of Huashan Mountain. (Central China.)

Shrines near the base of Huashan Mountain. (Central China.)

*At the Panda Conservatory
in Chengdu, China.*

WHERE I WENT AND WHAT I DID

BEIJING

I landed in Beijing on Monday, Oct. 30, 2000, on a flight from Seoul, Korea. I really like arriving in a new country, with its new language, currency and public transportation to figure out. Plus, there's the feeling of uncertainty and excitement. It's a sort of a "what's going to happen next?" feeling.

On the plane, I studied from my Mandarin phrasebook the basic words necessary for communication. Upon arrival, I forgot all of them and was forced to fend off aggressive touts using only English. The hawkers at the airport were aggressive and annoying. One lit a cigarette and blew smoke in my face as I sat trying to collect my thoughts and belongings. (That was hardly a good way to win my business.)

This was the only time that I allowed one of these folks to get under my skin. I think the combination of simultaneously computing high-order exchange rate calculations and how much money I should withdraw at the ATM, not speaking the language, hating cigarette smoke and hawkers, and not knowing how to get to my hotel, which I hadn't decided on yet, resulted in amplified frustration.

I moved to another seat and realized that my 45-pound pack was an excellent deflector as I sat on the end seat of the row and placed my bag on the seat next to me. Fortunately, he decided not to continue his sales pitch by squatting on the floor. I had visions of being arrested for clocking the guy with less than an hour in China under my belt.

I remember that one of the most striking first impressions of China was the language. Everyone was talking out of the backs of their throats. I heard lots of deep R's and other foreign sounds. I remember thinking, "Whoa -- Chinese." It sounded strong and aggressive. Heretofore, I could make most of the sounds of Korean and Japanese, or at least had an idea of what to try. With Chinese, I didn't know where to begin. This difficulty diminished over time, and by the end of the month a few goodhearted souls even gave me pronunciation compliments. (They were probably just trying to make me feel good.) But I still can't say *toilet* properly. Fortunately, most Chinese people understand the phrase, "W.C.?" (water closet)

So, with the help of the tourist information desk, I found a bus to the middle of the city and was then promptly ripped off by the first cab driver who approached me. (I did bargain him down, however, so that I paid only twice the normal price instead of three times.) But a trip to Beijing is hardly complete unless the taxi drivers rip you off at least once. The city is notorious for that.

My luck was to change, however. The manager of the fleabag hotel where I stayed was one of the most exuberant, self-motivated and friendly people I have ever had the pleasure of meeting. His last name was Liu (The Chinese go by their family name), but he asked me to call him Leo. He was really something else.

On my first night in Beijing, Leo took me to a fantastic little restaurant where I enjoyed my first Chinese meal -- kung pao chicken for $1 and a big bottle of beer for 45 cents. The food tasted so good I wanted to cry. We took the bus to Tiananmen Square (two miles north of where I stayed, about 30 minutes on the bus—a story unto itself). So my first view of the famous sights in central Beijing was at night.

Giant floodlights lit the colossal buildings, adding to their stature. I kept thinking, "Man, that's as big as all of China." It was a fitting introduction to the most populous and one of the most powerful countries in the world. That's what Tiananmen Square reminded me of. It was impressive. Imposing. Domineering. Intimidating.

Over the next four days I saw the Great Wall, the Forbidden City, a Chinese acrobatics performance, and the Temple of Heaven.

Those are the primary spots. I also took a trip by bus, subway (very nice), and on foot to the U.S. Embassy. Embassies are clustered in two locations. The area where the U.S. Embassy is located was clean and modern. That was in sharp contrast to the area I stayed in on the outskirts of the city. If the embassy neighborhood and some of the major sights were all that one saw of Beijing, one might walk away with the impression that Beijing is a well-to-do city. Certainly, the city has its bright spots, but there's plenty of poverty and grime as well.

One of the most visible distinctions of Beijing (and every other city I saw in China outside of Hong Kong, for that matter) was the traffic. I don't mean simply that there is a lot of traffic. I'm also referring to the actual makeup of participants and the traffic pattern. Bicycles are everywhere. Endless streams of bicycles and pedestrians along every street and alleyway inextricably mingled with motorized vehicles of all types. There were motorized rickshaws, cars, trucks, buses and motorcycles. If there's another type of vehicle that I'm leaving out, include it in your vision of Beijing -- I'm sure it's there.

The traffic pattern, on first glance, is crazy. People cross the street through such a morass of vehicles and bodies that, as a first-time observer, I often thought, "I can't believe that woman with the two kids made it." But after a quick breaking-in period (and it needs to be quick or you will perish), I realized the pattern works because everyone moves deliberately and predictably. Even though red lights are only advisory in certain parts of the city, as is the rule about driving on the proper side of the road, if you step into the street and slowly keep walking, you will eventually find yourself on the other side, no worse for the wear (but believe me, I still kept my head on a swivel).

XI'AN

My next stop was the terra cotta warriors in the city of Xi'an after an overnight 18-hour train ride southwest of Beijing. I suppose this is a good time to tell you about the trains in China.

They are loud, herky-jerky, sometimes kind of clean, sometimes gross and smelly, with frequent stops in the middle of nowhere (you don't get off -- the train just sits there) and grungy-looking food that I never tried. It was usually on time for departure, but plus or minus a half-hour or so on arrival after an overnight trip. It's hard to say because the ticket agent would tell me one thing and the conductor another. The train had a mind of its own.

I've done my best to be objective when writing about the places that I have been. I will make an exception for Xi'an, the most polluted city I've ever seen.

I never saw the sky, only the haze of who knows what kind of particulates that tainted my lungs for three days. No kidding, Xi'an made the haze of Phoenix and L.A. look like fresh mountain air. If Xi'an's air could be bottled, it would be used for chemical warfare. I pity the poor people who must live in that dump of a city. I felt my lifespan shorten with each passing minute.

The pollution was both airborne and grounded. I saw trash and dirt everywhere. And it wasn't confined to the city limits. Upon traveling to Huashan Mountain (one of the five sacred mountains of China), about 60 miles east of Xi'an, pollution continued to plague my existence. It is cities like Xi'an that make me realize why the Koreans and Japanese are upset with the filth that floats eastward via the winds to be deposited on their shores in the form of acid rain.

I'm probably being too harsh and my imagination has made it worse than it really was, but I got on a roll and just went with it.

While asphyxiating in Xi'an I saw:

- The terra cotta warriors. They are impressive, but it would have been more rewarding if a greater percentage of warriors had been unearthed. I estimate only 15 percent have been restored. The rest are still buried, and thus, all one sees is the dirt roof of this 10,000-strong underground army. (Actually, there are two armies and a command post. About 100 yards separates each site.)

- Huashan Mountain. Huashan is one of the highlights of my trip to China. It is so magnificently beautiful. I hiked with two fellow travelers and spent the night about two-thirds of the way up. After ascending to the peak, I reluctantly descended into the bile of pollutants to be transported back to the hell on earth known as Xi'an. Fortunately, the person I had ordered train tickets from on the black market had come through for me, and I was able to flee that evening.

CHENGDU

About 13 hours by train southwest of Xi'an sits the capital of Sichuan province, Chengdu. My reasons for stopping here were twofold. First, I wanted to break up the trip between Xi'an and the vacation city of Lijiang farther to the southwest, and second, I have always loved spicy Sichuan food. I subsequently discovered a third reason: Chengdu is home to the Panda Conservatory. (Sorry, I didn't get the official name, but *Panda* and *Conservatory* are definitely in the title.)

This turned out to be worth the trip in and of itself. About 25 pandas live at the conservatory -- more than any other captive location in the world. I was impressed with how close visitors were allowed to the pandas, as well as the quality of their habitat. The bears made for some great pictures.

Chengdu was a bustling city of several million people. There was air pollution, but not as bad as in Xi'an. I didn't see anything too amazing here. By the way, my trip to the Panda Conservatory was on the now infamous U.S. presidential Election Day, Nov. 8, 2000. (I saw one satirist call it Indecision Day.) I was able to watch the final two hours in my hotel room, although I suppose final is a misnomer.

LIJIANG

From Chengdu, I traveled to the quaint town of Lijiang in Yunnan Province. Lijiang is in southwest China, close to the border of Tibet and Myanmar. The south of China is where the vast majority of minority people live. Lijiang and the neighboring city of Dali, where I traveled to next, are pleasant cities where many Chinese go for vacation. Lijiang is the nicer of the two, with its narrow cobblestone streets, delicious food, and beautiful view of the majestic Jade Dragon Mountain. The minority group here is called Naxi. They have preserved a traditional form of music and its instruments that is performed each night in the old town. I took in a show, which was memorable.

While in Lijiang, I hiked, relaxed, read e-mail, and checked my stocks over excruciatingly slow Internet connections. Lijiang and Dali are places to relax and enjoy, as well as to meet other travelers and locals. I did all of the above.

DALI

Dali is similar to Lijiang but not as quaint. I took a boat trip across the nearby Erhai Lake to the town of Wase. Every five days, Wase has a market where people from the surrounding villages conduct trade. I thought of it as a good excuse to get out on the water and check out the scenery. The most notable thing about the excursion is that I found what I believed to be the grossest bathroom in all of China.

This is a good point to mention public toilets in China. To make a long story short, apply the tongue lashing that I gave to Xi'an. I guess most are not so bad (relatively), but believe me, there are some real stinkers (pun intended). The facility in Wase was so bad that I took a picture of it for explanatory purposes. I didn't think it could get any worse. I was certain it would take top honors for the worst toilet in China.

Alas, my choice was bested. Two Danish women at the market told me there was a dead pig in their facility. That's right, a *dead pig*.

KUNMING

Next stop was Kunming, still in Yunnan province. Kunming was about a four-hour bus ride east of Dali. What a change from Beijing, Xi'an and Chengdu! The city was, by comparison, sparkling clean. The downtown area had attractive skyscrapers, and the traffic pattern was far more organized than in any other city I saw in China. Wide bike lanes separated by dividers lined each side of the road in most areas. The hotel where I stayed was cheap, clean, and relatively friendly. All in all, I really liked Kunming. It was the first city where I said to myself, "If I live in China someday and have my choice, Kunming would be a nice location."

My roommate at the hotel was from Malaysia. His last name was Poh. After the standard exchange of pleasantries, Poh asked if I wanted to accompany him and the rest of his group (nine

One of the Chinese soldiers who helped me fix my flat tire.

people) as they toured the city the next day. I readily agreed, and the following morning I had a fantastic time just meandering around Kunming. Only three of the group spoke English (the rest spoke Mandarin as their mother tongue, although they are Malaysians by nationality).

For my final day in Kunming, I decided to tour the city by bicycle before my 10 p.m. train to Guangzhou. Basically, I rode six miles southwest of the city to Dian Lake. When I was about a mile away, my back tire went flat. That would be OK by itself, but the inner tube developed a huge rip, and I couldn't just pump it back up. Fortunately, with the prevalence of bicycles in China comes the ubiquitous bicycle repairman.

After fixing the bike the first time ($1), I continued to the lake, where I noticed the new inner tube had started to creep outside of the tire. That had probably caused the gash in the first inner tube. About 15 Chinese soldiers in uniform, cruising the shores of the lake on what I assume was liberty, stopped to help.

Although they spoke almost no English, we had a great time for about 30 minutes with the use of my phrasebook. I couldn't help but look into their young, confident and smiling faces and wonder if I was staring at a future friend or foe. They were genuinely friendly and inquisitive—helping out the American with a flat tire. Several wanted their picture with me, which we took, along with a few group shots.

GUANGZHOU

I took a 31-hour train to Guangzhou, an enormous city 60 miles west of Hong Kong. I stayed there for four days while waiting for my Vietnamese visa to be processed. (That's a story, too.) While in Guangzhou, I stayed on Shamian Island. This is technically an island in the southwest portion of the city, but it is separated from the mainland by only a thin canal and sits on the north bank of the Pearl River (famous for the trade that comes up the river from Hong Kong).

Shamian was beautiful. It is formerly a French/British territory, as evidenced by the architecture. Shamian also happens to be a fairly expensive place. (With clean, well-manicured grounds come pricey restaurants and hotels.) Fortunately, the one youth hostel in Guangzhou happens to be located here. It's a good deal for cheap travelers like me.

Things I did in Guangzhou:

- At Qing Ping market, merchants sell all kinds of animals. It's famous for that. Two of the more notable things that I saw were:

> - A huge basket of scorpions. (Yes, I saw someone purchase a container.)
> - Cats. (These poor animals were in horrid health and in filthy cages.)

I didn't see it, but someone else told me they saw dog carcasses hanging on hooks.

- I met the Chinese painter Gu Yuan and his wife, Wang Lujiang. He paints impressions of Tibet and has a studio on Shamian Island. This was a highlight for me. I stumbled across his studio by accident and out of curiosity. I spent about two hours the first day conversing with his wife and returned the following day to buy a print and then met Gu Yuan himself. He was recently featured at an international art expo in New York. Great stuff.

- The most notable thing about the Guangzhou zoo was how ironic I thought the experience was. The locals spent as much time looking at me as they did at the animals behind the bars. I should have been in one of the cages. I found generally poor conditions for the animals at this zoo.

- SERVAS is an international hosting organization that I joined prior to my trip. It is a Latin word that means "to serve". In Guangzhou, I was able to have dinner with fellow SERVAS members, Yi Changian and his wife, Pan Xiaoyan, who gave me insight into the changes taking place in China. I estimate they are 45 years old. Both remember Mao Zedong's Cultural Revolution well. Yi is an ophthalmologist, and Pan is a traditional Chinese-medicine doctor. It was fascinating to speak with them and listen to their views on the government, its policies and Chinese culture.

HONG KONG

I arrived in Hong Kong by ferry. What a way to approach Hong Kong for the first time. To say the skyline is impressive is an understatement. What I found interesting is the natural beauty located just a mile or two from the metropolis. Hong Kong and its Outer Territories look like the pictures I've seen of Southeast Asia (which, when I stopped to think about it, is where I was.)

The difference between Hong Kong and mainland China is conspicuous to every sense. Even the ferry ride indicated a change. The staff of the ferry was polite and almost friendly. The bathrooms had Western-style toilets that were remarkably clean. When I took the shuttle bus from the ferry landing to the train station, I realized we were driving on the "wrong" side of the road. "Oh yeah,"" I thought, "the Brits." But what cinched the deal was when I heard the polite female voice with a British accent on the train's public address system say, "Please *mind* the platform gap when *alighting*." I couldn't help but smile.

I stayed in Hong Kong for four days with another SERVAS member, Lo Ada, a gracious and helpful tour guide/host. She also provided some interesting insights into the turnover of Hong Kong from British rule (a mixture of excitement and apprehension). I shopped for electronic equipment (digital camera memory card) and was pleased to see that my item was about half the price that I had paid in the States.

The two visual memories that I took away from Hong Kong were skyscrapers in one view and beautiful bays and mountains in another. Both are equally strong. The other takeaway is the difference between Hong Kong and the mainland. Radical. People actually queue for the bus in Hong Kong. There's no spitting on the sidewalk. I experienced very little pushing and shoving. The buildings and shopping malls are clean and tidy. There are few bicycles, and people even wait for the Walk sign before crossing the street (usually). In China they describe the relationship as, "One country, two systems." I would add, "Two cultures."

I hope this serves to let everybody know what I've been up to. It's a fascinating trip, and I'm loving it. My health is great. Fortunately, the price of food is really cheap in Asia, so I've been eating well. I'm in Hanoi, Vietnam, now: New place, new money, new language, new everything. It's great.

9

Exuberant Leo – A Wannabe Capitalist in the New China

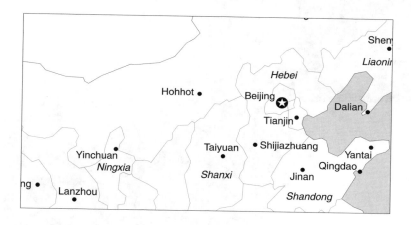

This is a story about a young Chinese man who managed the backpacker portion of the hotel where I stayed in Beijing. I decided to write about him because I think he exemplifies the new China that is developing rapidly while it clings to its old ways .

Liu Yue Lai (aka "Leo") was 24 years old, single (with a girlfriend he intended to marry), and lived in a decrepit portion of Beijing in the basement of a run–down hotel. He has what I estimate is the equivalent of a 10th-grade education, although he had taught himself English well enough that I understood about 90% of what he said. He was a personable young man, about 5 feet, 5inches tall and dressed sharply in the same black sportcoat and pants every day.

What I will forever remember about Leo is that he positively

Top:
A "Wild Wall" portion of the
Great Wall of China.

Center:
A typically energetic wave from Leo.

Bottom:
Leo inside one of the turrets
of the Great Wall.

radiated energy. That, coupled with the burning desire to own his own business and his grasp of capitalistic principles, makes him a case study for the changes taking place in China.

I met Leo within my first three hours in China, while sitting in the "plush" commons room of the Sea Star Hotel in south Beijing just outside of Third Ring Road. Leo bounded in from a quick trip to pick up lunch from the street vendors. He saw that I was studying a map of the city and quickly wished me a wonderful stay in Beijing with the hope that I would enjoy his country.

> "Thanks," I said. "By the way, do you know a good place to eat nearby?"
>
> (I wasn't hungry, but I figured this information would come in handy later.)
>
> "You want to eat? Now?" Leo asked.
>
> "Uh, sure," I said.
>
> "I take you to good restaurant," he said. "We go now?"
>
> "Whatever you say."
>
> "Here, try my food. It's good. Traditional Chinese street food."

I couldn't believe how friendly and energetic this guy was. "Where's the catch?" I kept thinking. "I wonder if he's going to expect me to pay for everything?" Over the next 24 hours, I would periodically ask myself, "When is this guy going to try to rip me off?"

But the rip-off never came. Leo was as genuine as they come. Although I had a natural reluctance to trust a stranger, Leo and I hit it off right away.

So we hopped a rickshaw for the short ride to the restaurant, and Leo paid for the ride. It was my first Chinese meal. Fantastic: Kung Pao chicken for $1 and a big bottle of beer for 45 cents. Finally some cheap, good food! I decided to pay for Leo's meal to say thanks and to cultivate good will.

After dinner, Leo decided it would be fun to take the bus up to Tiananmen Square to see downtown Beijing at night. The bus ride alone was an adventure.

First of all, passengers waited in a gaggle at the bus stop. This is the standard method pretty much anywhere in the world. The only problem here was that the buses were always -- I repeat, ALWAYS -- overcrowded. That, in addition to the uncanny and immensely powerful need for Chinese people to claim a seat, made for one heck of a battle when the door opened.

In all my years, I had never seen such pushing and shoving, like hooligan soccer fans storming the field after victory. Once I forcibly held back the crowd to allow a woman toting two large bags to regain her footing after being knocked down on the bus steps. Ridiculous!

After my first bus ride, as we walked along and toured the area, Leo taught me a few basic Chinese words. He must've been enjoying himself because he offered to take me up to the Great Wall the next day.

"Jason, I take you to REAL Great Wall tomorrow," Leo chattered enthusiastically. "No tourists! I have friend with car who lives there. Don't worry, he is very good friend. I call him and say, 'John, I want to visit Great Wall with my American friend tomorrow. Can you go and drive car?' He will say, 'Of course, Leo. You my very good friend!'"

"Is OK. No problem! I introduce you to my girlfriend too. She not very beautiful, but is OK for me. I love her. Tomorrow will be GOOD day!"

Leo often talked in bursts like that, with spontaneous and contagious energy.

The next day I awoke early and headed out with my new friend to see the fabled Great Wall of China. Three perilous bus changes later, I found myself in Yanqing, a small town about 20 miles northwest of Beijing. We met Leo's friend John (his Chinese name sounds similar to that) and his girlfriend, had a quick breakfast of rice soup and fried dumplings and departed for the countryside. Unfortunately, neither Leo's girlfriend nor John spoke English. They both enjoyed my poor attempts at speaking Chinese, however.

As we drove and talked, I learned Leo's ulterior motive for taking this trip to the Great Wall. After managing the basement of the Sea Star Hotel for a few years, Leo dreamed of running his own hostel. He wanted John, a Yanqing cabdriver, to purchase a small plot of land near the Great Wall and establish a business that Leo would help operate. Leo would provide the hotelier know-how and send business from the Sea Star in Beijing to "John and Leo's" at the Great Wall. John and his wife would manage the daily operations and live in their inexpensive bed and breakfast.

Then came another outburst from Leo (LOUDLY):

> "JASON! What do you think?!? Is this good spot? Do you like it? Will this be good? I think is good. REAL Great Wall. Not repaired like Badaling," a touristy part of the Wall.
> "I say to customer, 'Come to John and Leo's. You have problem with hotel, you call me 24 hours a day at 555-7383. I help you. Twenty-four hours hot water. GOOD food. Visit WILD Wall! See how Chinese peasant lives. Traditional Chinese living. Breathe FRESH air! ONLY 25 YUAN (about $3.00)!'"
> "What do you think, Jason?!? Is good? I think so."

What a salesman! I got excited for him as he touted the virtues of the location and his ideas. We chatted with some of the "peasants", as he called them, in the village. They seemed agreeable to whatever he said to them and smiled a lot at me, the foreigner. The sky was clear and the sun was shining. As he stood beaming in that moment, Leo felt there was nothing he couldn't do.

As we hiked along, Leo noted where he would place "danger" signs on the trail and timed the hike from his hostel to the Great Wall, about 10 minutes.

I asked him if the government would approve of his ideas

about signs on this portion of the Great Wall.

"Why not? My business will be good for the villagers, improve their life! Signs will keep the trail safe."

I also asked about the purchase of the land. Leo had not yet looked closely into that issue. He said one of the villagers would sell a plot with an old building on it for 10,000 yuan ($1,250), although a peasant makes only about $375 a year. Two days later he told me a local government official would need a bribe of several thousand yuan to approve the purchase. I got a sense that this type of corruption was normal.

After our trip, we headed back to town for lunch and a tour of Yanqing. Leo noticed that his cell phone was missing and looked distressed as he told me the price to replace it: about $300. I found out later that Leo had been illegally using a friend's phone. If China Telecom found out, there could be trouble for him and the phone's owner.

The next morning after our trip, I bumped into Leo en route to the hotel's common shower. He still looked upset because he would have to work for six months to pay for another phone. Not having a cell phone in Beijing for Leo was tantamount to solitary confinement. Apparently EVERYONE has one, so to be unconnected was crushing for such a gregarious personality.

But true to form, only hours later he bounced right back to normal. That night, on the walk home from a performance of Chinese acrobatics, I noted how happy he seemed. So I ventured a question about the cell phone.

His reply (with beaming smile): "JASON! Is OK! I will be all right. Something will work out. I LOVE LIFE!"

And then he sang a beautiful Chinese love song amid the rubble and dust of south Beijing.

Our outing to the Chinese acrobatics had been my introduction to the corrupt "Chinese system." Leo had told me about the Chinese acrobatics performance on my first day in Beijing, so I decided to take in a show but only if Leo went with me. Upon arriving at the theater after a 20-minute cab ride, Leo began acting peculiarly. First, he wanted me to wait around the corner and out of sight while he purchased my ticket. Next, he came back and said he wouldn't be able to attend because they wouldn't let him in. He would meet me after the show.

"What's the problem?" I asked. "I'll pay for your ticket, Leo. It's only $8. I don't want you to have to wait around out here for two hours. Plus, it'll be my treat, as a way to thank you for taking me to the "Wild Wall.""

"OK," he said hurriedly. "Let's go."

I handed him the $8, and then we rushed around the corner and through the theater entrance. But he didn't buy a ticket and didn't hand anything to the attendant. He just spoke to her, I think. It all happened so quickly.

As we sat inside, Leo pointed out the stern-looking female ushers guarding the "good seats" down in front.

Leo explained, "Jason, they know my face here. See that woman? I hope she doesn't talk to me. You don't understand. It's the 'Chinese system.'"

He crowded so close to me as he spoke that I thought he would crawl between the seat back and me. His surreptitious nature so piqued my interest that I pressed him for more information. Here's what I could gather from what he told me: (Remember, I could only understand about 90% of what he said.)

The government owned and distributed all of the tickets for this particular state-run theater. The tickets are sold to the general public, often through agencies such as hotels. Sometimes the people who work directly for the theater sell the tickets at reduced rates, but they don't tell the government about the sale and then pocket the cash. People like Leo act as middlemen between the original ticketholders and people who attend the performances. I paid a slightly inflated price over what Leo paid but still less than if I bought directly from the government ticket office. Hence, a black market.

Because Leo had come to know the ticket staff at the theater so well, they sometimes allowed him free entry. I imagined he took my $8, gave part to the attendant who let him in, and held on to the rest. Interesting, isn't it?

Looking back on my adventures with Leo, I'm surprised that in the midst of the capital of China, I found a young man with a vision and dreams. Dreams that rang of free enterprise and capitalism. Dreams that seemed so American to me.

In retrospect, I realize how special Leo was. As I traveled through the rest of China and stayed at other bargain-basement backpacker hotels, I could barely charm even a half-smile out of the sullen staff I encountered. Leo was exuberant, despite his lowly means and lack of formal education.

His gut sense for business concepts was in line with all that I had learned in business school. On a basic level, he dealt with pricing, marketing, bureaucracy and, most surprisingly, seemed a zealot for customer service. I loved his energy and motivation. If one could gather an army of Leos, *any* business could succeed. Heck, any ARMY could succeed. I told myself repeatedly, "I *must* work with people like Leo someday."

Yet for all the talk of free enterprise and ownership, I saw that Leo would have to overcome corruption and strict government control. Leo will require a knowledge of and familiarity with what he called the "Chinese system." Fortunately, he seemed adept at working within the system and had the energy and attitude to overcome adversity.

Before leaving the Sea Star, I wrote an advertisement for "John and Leo's" guesthouse. He in turn wrote some basic Chinese phrases and purchased a train ticket for me (on the black market, of course). I have since sent him a couple of e-mails, but haven't heard back. He may just be another face in the kaleidoscope that I'll never hear from again. But I hope not.

(Author's note) On March 26, 2003, I received a response to a holiday e-mail I had sent to Leo the previous December:

"hello, jason how are you . haven"nt see you for a long time . how are you doing ? this is leo your chinese friend . hope you luck , when you come to china just call me 13910030350."

After responding, I received this note:

"dear, jason nice to see you the email. hope you have a good time !

would mind send to me phto. take care and keep in touch! i got new job
. also basic hotel. but realy senter.(central) see you next time!"

10

A Black Suit and a
Bowl of Beef Noodle

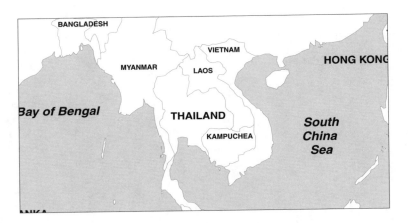

I spent three weeks traveling the length of Vietnam, starting in the north with Hanoi, and took a combination of trains, buses, airplanes and boats to arrive in the Mekong Delta, where I crossed the border of Cambodia. Vietnam, a beautiful country, was my introduction to Southeast Asia proper. The heat and humidity of the jungles near Hanoi let me know I had arrived.

I met both interesting locals and travelers. I would have liked to spend more time away from the travelers' circuit, but with the slow and uncertain nature of transportation here, I just couldn't do it in the time I allotted to this country. In fact, I spent almost a week longer than I had originally intended in Vietnam. I have the sneaking suspicion this will be a recurring theme as I continue my trip. The world is just a bigger place than I thought.

Top:
The gang at Diep-Shop No. 10. Hoi An,
Vietnam. (Na, Thao, Ms. Diep, Lee-Lee,
friend.)

Bottom:
The streets of Hanoi.

WHERE I WENT AND WHAT I SAW

HANOI

Hanoi exceeded my low expectations as a nice place to hang my hat for a few days. I stayed in the Old Quarter of town where the narrow streets are crowded with shops and the ubiquitous scooter and cyclo drivers. A cyclo is about the same thing as a rickshaw. It consists of three wheels, a seat for either one or two people, and a male driver in back who will offer you both prostitutes and marijuana. A typical exchange:

Driver: "Hey! Where you go?"
Me: (No response. Just ignore him, and do not make eye contact.)
Driver: "Where you from? You need ride?"
Me: (In the rare event that I acknowledge his presence) "America. I don't need a ride."
Driver: (Not hearing a word) "You need ride?"
Me: (In Vietnamese) "I don't need it." (They always seemed to understand the Vietnamese.)
Driver: (In hushed tone) "You want boom boom? Very nice. Beautiful girl. Very young."
Me: "No, that's OK. Thanks."
Driver: "No?"
Me: "No."
Driver: "You want marijuana? I get for you."
Me: (In Vietnamese) "I don't want it. Thanks."

(Proceed to next cyclo driver for more harassment.)

That was the thing about Vietnam; the vendors seemed needier than their Chinese counterparts. It took more energy for a simple walk about town than for the same walk in China.

One of the first things that I noticed about Hanoi, which turned out to be typical for all of Vietnam, was the number of scooters zipping about. China was bicycles. Vietnam is land of the scooter. Some common models: Honda Dream, Dream II, Superdream, Super Cub 50, Wave, and the Cadillac of scooters, the Spacy. The result of injecting scooters into the traffic pattern is a faster flow. You have to be a little more alert as you step out to cross the street.

A second difference from China: Most hotels and all of the package tours are priced in U.S. dollars. Even many of the restaurants accept U.S. dollars. I found that surprising. After consideration, however, it makes a lot of sense. The Vietnamese currency is so unstable that it's no wonder business owners prefer a hard currency like the mighty greenback. Why the U.S. dollar is used versus another currency I leave for others to ponder. But there's no question that the dollar is the standard by which all prices are compared. Many non–U.S. travelers have travelers' checks denominated in U.S. dollars.

A third difference from China: accommodations. The hotels in Vietnam are affordable so one doesn't have to stay in dorm rooms of three or four beds. A night's lodging costs from $5 to $12, depending on the city, location and quality. The price is always negotiable, and indeed a standard checking-in scenario includes a bit of haggling. Hotel operators understand the value of a U.S. dollar to Westerners and will try to use this in their negotiation. Keep in mind that for them, one dollar is a lot.

Upon my arrival in Hanoi, the first hotel I checked was full. The manager made a phone call, and soon a young man appeared at the door to walk with me to another hotel. The following negotiation ensued:

Manager:	"This room is normally $15, but I will give to you for $12."
Me:	"Hey look, I came down here from the last place with the understanding that I could stay for $10."
Her:	"Yes, but it's ONLY two more dollars."
Me:	"I don't care. $10 or nothing."
Her:	"Only two more dollars. That's not very much."
Me:	(Showing her my map) "Tell you what. Maybe you can show me another place here where I can find a $10 room."
Her:	'OK. $10."
Me:	(With friendly smile) "Thank you."

While in Hanoi I saw:

- Water-puppet theater. Water puppetry, an art form that is

thousands of years old, originated in the rice paddies of the north and is a distinctive Vietnamese art.

– The remains of the Hanoi Hilton. This is where American POWs were kept during the Vietnam War. The official name is Hoa Lo Prison, or Maison Centrale, and the French used it for more than a hundred years to house Vietnamese prisoners. Most of the structure has been demolished for a high-rise hotel and business center that now occupy the grounds. The museum only allots one room of the former prison to telling the story of American POWs. The signs about this portion of the building's history sounded like an excerpt of Communist propaganda.

To paraphrase: "The American prisoners held here were given very good treatment and food with plenty of exercise. They were even allowed to receive gifts from home even though they perpetrated great crimes against the people of Vietnam. They were not punished for their criminal acts."

I laughed when I saw a picture on the wall of five prisoners attending Catholic Mass. One of the guys was scratching his chin with his middle finger (giving "the bird") Many of the other photos were obvious propaganda shots. Examples:

– A prisoner sitting at a table laden with fresh fruit that was, oh by the way, untouched. He was smiling as he raised a glass for a toast with one of his captors.

– Prisoners smiling as they read Christmas letters at a table stacked with gifts.

– Prisoners smiling as they prepared a meal together. The photo showed full bowls of meat and vegetables (hardly a standard meal in the Hanoi Hilton).

– All the prisoners had fresh haircuts and clean, pressed prison uniforms. If that's all you saw of the treatment the prisoners received, you would think life in the Hanoi Hilton was pretty good. The photographs were exactly the kind of thing I was taught to recognize and try to avoid being a part of when I attended POW training in the Navy. Of course, that's not always possible.

HALONG BAY

Halong Bay, which is just north of Haiphong Harbor, the major port for North Vietnam. It was about a two-hour bus ride east of Hanoi. The scenery was remarkable. I read that it's a mountain range the ocean submerged a zillion years ago. Just the peaks of the mountains jut out above the water -- steep, craggy and beautiful.

The only time I had seen pictures of Halong Bay before going there was during a presentation given by a Vietnam War veteran at one of the training schools onboard Naval Air Station Oceana in Virginia Beach, Va. (where I was stationed for four years).

Phil Schuyler was an A-6 Intruder pilot flying with a Marine squadron off one of the aircraft carriers in the Gulf of Tonkin. Toward the end of the war, he and three other Intruder crews flew a daring daytime strike to destroy a factory in North Vietnam near Haiphong. The flight path took them over Halong Bay and then south to the target. Each carried about 20 500-pound bombs.

One of Schuyler's wingmen taped portions of the flight with an 8mm camera. Schuyler's jet was hit in the wing over Halong Bay as he flew inland. He was able to make it to the target, drop his ordnance, and then head east toward the aircraft carrier. The damage to his jet forced him and his bombardier/navigator to eject over the ocean. The bomb-damage assessment later confirmed a direct hit on the target. Both sides took their lumps that day.

Schuyler converted the 8mm video to photographs and prepared a brief for young aviators like myself. I remember seeing the pictures of Halong Bay and marveling at its beauty.

On the day I toured the bay, we stopped at a former Vietnamese anti-aircraft fortification on one of the many islands. The non-English-speaking guide described how he had lived there for his entire life and was responsible for defending the secret base. He sang a song about the war. I could understand only the boom-boom part with the accompanying anti-aircraft hand motion, followed by an airplane flying into the ground. He was a really pleasant guy and quite hospitable to all of us.

I flew A-6 Intruders also. Thirty years earlier, it could have easily been me whom this guy and his friends were shooting at. I was, of course, happy to just be on a tour and visiting with this smiling guide. What a feeling.

HUE

After Hanoi, I headed down to central Vietnam and the city of Hue. Hue was the capital of Vietnam for a long time and has a couple of sights worth seeing. One of the primary reasons to stop in Hue is that it is a launching site for Demilitarized Zone (DMZ) tours. In general, Hue was unfriendly and filled with aggressive cyclo drivers. The weather happened to be gray and rainy, and that didn't improve the setting.

One place I found interesting in Hue was its forbidden city. Just like Beijing, Hue had a palace and forbidden city that was off limits to most people. Unfortunately, almost all of the buildings are rubble today. I could get the general sense of how large it was and how things were laid out, but that's about it. The model in the museum showed that it had been a grand place in its day. I realized that China was not the only country to build lavish facilities for its emperor.

DMZ TOUR

Much like my visit to Halong Bay, I found the DMZ tour interesting in both a historical and personal way. There is not much left of the bases that were once featured in headlines during the '60s and '70s. Of the places I saw, only Khe Sanh had anything recognizable, and that was just the outline of the runway where trees don't grow. Nonetheless, I got a feel for the terrain, vegetation, distances, and views of the area. All of these will enrich any later reading.

HOI AN

I traveled by bus to Hoi An, a quaint town just a short distance south of Hue that is known for the tailors who incessantly pester tourists to shop at their stores. Heavy rain greeted me on the day that arrived. I don't think the fires of hell itself would deter those shop owners from seeking travelers' business, so certainly a little rain did not stand in their way. Two young women with jackets over their heads approached me as I hustled with my backpack through the rain to a hotel in the market district.

Right away, I sensed something different about one of them. It's amazing how quickly you can get a sense for someone's character after having been approached a million times by salesmen. I still gave only a half-hearted "Yeah sure. I'll come to your shop later. Let me get out of the rain and check in to my hotel." I figured she could see where I was staying and would have no trouble finding me later.

Not to be disappointed, about two hours later as I sat eating lunch across the street from my hotel, the woman appeared with friend in tow.

Hua Thi Nhan "Na"" is 24 years old and married with a young son and works in one of the large tailor shops in Hoi An. The name of her store is Diep -- Shop No. 10. According to Na, "Numbah 10 is Numbah One!"

A few days later, I wrote this in a comment book at her shop: "Na has the best smile in Vietnam with the personality to match." Her smile came from deep within her heart. Every fiber of her being exuded joy when she laughed or smiled. She was such a pleasure to be around that I agreed to visit her store.

I'm not a big-time shopper, and I generally do not like shopping for clothes, which I view as a necessary evil. I can't stand pushy salespeople and count the minutes that I am forced to spend inside clothing stores. It's only rarely that I have moments during which I enjoy the clothes-shopping experience.

But I could have spent all day sitting around with Na and the gang at Diep -- Shop No. 10.

Ms. Diep, who owns the store, is clearly the woman in charge. Na's cousin, Thao, takes measurements and orders from the customers. Na is a seamstress who occasionally pulls people in from off of the streets. Lee-Lee is a girl of about 12 who does odds and ends around the store -- primarily, it appears, talking with patrons.

The process was simple. Choose a fabric from large bolts of cloth (I asked for the best-quality material they had, which was a nice wool weave). Pick the style of suit that you want from a couple of large designer catalogues (I picked a three-button number). Specify whether you want pleats, cuffs, or extra buttons on the sleeve and return the next day to try it on and make adjustments. Piece of cake.

I wound up buying two suits and a tuxedo for $138. I really wanted only a black suit, but the price of the tuxedo was close to what I'd pay to rent one back in the States, and the blue material for the second suit was a really nice color. While chewing the fat with the folks in the store, Na offered me a bowl of beef noodle soup that was being served to the staff. My friend in Saigon, Mike Kleine, later wrote to me, "A black suit and a bowl of beef noodle. That's beautiful. Just like Brooks Brothers, huh?" Well put.

The shop in Hoi An was the highlight of Vietnam for me. I've already e-mailed the shop and received a response. What's great is they have my measurements. If I see a suit, shirt or pants that I like, I can mail a picture to the store and have it made: custom tailoring for pennies.

HO CHI MINH CITY (SAIGON)

I decided to fly from Hoi An to Saigon. I wanted to save time, and the flight was cheap ($69). I stayed with an old fraternity brother from college who now works at the U.S.

Consulate in Ho Chi Minh City as a Foreign Service officer.

Mike Kleine met me at the airport, and we hopped a cab back to his apartment in central Saigon. I was immediately impressed with Mike's ability to speak Vietnamese. The State Department does a good job of preparing its officers with language training, but Mike has made the effort to take his language skills a step further. So it was great to have a translator for a few days, as well as to spend time with an old friend.

I was happy to see that Uncle Sam had set up his overseas servicemen with nice accommodations in Saigon. For five days, I lived in the lap of luxury: air conditioning, instant hot water from the shower, and that thing called water pressure. It was medicinal.

Saigon was hotter and more humid than the other areas I had been. Mike said it stays like that all year - hot and humid. The places I toured:

- The U.S. Consulate is next door to the old embassy, which is now a swimming pool. You can still see the outline of the embassy, however, with its gun turrets on each corner. The new consulate is a modern and comfortable building. Across the street sit many vendors and scooter drivers. What are they selling? "Genuine" birth certificates and marriage licenses for people seeking entry to the U.S.

When the consulate opened, so many people wanted to immigrate to the United States that the crowds in front of the building became unsightly. The consulate was forced to allocate a room inside the compound to get people off the street. After waiting inside, applicants are led in groups to the front gate, where they wait for admittance to the secure area of the compound. In effect, they wait to wait.

The security at the consulate is tight. (My pocketknife made it through the first checkpoint, however, but was discovered at the second. It was an honest oversight on my part, not a test.) I was pleased with the level of professionalism and courtesy of the Vietnamese security guards and would feel safe working there.

- Reunification Palace is where the head of the South

Vietnam government ran the war. At the time, it was called Independence Palace. The famous scene of a tank crashing through the front gate occurred here. Touring the palace is like taking a trip back in time. Everything is quintessential early '70s, from the shag carpet to the style of furniture, even some of the artwork. Very *Brady Bunch*.

- The War Remembrance museum was the most penetrating sight in Vietnam. This was primarily due to the exhibition on display called "Requiem," a collection of photographs taken by journalists during the war that was collected in a book of the same title. I believe, although I'm not positive, most of the photographers were either killed or are missing in action. The photos were phenomenal. A few had captions such as, "Last frame in black and white taken on roll of film," or "Last color frame shot on roll of film" (photographer stepped on land mine in dike on right of photograph). I have seen this book on my parents' coffee table in Atlanta. To see the photos framed on the wall in Saigon added to their effect.

In the rest of the museum, I saw horrid pictures of death and destruction, as well as a historical accounting of troop movements and the effects of war on civilians. I'd be lying if I said I didn't bristle at a few of the captions under pictures of Americans. I thought it was another example of selective truth and assumptions at play. But all in all, I think I did a good job of keeping my emotions in check and trying to be more objective than the caption writers.

After enjoying the high life and Mike's palatial apartment, I headed out for a three-day tour of the Mekong Delta that would end in an overland crossing into Cambodia and a boat/minibus ride to Phnom Penh. That was a great deal at $40.

The Mekong Delta was a fascinating place to explore. Our guide said it has more than 1,500 miles of waterways. Some passages are wide, while others could be pole-vaulted. We toured two floating markets, a rice-processing plant, a puffed-rice cake making place (don't know what else to call it), a rice whiskey place (rice is used for a lot down here), a tribal village and a stork preserve.

But the coolest part of touring the delta was just riding along in the boat, watching how the local people live. Pigs, water buffalo, chickens and dogs meander about. People bathe, swim, and wash dishes in the river. Almost all of the children greeted us with smiles, waves and yells as we motored by in our narrow Vietnamese version of a johnboat. The adults were generally less smiley, although a few waved and grinned. Almost everyone would respond to a quick nod-of-the-head greeting. It was a lot of fun. And I lucked out with the weather. It rained for only about an hour one day, which happened to be the only ride I took in a large boat with a sheltered cabin. Perfect.

I highly recommend a trip to Vietnam. The people are friendly, the cost is cheap, and the sights both historic and exotic. I quickly noticed the people in Vietnam have darker skin and somehow softer features than the Chinese. In my humble and personal opinion, the women of Vietnam are, generally speaking, the most beautiful I have seen in my travels so far. Their warm and open personalities complement their beauty.

Another thing: The sights and sounds of Vietnam are exactly as one would expect. The abundance of conical hats, water buffalo, appeals from cyclo drivers touting "boom-boom," rain, mud, flooded rice fields, lush vegetation, heat, and humidity were all just as I had imagined. Vietnam did not disappoint.

I'm in Cambodia now. I plan to make it to Thailand for Christmas and New Year's Eve.

Lots of times people ask if I feel lonely yet. Far from it. Sure there are some down times, but there's way too much to see and do for those to last very long. Plus, I meet a lot of people in my travels. But another important factor is that I know I can always check my e-mail and usually find a few messages from people back home. That knowledge gives me a constant sense of contact with familiar folks.

11

Making Peace With a Rodent Roommate in the Mekong Delta

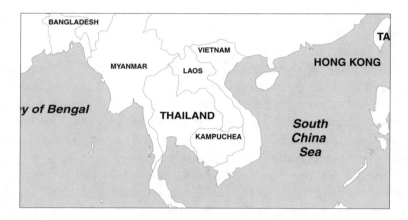

This is a quick tale about some of the fun you can have while staying in the Mekong Delta. It should give you an idea of the environmental factors one must occasionally endure on a low-budget world trip.

As part of the $40 price tag for my three-day minibus/boat trip through the Mekong Delta of Vietnam, I was guaranteed two nights of lodging. The first was to be in the town of Can Tho and the second in the Cambodian border town of Chau Doc. Both locations offered the option of upgrading to an air-conditioned room: The Can Tho room would cost an extra $5 and the Chau Doc room $2 more.

Because the weather was reasonably cool at night, certainly a relative phrase, I opted to save the $5 and stick with the fan room for the first night. I figured I had been living it up in AC for the

*Life along the
Mekong Delta.*

previous week at my buddy's place in Saigon. Surely I could handle a couple of nights without the luxury of a chilled room. Plus, it would be a chance to go native in some small sense, try to feel what the locals feel, experience what they experience. I realize that's a bit laughable considering I would have a large room and double bed to myself with running water and a private bathroom. But it was at least a small effort.

The one thing I did not consider, but will forever appreciate, is that air conditioning doesn't provide the guest with just a refrigerated environment. Another benefit, and arguably more important in this region of the world, is that air conditioning seals off the occupant from the outside world. An air-conditioned room is insulated (I would now say *protected*) from the great outdoors by design. The seal keeps cool air in, and by default, hot air and everything else *out*.

After our motorized Vietnamese johnboat pulled up to a waterside restaurant, we disembarked. I crossed the street to our hotel, checked in at the front desk, and walked to my abode. "Nice place," I thought, as I made my way along the canal-lined pathways. The hotel was about 10 miles outside Can Tho and appeared to be geared toward affluent Vietnamese. I say this because of the resort-like grounds. There was a "get-away-from-it all-for-the-weekend" kind of feel.

I quickly found my bungalow and climbed the steps. The neat bungalows looked like bamboo cabins with thatched roofs on stilts. (Handy when the nearby Mekong floods. Two months prior to my visit, the river rose to its highest level in more than a half-century. The ground was still wet everywhere.) I dumped my bag in the room and explored the hotel grounds to find rows of cabins and several artificial islands created by the network of canals, further adding to the "R&R" feel.

The tour group met for dinner that night. Our guide kept pushing the "snake wine" (spelled "snack wine" on the menu). Snake wine is wine in a large glass jug with a big snake coiled up inside. I can't determine if it's simply a tourist gimmick or if the locals actually drink or even like the stuff. I think it's just rice wine with maybe a little coloring, but I suppose it would take a chemist and some litmus paper to find out for sure. Whatever it is, the tour guide brought out a plastic water bottle full of the brew and started passing around shot glasses. Then he began singing praises for the snake wine.

"For strength," he said. "Snake wine will make you smart. If you are lonely man, beautiful girl fall in love with you. I drink snake wine every night."

That was ridiculous, of course, but I swear he said it all with a straight face. It reminds me of the Irish and their love of Guinness (mine too).

I passed on the "snack wine", but a couple of the other tourists tempted fate and had a little of the nectar. The British guy I had befriended earlier said it was pretty good, but I still wasn't sold. If I had known what the rest of the night would hold in store, however, I probably would've had a shot.

After dinner I retired to my quarters instead of staying up and playing pool. I wanted to get a good night's sleep. Tomorrow would be another long day, and I would need my energy. I remember walking into the room, looking at where the wall met the roof, and thinking, "Hey, there's a gap there. Anything can just climb right in."

Not ten minutes later, I heard loud banging and fluttering from behind the bathroom at the back of the cabin. Part of the wall was made of sheet metal, which really caused a racket.

"What the . . .?" I wondered, alarmed.

After the initial surprise wore off, I figured it must just be a bat.

"Good. Get him out of here before I settle in to sleep."

A few minutes went by, and I heard it again.

A little bit upset, I then thought, "What in the world is that?"

Wanting to flush whatever it was out of the house, I bolted for the bathroom and flung open the door only to catch a glimpse of fur streaking through the gap between the roof and the wall.

"That ain't no bat."

I found my flashlight and boldly walked outside to confront my enemy in the dark. I figured it was better to have it out right then and there instead of wondering when I would be attacked during the night.

Picture the scene: I'm in the middle of the Mekong Delta. The air is thick with humidity and the ground soaked from rain and flooding. The canals that criss-cross the complex are thick with mud, carp, and who knows what else. And the vegetation is thick enough to restrict your view to less than 10 feet in any direction.

I walked around the back of the cabin and shined my light on the corner near the bathroom. Sufficiently flushed, a furry creature scurried away from the building and through the tree branches in my direction. Why toward me? Aren't wild animals supposed to be *afraid* of humans?

I followed the movement through the leaves, still not able to get sight of it. Suddenly it stopped, directly in front of me, not five feet from my head. The beam of my flashlight found its mark. There, in all his glory, sat a big fat brown rat with a glistening white belly.

"Just what I was afraid of."

When I hear the word rat, a couple of things come to mind. Let's play word association:

Rodent = black plague
Rodent fur and saliva = conduit for disease
Rat = dirty, evil harbinger of death

I panned down to confirm it wasn't just an overgrown mouse. There was no mistaking that distinctive rat-like tail. He was a big one too, beautiful specimen actually, healthy.

We sat there for a moment in a stare-down, round eye to beady eye. Then, with no provocation, he squealed at me. LOUDLY.

"The nerve!"

I wasn't going to take any crap from a Mekong rat and looked around for something to throw at him. I figured if I could let him know who was boss, he'd leave me alone and I could rest in peace. I searched around for a rock or other hard object but could find only an empty pack of Marlboro Red cigarettes.

I crumpled up the cowboy killers and winged it at the rat for an indirect hit through the leaves.

I grew up playing baseball. I started T-ball when I was 5 years old, and my favorite position was pitcher. So when I throw a strike, I'm pretty darn happy.

"That ought to do it," I thought, pleased with my aim and with a hint of hostility.

Yeah, that did it all right, so well that he went running up the tree, crossed above my head, and dropped easily on the roof of my bungalow.

"Expletive!"

Then I didn't know *what* to do. He obviously had the upper hand. I could see that this was his turf and I was the invader. I trudged inside my room, looked up at the wall, and saw several lizards dart for the gap.

"Oh well," I sighed. "Looks like it's me and the boys, hanging out in bungalow No. 5."

I made a quick decision (although one that took a little getting used to). I decided that all of these guys were going to be my friends. The geckos never really bothered me because I know they eat the bugs (nice work, guys). And since there was nothing I could do about the rat, I resolved to just deal with it.

So I hopped in bed, dropped the mosquito net around me (which I admit was a security blanket), and lay on my back to do some reading. About 20 minutes went by undisturbed. I was just getting comfortable with my resolution and proud of my ability to cope.

Then I heard some rustling. I looked up past my book and

noticed the large gap where the roof met at a V. Skillfully zigzagging his way along the central beam was my friend the rat. My skin crawled.

"I wonder if he's gonna drop down on me?"

On his second pass about five minutes later, I was emotionally prepared. Instead of worrying about whether he would get me or wondering if he would crawl up under the mosquito netting as I slept, I started to appreciate his dexterity and the fact that I was a visitor in his home. Heck, this is how many of the locals live all of their lives. I should be able to hack it for one night. I don't know how I did it, but I wound up getting a good night's sleep. I didn't wake up once.

But I'll tell you what: I kept one eye peeled on that gap in the bathroom by the sink as I brushed my teeth the next morning.

And I spent the extra two bucks on an air-conditioned room the following night.

12

Basking in Smiles as "Chief" Shepherds Us to the Cambodian Border

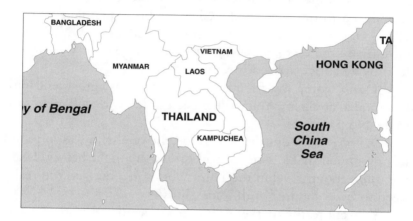

Occasionally, I have a day that is exceptionally rich. The day I crossed the border of Cambodia was one. Here's what happened.

After spending the night in the Vietnamese border town of Chau Doc, I woke up prepared for a long day of boat rides and border guards. I would cross into Cambodia sometime in the afternoon. The day started with a boat trip to a tribal village (the Cham people) and then a stop at a floating fish farm. The farm was a floating house with a net underneath that hemmed in well-fed fish. We watched a morning feeding and headed back to the hotel to pack up and check out.

Out of nine people on our three-day tour of the Mekong Delta, seven would continue from Chau Doc to Phnom Penh. Let me describe the group:

There were four Israelis, Ronen (male) and Sagit (female) were a couple, about 22 years old, and Adi and Nama (both female, about 22), who began traveling together a month earlier when they met in Thailand. There were also two Brits, Nick and his wife, in their mid–30s, I estimate. They were from Leeds, England, and upset because I didn't know they had a "football" team. "Have we got a *team?!?*" he replied in flabbergasted fashion.

And I (31) was the sole American.

We sat in the open-air lobby of our hotel and were officially introduced to our new guide, Chang, who would take us from Chau Doc to the Cambodian border and assist with border crossing on the Vietnamese side. It wasn't quite clear who would help us when we arrived in Cambodia.

"Don't worry, my friend. My company has agreement with Cambodia company. You will meet guide who will help you there. No problems."

That was from our original guide, the one who was so proud of how much snake wine he had drunk the night before. That's the thing about travel in the Third World on a budget: You really need to have comfort with uncertainty.

We went to the market to buy fruit, bread and water for our trip. There was no telling when we would have the chance to eat during the day. I bought an egg sandwich (scrambled eggs stuffed inside a baguette does the trick) and a bottle of water.

Chang led us to the port area of Chau Doc, and we boarded the first of what was to be several boats that day. It was a long, narrow vessel with the characteristic extended propeller shaft jutting from the stern. I have read these are called "longtails" in Thailand, but I'm not sure what the locals call them here. It was long, skinny (we had to sit single file), and low to the water and went only 15 miles per hour at full speed. We tended to cruise at about 10 mph. That speed was pleasant at first, but painful after the novelty wore off.

By happenstance, I wound up sitting in the front of the boat. I had been testing my limited Vietnamese with the locals and

*Me and "Chief" enroute
the Cambodian border.*

trying to say, "What a beautiful baby!" while everyone else boarded ahead of me. I got on last, placing me next to our guide, Chang.

Chang was 50 years old, but like most Vietnamese, he looked 10 years younger. He had catlike eyes and dark skin with an ever-present smile. His personality was earnest and comfortable; he was eager to please. I felt fortunate to be sitting next to him. Though his name was Chang, he quickly informed me I could call him "Chief." He seemed to like that, so I called him Chief for the rest of the trip.

We putted along at 10 miles per hour for quite some time, giving me the opportunity to chat with Chief. I noticed a deep scar on the underside of his left forearm and wondered aloud how he got it.

"From the war," he said. "I fought with the South. This happened near Cai Be" (a town in the Delta, not far from Saigon).

"Oh really?" I responded.

"Yes. I remember many Americans. I remember how the black man shook hands. Like this " he said, showing me.

We slapped our hands back and forth and clasped palms in a soul brother kind of way. "That is so '60s," I thought.

I also noticed a couple of tattoos on his arms. He couldn't remember how he got those. Said he got drunk one night and woke up with them the next morning.

Chief was learning English at a rapid pace. He had begun lessons only one month earlier and could already carry on a limited conversation. Earlier that morning, I had given him my *Lonely Planet*–(Vietnam) book I thought he might appreciate the chance to read about his country and practice reading English. I also thought it was a good opportunity to expose him to the history of his country from a source other than the Vietnamese government. (Albeit the history written in the *Lonely Planet* was colored by the writer's assumptions and opinions, which I took issue with in several instances).

As we motored along and conversed, I made use of my Vietnamese phrasebook. Knowing I would have limited use for it in Cambodia, I decided to give the book to Chief. His expressions of gratitude were effusive. The books I gave him were worth about $25 purchased legally. Even on the black market, photocopied versions would cost about $7. But that was a small fortune for Chief.

In another sense, the gift is hard to measure. Chief was better at writing words than speaking them. Here's what he wrote in my notebook (verbatim):

> YES NICE TO MEET YOU
> I HOPE THAT ONOTHER DAY WE WILL SEE,
> VIETNAM AGAIN.
> ALL THE BEST TO YOU.
> WHEN RETURN HOME GIVE MY REGARDS
> TO YOUR FAMILY.
> ALWAYS DON'T FORGET YOU.
> MY FRIEND COME FROM AMERICA.
> ALLRIGHT HAND IN HAND MAKE FRIEND
> TOGETHE. CHIEF.
> MISS A LOT
>
> Signed "Chief"
> CHAU DOCTOWN

Touching.

ANGIANG PROVINCE

As we got close to the border, Chief told us that we had to put our cameras away: "Border security."

The canal in this part of the river was about 100 feet wide. On either side were elevated dikes, 50 feet wide, that supported houses, trees, people and various animals. Occasionally, we saw buffalo along the edges of the riverbank cooling themselves in muddy water up to their backs. Large bamboo structures with nets for fishing extended from the banks and hung over the river in various places.

Chief told us that this particular border crossing had been officially open to foreigners for only 20 days. I don't know if he meant only 20 days recently or 20 days ever. I think the latter is more likely because my guidebook does not mention being able to cross here. If it's not in a Lonely Planet guidebook, it probably doesn't exist. Chief knew, however, that border guards had been bribed in the past to allow foreigners to cross at this location.

In any event, the people in this region are far less familiar with foreign faces than in other parts of the Delta. That means more stares, more smiles, and more shouts from children. Everywhere we went the children would wave, yell, and run along the bank chasing our boat. It was a lot of fun.

Our first stop on the Vietnamese side was brief. Chief got out of the boat with our passports and quickly ran up to the building. We waited in the shade of our boat for about ten minutes until he returned.

"Not too bad," I thought. Little did I know that was the first of seven visits to various border stations, the longest of which would last more than two hours.

The next stop was after ten more minutes of river cruising. This one took some time. We approached the building, set amid trees and surrounded by a wall, about 50 feet away. The guards looked as if their shoes were too tight: stern faces and grimaced looks. Fortunately, we didn't have to interact with them too much. Chief handed our passports to tough guy No. 1 behind the desk. The rest of us waited outside, wondering what was taking so long.

They had our passports for at least 45 minutes. What could they possibly be doing in there?

As we waited, the children of the nearby village behaved as children will and called hello to us from beyond the wall. We waved and smiled back, responding in Vietnamese to their English. As time wore on, they gained courage and slowly worked their way closer to our position in front of the building. The most brazen of the bunch actually made it to within arm's reach. I extended a hand to shake with one of them, but she was shy and scurried away, giggling.

Suddenly Chief came up from behind and shooed them all away. We didn't know if he thought they were bothering us or if it was a "security issue" with the border guards. I made a crack about the children "catching democracy through osmosis," and it got a laugh from Nick, the Brit.

Finally we finished with the guards, only to wait beside the river for another hour. Our next stop was the actual border station on the Vietnamese side, followed by a short walk to Cambodia. We didn't know that at the time. We didn't know much at all, frankly. The whole day was a series of, "No problem, my friend. This way. Not too much longer."

I wasn't one to ask too much about what was coming up next. I figured I was in for a long day of hurry up and wait, for which the Navy had prepared me well. But a couple of the Israeli women? Forget about it. They wanted to know *everything*.

"How long will this take? Who will be our guide? Will you take us to the border? Is it OK to leave our bags here? Where can I change money? What is the rate? When will he be here? What is the rate again? I want to change money. How much longer? Why do we have to pay again for a boat? We should not have to pay."

Oy vey!

Our tour price included transportation to the Cambodian border and a walk from Vietnam's second border post (where we currently were) into Cambodia to meet the boat that would take us to a point near Phnom Penh. That was a new crossing arrangement between companies in Vietnam and Cambodia, and all of the kinks hadn't yet been worked out.

No one told us the part about walking across the border. Indeed, the people in Saigon who sell the tickets probably have no idea what happens way out here. Our guide and my friend, Chief, was willing to arrange a small boat to take us from Vietnam to our transportation in Cambodia (there was a small and required walk across the actual border). It was only 33 cents more for this service, but the offer was met with a barrage of questions and mistrust.

In their defense, I can understand the initial misgivings. Travelers are ripped off all the time, and you get fed up with it. But in this case, we weren't being ripped off. It took some time to persuade the others of that.

After settling the boat dispute, we sat in the shade of a riverside restaurant waiting to acquire some Cambodian riel (unit of currency). Several of us had extra Vietnamese dong to exchange, and doing so outside of Vietnam would be difficult.

As we waited, we entertained ourselves by yukking it up with the children. There must have been 20 of them along with several adults. Nick spent an hour counting to five and then to ten in both Vietnamese and English: Forward and backward, backward and forward, counting noses and holding up fingers, quizzing and being quizzed. It sounds as if it would get old, but I promise it never lost its appeal. The smiles and laughter of those children were priceless.

Ronen had a little magic trick that never ceased to amaze his audience of both children and adults. He would take a small handkerchief and stuff it into his clenched fist. After blowing on his hand two or three times, he would slap his palms together, raise them above his head, and exclaim, "Wah-lah!" The cloth had disappeared. Cries of wonder and excitement erupted every time.

What could have been a hot, boring afternoon turned into a memorable experience.

Eventually we boarded another wooden boat, this one deeper and more beat-up than the last, and headed for the border. After leaving our bags in the boat, which always made me feel vulnerable, we walked up the riverbank to the final checkpoint on the Vietnamese side. The stoic guard took a quick look at my passport and handed it back.

> "OK?" I asked.
> The guard (expressionless) nodded, "yes," paused, and then nodded in the direction of Cambodia.
> "Thanks for the help, pal," I thought.

The next portion of the crossing was unnerving. I cautiously stepped forward into the no man's land that separates Vietnam from Cambodia. I remembered that these countries had been fighting over this land for hundreds of years. In fact, many Khmer people refer to the Mekong Delta as Lower Cambodia. The region was part of the Cambodian empire at one time and was annexed by the Vietnamese as the price tag for help fighting against Thailand. The two countries were at peace currently, but I still felt naked as I walked unprotected for the 50 yards or so to the first Cambodian guardhouse.

To make matters worse, our group looked hesitant and awkward as we ventured forward together. In contrast, Vietnamese and Cambodians crossed unimpeded as they pushed bicycles, rode motorbikes, and carried packages. We stuck out like a sore thumb.

I didn't like the feeling. I feel more comfortable showing confidence and certainty. I had been leading the way as we approached each station and decided it was time to pick up the pace.

This is my take on crossing borders. I think it's important to be direct, honest and respectful when dealing with officials. I

answer their questions in clear English and in a friendly tone. I generally try to wear a collared shirt, but I haven't been too good about wearing long pants. I don't want any trouble with these guys and so far have not had any. On this day, I took off my hat and sunglasses (it was hot and bright) and strode right up to each station.

Upon marching up to the first Cambodian border guard, I handed over my passport.

"Where going?" he asked.
"Phnom Penh," I replied.
"What is your purpose?" he asked.
"Oh, just tourism."

He handed my passport back and waved me on. I walked 30 feet more through the dust and growing crowd of locals to the next station, customs.

The man at this station was one of the more harsh-looking fellows we had the pleasure of meeting that day. He wasn't rude or mean; he just looked as if he wasn't in the mood for any nonsense and never would be.

I was told to retrieve my bag, which had not yet disappeared from the boat. I hauled it up from the river to the tiny guardhouse and plopped it down on an inch of dirt. The shack was just big enough for three people and a bag on the floor. While a woman at the counter processed the rest of the group one by one, I labored at opening my pack and pulling out whatever the customs guy wanted to see. We went through only a few items before I was given the green light to move along.

Outside I repacked my belongings and carried the bag back down to the boat. Next I hauled the even larger and heavier bags of Adi and Nama up to the guard shack. It took a while for everyone to clear customs. During this time, I took the opportunity to stare back at the crowd that had formed. Immediately upon approaching the first border guards, I noticed how dark their skin was. Some of them were *much* darker than the Vietnamese. And now, as I looked at the locals, I could see a difference in the facial features. It's hard to describe, but there is definitely a difference.

One or two of the locals looked downright scary. I know that's an unpleasant thing to say, but my overactive imagination pictured the Khmer Rouge chasing me through the jungle with hatchets and machetes. On the other hand, these same faces changed dramatically as soon as they returned my smile. I don't think they knew quite what to make of us. We were such an oddity for them.

I asked our new Vietnamese guide (different from Chief now) how to say "hello" and "thank you" in Khmer. As I mimicked him, I could see smiles cross faces and several lips mouth the words I had just said. I started feeling a little more comfortable.

We went through two more stations before finally passing muster. The next one was a boat ride up the river for about 30 minutes of processing passports. These guys were a little friendlier, but there weren't any villagers around to rub elbows with.

The final station was a lone official sitting in the shade of the riverbank. We didn't even get out of the boat. Our Vietnamese guide came running down to the river's edge saying, "I told him you had been checked through, but he didn't believe me. Let me show him your passports."

At a previous checkpoint, we had boarded the boats that would take us upriver to Phnom Penh. I'll describe them as oversized rowboats with large outboard motors: finally, an engine that could actually propel a boat with some gusto. I estimate we cruised at 40-plus mph, which felt like upgrading from a paddleboat to the Millennium Falcon.

We were liberated from the labor of crawling along in painfully slow Vietnamese boats and dealing with border officials. To be cut loose on the river was invigorating: freedom! This was one of the best moments on my world trip.

The weather was perfect for a river cruise. We had escaped rain all day with a view of blue sky and white puffies on an empty, glass-like river. The temperature was hot at a standstill but undetectable while moving, a feeling known to boating people everywhere. You can tell that you're moving because your hair is blowing, and you can see the water race by, but you can't "feel" the air on your skin.

I had a pretty Israeli girl sitting next to me and the sun at my back. Beside us, our playmate weaved back and forth in a waterborne game of chase. For the next hour, we laughed, waved, took pictures, and felt happy to be alive in the world.

I was enjoying the moment, rocketing up the Mekong.

13

In Poor Cambodia, a Palace Rivals the Forbidden City

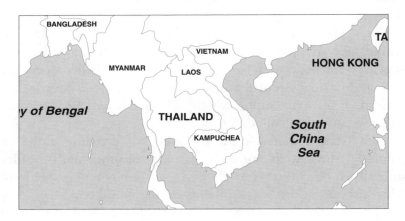

Hello from Indonesia, where I'm stationed for a couple of days in the cool mountain town of Bukittinggi, in western Sumatra.

This update covers the one week I spent in Cambodia. I arrived in Phnom Penh under the cover of night. My first impression as we drove through town was, "Hmm, looks like another dirty, trash-strewn city." Daylight did not improve the view. It wasn't awful like a few of the Chinese cities that I visited, just plain old dirty with litter cast about. Most of the roads are paved, but several are just dirt, or roads with scant signs of the asphalt that once was.

Let me backtrack for just a moment. Keep in mind as I walk through my Cambodian experience that this country only recently found itself at peace. It was just 1998 when the last

Top left: Royal Palace Complex. Phnom Penh.

Top right: Central Stupa at the Killing Fields just outside Phnom Penh. It is a solemn and chilling sight.

Bottom left: Gateway to Banteay Kdei temple. One of the many Temples of Angkor.

Bottom right: The jungle overtook Ta Prahm temple.

organized force of the Khmer Rouge was finally disbanded. Although there are still remnants of this organization in parts of the country, it is for the most part no longer a threat to national peace.

Cambodia is one of the most corrupt and poor countries in Southeast Asia. The police are rumored to extort "security fees" from cars as they travel the national highways and to resort to banditry to legitimize the need for their protection. Thousands upon thousands of landmines are buried across the country and continue to kill and maim the populace. Several local people told me to be careful where I went at night and to keep only small change on me in the event that I was robbed.

I don't mean to exaggerate my description of the security risk in Cambodia, but I think it's fair to say I had a heightened awareness during my short stay.

PHNOM PENH

I spent my first day in Cambodia exploring Phnom Penh. The two most interesting things I saw were the Royal Palace (whose grounds contain the popular Silver Pagoda) and the flight of bats exiting the roof of the National Museum at sunset.

The Royal Palace is one of the most impressive sights I have seen in Southeast Asia. I loved it. Actually, the Royal Palace is off-limits. But it's OK to tour the surrounding buildings. For me, the architecture and opulence were beyond what I had seen to this point. This might upset some Far East culture stickler somewhere, but I thought it edged out the Forbidden City in Beijing. The Forbidden City is grander, but this had greater beauty. If I had my way, I'd enlarge the Royal Palace complex and move it to Beijing so that I could live in these buildings but be in charge of more people.

This was the first time I had ever seen buildings with the distinctive curls of Cambodia and Thailand at the ends of the roof. The colors and materials used on the exterior, as well as the gold and silver and jade and bronze and whatever else that adorned the statues and baubles on the interior, were astonishing. There were intricate patterns; the buildings were exceptionally well-maintained (other than the silver floor of the Silver Pagoda needing a bit of a polish).

By the way, I was busted for taking pictures without purchasing a camera ticket. I hadn't realized how beautiful and exotic the buildings would be. (At least the security guy didn't take my camera.)

One night I went with two of the Israelis I had been traveling with to watch the "bat show." About 10 million bats live in the roof of the National Museum in downtown Phnom Penh. Each night at sunset they exit the building en masse for a night of feeding. For anyone who has seen a similar sight, maybe in Austin, Texas, you know what a spectacle it can be. Supposedly, the bats are of a rare kind that lives only in this one place. In general, bats are common throughout the region. In fact, I saw small groups of bats hanging upside down inside many of the temples of Angkor.

After the show, I navigated our trio back to the hotel on the other side of town. It was only a 25-minute walk, but turned out to be one of the only times I felt unsafe on my trip. Phnom Penh does not have streetlights in most of the city. That makes for an awfully dark walk in residential neighborhoods. Even in areas where there are hotels and other businesses, the streets are devoid of bright lights. Other than major roads, you're taking your chances on whom you'll meet or, more precisely, who will seek you out in the dark.

Scooter drivers would sidle up alongside and ask the standard, "Where you going? Motorbike? Where you from?" During daylight hours, the drivers were more likely to move along after being ignored or told, "I don't need it," in Khmer. But the cloak of darkness seemed to embolden the same guy who would have been on his way only hours earlier. Now, instead of motoring off and minding his own business, the scooter guy simply fell in line about 10 feet behind. Maybe he hoped you would change your mind, maybe he was waiting for a dark spot to make his move, or maybe he just didn't have anything better to do. I don't know. But I do know this: it made the hair stand up on the back of my neck. And I didn't like it.

Phnom Penh was the first city where I saw children walking around naked. Often, I saw kids playing in groups on the side of the street. Usually most of them would be dressed, but it was not uncommon to see a couple of them without a stitch of clothing. I don't know where the adult supervision was, if any. I suppose an adult could've been nearby, as when a child beggar scurries back to a parent waiting in the wings. Who knows?

One evening I sat checking e-mail while a vicious thunderstorm raged outside. A boy of about 10 came running by, naked and screaming with laughter as he played in the rain. He kept zipping back and forth, laughing and yelling. I was in downtown Phnom Penh, not in the suburbs, not in the country, and certainly not in Kansas anymore.

While visiting one of the large Wats (Buddhist temples), I happened to meet a few of the young monks-in-training. Many Cambodian males join a Wat for a few years and then return to a secular life. One of the most conspicuous benefits of such a system is education.

According to "Chone," who is 21 years old and speaks excellent English, the degree he will receive from his temple is more esteemed than that of the public education system. He listens to Voice of America and a BBC program, both of which are broadcast only once per week, to improve his English. Chone flunked out of public high school, but is doing well studying under the guidance of senior monks. Chone also told me that in the western part of Cambodia the Khmer Rouge is still strong. It is dangerous for him to visit there. If questioned by a party member, he would have to feign ignorance and an apolitical belief system in order to avoid harm. "But it's safe for tourist," he said.

THE KILLING FIELDS

The most penetrating memorial I have seen since Camp Dachau in Germany was the Killing Fields, 10 miles south of Phnom Penh. The area that makes up the Killing Fields isn't large, maybe an acre or a football field. The mass burial site is probably 75 yards long and 20 yards wide. That is a long strip of awful history.

To give you an idea of what happened here, I'll cover the history briefly. During three years in the early '70s, the Khmer Rouge, led by Pol Pot, took over Cambodia in a reign of terror with few equals. No one knows how many Cambodians were killed as "enemies of the revolution" during this time, but the most conservative estimate is 1 million. The upper estimates are more than 3 million. The Killing Fields was a place to bury bodies in the Phnom Penh area. About 18,000 remains were found there.

The first thing you see when approaching the Killing Fields is a 75-foot high stupa, a memorial to the people who were buried here. The stupa looks like a tall, slender building with the characteristic curls rising from the ends of the roof. As you walk a little closer, you realize objects are visible through the glass, stacked all the way to the top. Upon slightly closer examination, it is possible to see what those objects are: human skulls. Thousands of them.

The sight is chilling.

I stood for a moment in silence, allowing my eyes and mind to soak it in. I was surprised that you can enter the stupa and view the bones without a barrier. After leaving the stupa, it is only a short walk to the mass graves. I walked among the gravesites, which look like five-foot-deep craters. There are well over one hundred of them. A few have signs that describe the victims found there:

"Site of 100 bodies, each found missing their head."
"Site of 50 bodies, each found blindfolded and hands tied behind their backs."
"Site of 150 bodies, all female."

After the Killing Fields, I toured Tuol Sleng Museum, otherwise known as S-21 prison. S-21 was one of the area prisons where the Khmer Rouge interrogated and tortured. After having been tortured to death here or dying in their cell, prisoners were transported to the Killing Fields for burial. Some were taken to the Killing Fields alive then and murdered.

The prison was a converted high school. Very little has changed in the 25-plus years since it ceased operation. The bottom floor served as the interrogation chambers. On the wall of each chamber are pictures of the last victim to die and then be found there by the Vietnamese who liberated Phnom Penh in 1975. The photos are absolutely gruesome.

I took the Killing Fields and S-21 prison as a reminder that the world holds some unbelievably horrible people who do not share my own sense of right and wrong. I remember walking away and thinking, "God, I hope that doesn't happen here again." But now I wonder, "What will it take to help prevent that from happening? Where will this happen next? It happened recently in Kosovo." Seeing the atrocities of mankind firsthand makes the strongest impression. It also provides mental ammunition against the argument that there's no need, or we just plain shouldn't worry about evil elsewhere in the world. At least, that's what it does for me.

SIEM REAP

Enough of the soapbox. The next adventure was Siem Reap, home to the temples of Angkor. I was transported by high-speed ferry up the Tonle Sap River and over Tonle Sap Lake. It took about four hours and was far preferable to the grueling bus ride that I could have taken. Upon arrival at the dock, three men from a hotel who would drive us to town on scooters met my traveling partners and me. We passed more naked children on the five-mile journey. They're everywhere!

Before describing the temples of Angkor, I'll just mention the Hanukkah ceremony I was allowed to participate in. For about 10 days or so, I had been traveling with four Israelis. They were all concerned with events back in their home country and were interesting to talk to about life in Israel. Since it was December, Christmas decorations were everywhere. Once two women dressed in Santa costumes wished us a Merry Christmas as they placed advertising on our restaurant table. The two Israeli girls murmured, "We're Jewish," under their breath. I suppose it was getting to them.

On Dec. 29, the first night of Hanukkah began at sundown. For a few days, my friends had been making a fuss over lighting candles on the Menorah. I shared their enthusiasm, for I respect anyone who is dedicated to his faith. As we sat at the hotel restaurant, three other Israelis from a nearby hotel joined us for the ceremony. A candle was placed in a water bottle, and we all gathered 'round. One of the guys read from a book of religious writing in Hebrew. He wore a yarmulke, and the rest of us placed napkins on our heads. The candle was lit, and a song was sung. This, too, was in Hebrew. I was happy to be included in their celebration and didn't feel it compromised my own beliefs in the least.

THE TEMPLES OF ANGKOR

These temples include scores of religious and royal structures spread across a wide region and built over thousands of years. The jewel of these sites is Angkor Wat. I viewed Angkor Wat at sunrise, followed by full day of temple touring, an exhausting enterprise. Briefly, here are the highlights:

Approaching Angkor Wat is like walking straight into the pages of National Geographic. It is everything the photographs would lead you to believe. The temple lives up to its billing. First you cross a giant causeway above an enormous moat (think small lake). Inside the first gate, you continue on the elevated walkway for at least 100 yards to the temple complex. The characteristic five domes rise up to greet you in majestic fashion. It's really a sight.

One of the most interesting things was the bas-reliefs that circumscribe the exterior wall of the temple. These are some of the most famous carvings in the world. I was eager to follow along with my guidebook's description of each relief. Upon viewing the first of several, my jaw dropped as I stared in surprise: "Man, that looks familiar!"

I'm nearly certain that part of the relief on the southwest face of Angkor Wat has been hanging on the wall of my home in Atlanta for my entire life. Not the actual bas-relief, of course, but a temple rubbing from this portion. What's more, there is another relief on the south side of the temple that stirred some memory files in the back of my mind. I took pictures for later confirmation.

The most notable thing about Ta Prohm is the way the jungle has overtaken this temple. The tree roots have engulfed 10-foot walls, making an exotic scene. It's amazing what the jungle can do.

Bayon is known for the staring faces of its bodhisattvas. No matter where you walk, it seems there are at least four faces smiling down upon you. People have described them as enigmatic or inscrutable smiles. I can't think of an original way to put it. That's how they look.

Finally, the town of Siem Reap is a nice little place, a dusty, quiet little town with a charm of its own. The hawkers seemed to take "No" pretty well and didn't pressure too much. It wasn't spotless, but I've seen dirtier towns. It wasn't a bad place as a base for visits to one of the most impressive archeological sites in the world.

A few observations:

- The owner of the hotel where I stayed in Siem Reap was afraid to go to Thailand. He said it was dangerous for him there. "The police might hurt me." He was a well-educated guy with a rational aura about him and didn't seem to be one to cry wolf. Later I met some Thais who fit the same mold. They told me it was not safe for them to visit Cambodia. "It's too dangerous for us." What a shame it is that good people in countries right next to each other can't visit and share because a minority of the population makes it unsafe. I try to imagine what it would be like if I thought it would be too dangerous to take a trip to Mexico or Canada, or, for that matter, to visit California from Arizona or Florida from Georgia.

- The Khmers have a distinctive look, their skin color noticeably darker than the Vietnamese's.

- Cambodia is a visibly poor country. Road maintenance is almost nonexistent. I can only imagine that other public works projects get short shrift as well. But for some reason, the cost for a traveler is higher than in Vietnam. The hotels, water, food, and Internet access, for instance, are all more expensive.

- The number of amputees I saw increased dramatically as compared to the rest of Asia. I had seen a few begging in other Asian countries, but not in nearly the numbers as in Cambodia. It seemed that every tourist site had its cadre of amputees. I suppose that is testimony to Cambodia's wars and the prevalence of landmines.

- Although hotels are still the standard for budget traveler accommodation, as opposed to dorm rooms, hot water is definitely not. It was cold showers for the week.

14

Cambodia's National Highway 6: Oh, the Horror

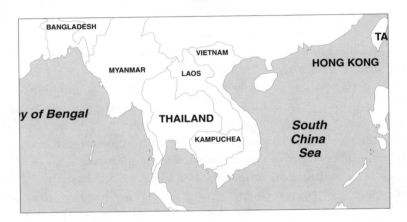

Cambodia has a limited national highway system that stretches through its jungles to connect the major cities and border towns. There are six or seven of them, simplistically numbered, "National Highway 5" or "National Highway 6," for example. I don't know when they were built. But I can make a good guess at how often they've been maintained: never.

This is an account of my overland journey from Siem Reap to the border town of Poipet as I made my way west to Thailand. They call the road I took National Highway 6. I can think of several more names for it.

I had a choice: Fly, or take the truck from Siem Reap to Bangkok. I didn't mull this for very long. A flight from Siem Reap, Cambodia, to Bangkok, Thailand, easily cost more than $100. The overland route via truck and van was only $14, $16 for

The truck we crammed 20 people into for our 7-hour exodus from Cambodia.

a seat inside.

"Inside?" you ask. Yes. The trucks heading for the border pack people onboard wherever they can fit them. Luggage and humans are piled in the truck bed, subject to the dust and sun (and falling off, but who worries about that?).

I had read and heard horror stories about the highways in Cambodia. For example, my guidebook had a special section that described the awful condition of the roads. The writer seemed to delight in the debate over which stretch of road was Cambodia's worst. It appears there is some disagreement among seasoned travelers.

My other source of information was an Australian man I had met at the bar of a restaurant in Hoi An, Vietnam, two weeks earlier. At some point the conversation turned to his trip from Thailand east to Siem Reap.

> "How are those roads?" I asked. "I've read some pretty bad stuff about their condition."
> "If you can find another way to Thailand, take it," the

Aussie said.

"Why?" I asked. "Is it really that bad?"

"I've still got boils on my arse from that bloody road!"

OK. I guess there's some pain involved. But how bad can it really be? A lot of other people do it. Heck, the drivers of the trucks make the journey for a *living*. The two Israeli women I've been traveling with think they can hack it; certainly I can match their energy and tolerance for pain. And the cost savings, given my budget, is significant (even if I did pay the extra two bucks for an inside seat). "Aw, to hell with it," I thought, "I'm takin' the truck."

How could I have known the extent of the pain I would endure?

The trip started at 7:30 a.m. in front of our hotel. The Israeli women didn't have an alarm clock and had relied on the hotel staff to awake them on time, unsuccessfully. One of the two has a penchant for letting people know when she's not happy. Great. We have a 10-hour trip, and Ms. Grumpy has already made an appearance.

We walked outside to greet our chariot (which had been waiting a half-hour because Ms. Grumpy needed 30 minutes for breakfast). I wasn't thrilled with the small Toyota pick-up truck with extended cab. The truck bed was piled full of luggage, about five Japanese travelers, and three Cambodians. I peeked inside the cab. "Man, there's really not too much room in here," I thought.

At times like these, I'm happy to be skinny.

At times like these, I'm not so happy to have long legs.

I crawled inside and braced myself for pain. I shared a hump seat in the back with a Japanese girl: One cheek on, one cheek off. To my left was a French guy, and on the far right of the backseat was one of the Israelis. The other had her own hump seat up front with a Swiss guy on the left and the Cambodian driver on the right. The cab body count was seven. Cozy.

Unbeknownst to us, the plan was to stop for lunch in Sisophon and twice for water and bathroom breaks. We had no idea when we would stop and only a rough idea of how long the trip would take. Six hours to the border was the estimate.

As we drove out of town, the truck occasionally stopped to pick up more passengers. I couldn't believe it. They must've crammed three or four more people in the back. So the passenger count was seven in the cab and 10 to 13 in the back. There were 20 souls on board, plus luggage. Safety first, right?

The trip didn't start out so badly. Although we were without a radio, we had air conditioning inside the cabin that, amazingly enough, worked pretty well. I was squeezed, but felt OK and kept reminding myself of the savings of the surface route. Everyone in the truck was making small jokes and chuckling about our cramped quarters. But that didn't last long. It was only a matter of time before joviality gave way to clenched silence.

The road condition was poor in the early going, to be sure. But it was a mere shadow of the violent thrashing that we would take after about an hour of travel. It was at that point that my joints started to ache and my feet went to sleep. We couldn't sit up straight in the back of the cab because it wasn't wide enough for our shoulders. So we took turns leaning forward and back. I had lost some weight on the trip and wasn't a really thick guy to begin with. So I didn't have much padding on my backside. What's left was thoroughly compressed by the repeated bouncing. That allowed me the good fortune of feeling even more of the road than I would have otherwise.

Somewhere outside Siem Reap, the road began to steadily deteriorate. I don't think mere words will do justice to how the highway looked and felt.

National Highway 6 is a variegated instrument of torture. Some stretches are former asphalt, peppered with potholes and other large divots. Other parts are made of dirt and susceptible to the wind and rain that create large holes to bend an axle or pop a tire. Portions are covered with crater-sized depressions that looked as if a string of bombs had been dropped neatly in a row. Those are actually favorable because the entire truck can smoothly descend into the hole and back out again. Finally, there are the rare stretches of actual pavement to tease you with suggestions of smooth sailing.

How did National Highway 6 feel? Imagine seven hours of the most bone-jarring, tooth-rattling, hemorrhoid-inducing travel possible. I wondered if I would chip a tooth or knock a filling loose. Picture hours of jolting and pounding combined with the centrifugal force of our driver swerving erratically in his poor attempt to miss the worst holes. I didn't think he was very good, frankly. I kept thinking, "This guy must be new. Come on, rookie, get your head in the game! You're killin' me!"

My back and butt hurt so badly after the first two hours that I actually tried to escape my body by thinking pleasant thoughts. It was truly a test of pain tolerance and endurance. It was also a great example of how highways can deteriorate when left to the elements and continued use without maintenance.

One of the scariest parts was the bridge crossings. Fortunately, these were infrequent, but each one made me think, "Man, I don't want it all to end here."

Now and then the highway would cross a small stream or wetlands area. The bridges were in the same condition as the roads, pathetic. Some were made only of wood, while others had remnants of steel. All of them had gaping holes. Usually, two planks of wood were placed across the span for the wheels of the truck to carefully tread.

"I hope Rookie's got good aim," I thought

I looked out the side of the truck to see the water below through the holes of the bridge. "There's no way I'll make it out of the cabin if this baby flips," I thought. More probable was to become stuck on the bridge and block *all traffic* moving east and west across Cambodia. That would really make some Khmers happy. Who knew how long it would take to dislodge the vehicle from a precarious position on one of these bridges? And the weather wasn't nice and cool. And remember the tales of banditry and the Khmer Rouge.

My dad said jokingly, "At least you weren't held up or otherwise harmed by the Khmer Rouge."

My retort: "That's the only way it could've gotten worse."

After seven hours of torture and a fly-covered lunch in Sisophon, we finally reached the border town of Poipet. I was sweaty, dusty, and in pain and could no longer feel my butt. As if to play a cruel joke, a road crew was making repairs on the final 50 yards of the highway.

Talk about salt in the wounds.

Disgusted, I nodded toward the crew and deadpanned, "Road construction."

The French guy next to me was the only one to chuckle. I thought it was a particularly wry observation that somehow eased my pain.

So how would I summarize my travel experience between Siem Reap and Poipet? I'll refresh your memory with what the Aussie said to me in Vietnam:

"I've still got boils on my arse from that bloody road!"

I can say it even more succinctly. National Highway 6, Cambodia:

Ouch!

15

Exploring Khao San Road, Mecca for Backpackers in Asia

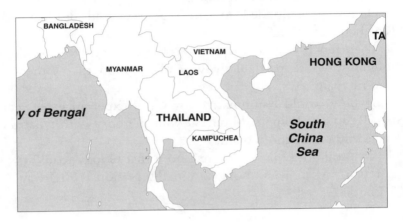

After leaving Cambodia, I spent four days in Thailand before jetting down to Indonesia. My plan was to work my way north, up the Malay Peninsula, as opposed to down. Considering my itinerary, either direction of travel would involve a plane flight at some point. Because of timing considerations, my choice allowed me to meet up with some friends in Malaysia over the Chinese New Year.

BANGKOK

My first stop in Thailand was Khao San Road, Bangkok. Khao San Road is, of course, just that, a road. But even more, it's an area of the city that is well-known on the travelers' circuit through Southeast Asia. In fact, Khao San Road is best described as the Mecca of haunts for backpackers from all over Asia, even the world.

Top:
Temple embellishment on
Wat Pho. Bangkok.

Center:
Monsters holding up Wat
Arun. Bangkok.

Bottom:
A typical temple roof.
Nearby Wat Arun.
Bangkok.

Hordes of travelers, cheap hotels, open-air restaurants, and hawkers of every sort line the streets of this neighborhood. The entire place is devoted to the budget traveler. Tickets, tours and visa arrangements are easily made. Internet cafes and regular cafes are abundant. Khao San Road is at the extreme end of easy on the easy-to-hard scale for a traveler. And speaking of travelers, the place is packed. People of all shapes and sizes stroll along the boulevard, hopping in and out of shops and food stalls and haggling with vendors and hotel staff.

I found the scene a little much: A little too young, a little too noisy, a little too crowded, a little too backpackerish. But that's just me.

I arrived on Christmas Eve to find decorations everywhere. Music from a Christmas Eve concert filled the air as I walked about and looked for a place to eat. Of course, I had to have some Thai food, right? I found a nice little place and tried the shrimp with red curry. I was delighted with the flavor, but disappointed with the portion. Then I filled up with Swensen's ice cream next door.

I had made contact with Amporn Youngmod, a SERVAS member who lives in Rayong, about 50 miles southeast of Bangkok. She told me this would be a good time to visit, before New Year's, when she would be with family in Bangkok. So I decided to head down and stay for a few days.

RAYONG

Amporn Youngmod is 52 years old and married with grown children and has worked more than 30 years for the Thai equivalent of the U.S. Department of Agriculture. She is the senior administrator at the Rayong Field Crops Research Center in charge of payroll, personnel issues, and other administrative tasks. The primary crops studied at the facility are sugarcane and cassava. The land area there is large enough to support several fields and research buildings. Examples of their studies include the effect of fertilizer, planting seasons and harvest times on crop yields and nutrition content. The scientists also study production methods and additional uses for the plants.

What the heck is cassava? It's best known in the West as the primary ingredient in tapioca. Cassava is a tuber grown primarily in Africa and South America. Although a few varieties are naturally edible, most are inedible in their raw form and must be processed to make flour that is safe for consumption. Cassava is resistant to both pests and harsh environments. Some scientists estimate that this plant sustains 500 million people around the world. And to think that I had never even heard of it.

My first full day in Rayong was so filled with stories to tell that I will have to write another anecdote to capture it all. So I'll skip it and tell you about the next couple of days. Amporn introduced me to her niece, Bo, and an entomologist at the center, Prapit. Bo is approximately 13, and Prapit I estimate to be in her mid-30s.

Prapit is performing an interesting study. She wants to determine if a certain species of spider can be used to eat other spiders to control the damage they do to cassava leaves. Isn't nature fascinating?

Our foursome spent one afternoon touring along the Gulf of Thailand in this region. A summary:

Beach on Navy Base — No one comes to this beach because they think the Navy will be too strict. Amporn says it's just like any other beach, only less crowded because of that erroneous assumption. The beach had a private feeling that reminded me of my Navy flight-school days living on Perdido Key, Fla., near Pensacola. We found a table and lounge chairs underneath pine trees on the beach to relax and enjoy the view of the crystal blue Thai water.

Temple of Saints Museum —There is a fantastic array of artistic styles from all of Asia on display. Most of the statues and paintings were, of course, religiously oriented, but others were historic or literary. Some were originals, such as the terra cotta warriors from Xi'an, China. Examples of waterside amphitheaters and temples from several countries of Asia were displayed on the enormous grounds outside. If you get to Bangkok, or more conveniently, Pattaya (a popular beach resort nearby), I highly recommend a day trip.

At dinner that night, I found out how hot the Thai people like their food. Understand that I'm a hot-sauce nut. At the grocery store, I sometimes just stand and stare at all of the bottles in the condiment aisle. So many colors, so many flavors, so tempting. I wonder how each one would taste and always check to see where they're made. I rarely leave the aisle empty-handed. I go home and spice up whatever it is that I'm cooking with my new purchase. I remember an advertisement in which Dan Akroyd was asked what he likes to put Tabasco hot sauce on. His reply: "Anything edible by humans." Hear, hear!

I like it hot, but I don't hold a candle to Ms. Prapit. I watched in amazement as she literally peppered her food with hot peppers. I tried a few, and they were good, but I just couldn't handle the quantity that she slurped down with a smile. Amporn had her share, too. Impressive.

BANGKOK (revisited)

I returned to Bangkok for a day to catch a flight west to Nepal. While there I saw two things of note:

Jim Thompson house -- Jim Thompson was an American member of the OSS (precursor to the CIA) who was stationed in Thailand during World War II. He stayed after the war and eventually rekindled the Thai silk industry, which had sunk into obscurity. Thompson was beloved by the Thais for reviving a cultural art that has become a point of pride for this country. Consider the Thai Airways slogan: Smooth as Silk.

His house is now a museum. It's a small place made entirely of teakwood in the style of traditional Thai homes. The inside is filled with priceless artifacts such as statues, paintings, and among other things, a Buddha head (so that's where they go!). The tragedy of the Jim Thompson story is that he disappeared on a vacation to Cameron Highlands, Malaysia, when he was about 60 years old. He was never found, and no one knows what happened.

Movie at the mall -- That doesn't have an exotic ring to it, but

I must tell America about how organized my "movie theater at the mall" experience was. I needed to buy a new camera (the humidity of Southeast Asia did in my digital camera), so I set aside a few hours at the mall to pick one up. After making the purchase, I realized the day was almost over and all I had to look forward to was a night's sleep in my fleabag hotel.

I walked by the movie-theater section on the sixth floor just to take a peek at what was playing. I couldn't find a list above the ticket counter or on the wall nearby. Frustrated, I approached the ticket-taker guy. He was no help -- too little English for us to understand each other. But another Thai walked up and offered to help. He recommended a new Thai movie about a village in western Thailand that held off the Burmese army in 1765 as it made its run on the ancient capital of Ayuthaya (30 miles north of Bangkok). The title was "Bang Ra Jan," the name of the village.

The advertisement showed an angry crowd of villagers in loincloths wielding hatchets and spears. They practically leapt out of the poster and into the lobby. Leading the way was a screaming warrior atop a huge water buffalo.

"Looks gory," I said.
"Just came out today," he said. "It's a big event. I recommend it."
"Does it have English subtitles?" I asked.
"Yes."

I was sold.

I crossed to the ticket counter, where there was no line. The woman behind the glass smiled politely and asked, "Which movie, sir?"
"Bang Ra Jan," I said.
"Where would you like to sit?" she asked.
"Excuse me?" I said.
"Where would you like to sit, sir?" (She showed me her computer screen with a diagram of the theater and boxes

around the available seats.)

"How about there?" I said.

The next thing I knew I held a reserved seat to a movie that would start in two hours. What a breeze.

I returned to the theater about 15 minutes before showtime. I was bored with the mall and looking for a cool place to relax. Aware of several moviegoers sitting on benches, I searched for my theater, found the big red door and marched up to give it a tug. It was locked.

It turns out that the theater doesn't open the doors until the time printed on your ticket (what I thought was showtime). After the doors open, it's about a 10-minute wait until the lights go down and the roll'em starts. Because you have a reserved seat, there's no mad rush to the door. No one tries to show up early to claim a good seat. All the fuss is obviated at the ticket counter when you handpick where you want to sit. In the meantime, when you arrive, you conveniently wait in a comfortable lounge known as the concession area.

That has to increase sales. Clever.

Before the previews, an austere voice on the public-address system said, "Please stand and show your respect to His Majesty, the King of Thailand."

Everyone stood as if the national anthem would be played. Instead, a two-minute feel-good flick about the king came on. No words, just music and photographs of the king in various settings. The Thais take their royal family seriously. The king's picture is everywhere. Billboards, posters, banners on the outside of office buildings, calendars inside the office buildings. So it was no surprise that homage was paid at this public gathering.

A couple of general observations:

- The Thai people go by their first name and then last name. This is the reverse of everywhere else I've been in Asia.
- I didn't see many chopsticks in Thailand. Amporn said when

noodles are served, chopsticks are used, but not for much else.

- Bangkok is the first place in Asia where I've noticed homosexuals. I wouldn't mention that if it weren't so apparent. They were conspicuous in the Khao San Road area.

- Thai hawkers are much more polite and back off more quickly than their counterparts in China, Vietnam and Cambodia.

- Thailand, like Cambodia, does not offer hot water for the showers in budget hotels.

Occasionally as I travel, I see something that reminds me of how different things are from America. A drive in Rayong illustrated this tendency.

As we drove along a major thoroughfare, I noticed an elephant walking by with a rider on his neck.

"Hmm," I thought. "Now there's something you don't see every day."

Not five minutes later, we passed a man standing on the side of the road with his fly undone, urinating in the wind. There was no attempt at discretion, no shame. And no one in the car seemed to notice.

All part of a normal afternoon drive in Thailand.

16

Rumbles in the Jungle: A Volcano and White-Knuckle Ride in Sumatra

After making ticket reservations for a flight to Jakarta, Indonesia, and deciding to travel northward on the Malaysian peninsula, I received e-mails from my father and a friend warning me of violence there. Here's an example of what I received:

> "The Department of State urges American citizens to defer nonessential travel to Indonesia and all travel to Aceh, Maluku, Papua and West Timor. Those who must travel to Indonesia, or who are resident there, should exercise extreme caution. Bombings of religious, political and business targets have occurred throughout the country, culminating in several dozen explosions at churches on Christmas Eve. Serious violence has broken

Top:
Prambanan Temple. One of the most
famous Hindu temples in SE Asia.
(Central Java, Indonesia.)

Center:
Prambanan Temple.

Bottom:
Gunung Merapi in Central Java,
Indonesia. The name means,
"mountain breathes fire."

out in the past year on most major islands. Events in the Middle East have increased the possibility of further violence."

I must admit that gave me pause. My health insurance policy has an important caveat, among a myriad of others, of course: Coverage is not extended during travel to countries that are under a State Department travel warning.

So it looked as if I wouldn't be doing any bungee jumping in Indonesia.

Cautious but undaunted, I boarded the plane in Bangkok and set off for my first trip south of the Equator since I was a small child. From 1970 to 1972, my family lived in Singapore while my father covered the Vietnam War as a correspondent for NBC News. So, touching down in Singapore for an hour had more sentimental value than your standard layover.

Sitting in the terminal awaiting the next leg of my flight, I felt awkward for the first time that I was wearing shorts. I don't know if it was the State Department warnings, having worn only long pants for the past several days with my hosts in Thailand, or the fact that after four months in Asia I was finally adapting to the culture. Whatever the cause, I felt my bare legs screaming, "American here! Shoot me first!"

That's an exaggeration. But it is true that I had a heightened sense of self-awareness on this flight.

I landed in Jakarta without being hijacked, bombed or shot, and caught a cab to my friend's house in the suburbs. Mark Lacy and his family have lived in Jakarta for two years. Mark is a physician in the U.S. Navy doing infectious-disease research, primarily on malaria. He and his wife, Marlene, are raising three children: Marian (15), Rachel (12), and Nathaniel (8). Mark has been in the Navy for only two years, so this is his first duty station. I was their recruiter. How's that for checking up on your 'placement'?

Here's some of what I saw in Jakarta:

On the northern edge of present-day Jakarta and where the

city was originally called "Batavia" is the Old City. It is very close to the 1998 riots where several buildings were burned and shops looted, mostly Chinese. You can still see obvious signs of the violence. The Dutch colonized Indonesia (along with a few other Far East countries) in the mid-1600s -- the Dutch East Indies. Remnants of their presence are easy to spot in the architecture of the Old City. The most notable sight here is the Macassar schooners found in the port. A long line of these low-slung vessels rests by the pier between journeys throughout Indonesia where they transport wood and other goods from the outer islands.

The National Monument, which looks like the Washington Monument with a gold flame on top, is right in the middle of downtown. The most eye-catching thing isn't the monument but the number of people lying around litter-strewn lawns. The most conspicuous member of the trash family in this part of the world is white plastic bags. Such an eyesore they are. There's one thing the eye won't see, however—trash cans.

Although Mark and Marlene are not Baptist, the family has joined a Baptist church in Jakarta. I was invited to attend both Sunday school and the main service on New Year's Eve and happily joined them. Having spent the past four months visiting Buddhist temple after temple as well as worship places for Tao, Shinto, Hindu and other religious creeds, I welcomed the chance to touch base with Christianity—my own religion.

One of the subtle benefits of a trip such as mine is the chance to read. Long train and bus rides as well as afternoons in the park have afforded me the time to delve into some subjects whose exploration is long overdue. Among other books, I have nearly completed the New Testament. A number of pages are devoted to the persecution of early Christians at the hands of both Jews and Romans. The apostles, especially Paul, wrote letters to encourage the spirit of church members as they faced religious hostility.

As I stood in the courtyard between the Sunday school building and the sanctuary, I thought about the church bombings and the fact that several cathedrals were targeted in Jakarta. The recent Bible study and my defiant nature concurred to make me think, perhaps in a not-so-Christian-like manner, "To hell with it, I'm going to church."

The pastor mentioned the topic briefly, and some attendees sat closer to the pulpit than usual (farther from the front door and presumably safer from a car bomb). Other than that, there was nothing unusual about the service, and the hour passed peacefully. In fact, I really enjoyed sharing fellowship with the Lacys and other members of the congregation. Spending so much time discovering other religions gave me a greater thirst for learning about my own. That's another benefit of world travel.

I branched out from Jakarta for a few days to explore cultural capital of Java, Yogyakarta. Yogya, as it is commonly called, is a nine-hour train ride east of Jakarta to the center of Java. The city has the highest concentration of universities in Indonesia. It is from here that people make day trips to the two most famous temples in this part of Southeast Asia. Borobudur is one of the largest Buddhist temples in the world, and Prambanan is the local Hindu masterpiece. Both are close to Yogya and easily toured on the same day.

The most impressive thing about Borobudur, a massive temple, is that almost half of its 504 Buddha statues still have their heads! That is a striking sight after seeing so many decapitated statues and reliefs at the temples of Angkor in Cambodia. This temple does not have an inside. Instead, the structure consists of nine tiered layers of stone, each with several Buddha figures sitting on top of walls covered with bas-reliefs. Imagine a square wedding cake with nine short stories.

Prambanan is actually the name of a temple complex. The primary drawing card is the Shiva temple, the first Hindu site visited on my world trip. At 150 feet tall, the temple is impressive for its size. It is a great introduction to the gods of this religion.

One of the things I didn't expect when I left my hotel for a day of temple viewing was to become part of the attraction.

Upon reaching the top of Borobudur, I was accosted several times (and later at Prambanan) by Indonesian tourists wanting to take my photo with them. I must be in photo albums all over Java by now.

The last time I felt that way was walking through downtown Phoenix in my white Navy uniform. As my buddy Adrien Sanchez put it, "People look at us like we're from the moon." It was the same effect in Indonesia. I guess the Western look is as interesting as 1,000-year-old temples, and sailors in Phoenix are as common as a man from the moon.

Another side trip from Yogya was a hike to Gunung Merapi, meaning, "mountain breathes fire." Merapi is one of the 10 most active volcanoes in the world and was on a heightened state of alert. I wasn't aware of the alert status when I took the 15-mile, 33-cent van ride in pouring rain to Kaliurang, where the volcano hike began. But I was thrilled with the idea that I might get to witness some volcano action on my hike.

In order to see Merapi before clouds obscure the view, an early-morning start is required. I arose at 3:30 and lumbered to the restaurant/lobby of my hotel for the group pre-hike briefing. The owner of Vogels hostel, an Indonesian man named Christian, has been a mountain rescue-team member and tour-guide operator for 10-plus years. He has a calm and intelligent persona; he's the type to conserve his energy until things hit the fan, then take action. There's not a lot of frivolity in his forthright manner. I liked him immediately.

The brief was concise and even-keeled. There was no hype to Christian's description of the dangers inherent in an active-volcano trek. I'll paraphrase what he said:

> "Your hike will begin here at Vogels and take about three hours. You will walk for two hours, take a five-minute break, and then walk another hour to a viewpoint here (pointing to the map). The area outside of this dotted line is considered the forbidden zone. It is very dangerous to hike there. The area is forbidden unless you have a special

permit that allows you to enter. We have that permit.

"This morning my brother will accompany you. I must go to a meeting to discuss the current alert status. We meet every two weeks to talk about the level of activity on Merapi.

"Currently, the mountain is very active. We are on a level 2 alert. Level 1 is normal active. Level 2 is, Start making plans for evacuation. Level 3 is, Bags are packed, cars lined up on the side of the road, ready to go. Level 4 is, Evacuate. Right now Merapi is at level 2.

"There is no need to worry. The mountain will not erupt today. If you are lucky, you may see some gases or ash, but I can't promise anything. If something starts to happen, follow my brother back down the mountain. Listen to what he says. OK? Let's go."

And off we headed. It was pitch-black walking through the jungle. I stayed directly behind our guide, figuring that if I followed his footsteps I would avoid pitfalls. At one point, he stopped in front of me and shined his flashlight on the dirt between us.

"Wild pig," he whispered. "Fresh tracks!"

At least he didn't say, "Tiger."

Part of the trail was narrow with a steep drop on one side. Other sections were open, like meadows beneath large pine trees. Most of the way I could feel morning dew on the branches and leaves of trees as they brushed by my neck. We whisked by tall grasses and enormous bamboo reaching 100 feet to the sky. Their trunks were as large as my leg. I felt as if I were walking through a primordial picture book.—It made me think of dinosaur books with illustrations of prehistoric forests: A brontosaurus munches on incredibly oversized ferns while dragonflies the size of eagles buzz overhead.

The sky started to lighten, and we turned our flashlights off. Our guide said to me, "Go ahead. Wait for me up there (waving a hand up the hill). I will wait for the others."

Sensing the nearness of Merapi, I picked up the pace and hustled up the hill. This is a cliché, but it needs to be said: There's something primeval about seeing an active volcano. I clearly remember my first view of Merapi, as I finally broke free of the jungle and its obscurations. An imposing volcano sat quietly puffing thick white smoke in front of a beautiful blue backdrop. It looked surreal, like the cover of Jimmy Buffett's "Volcano" album.

We sat staring at the black cone for quite some time. We walked a little closer to what looked like dry riverbeds that mark the path of lava flows, spewed forth during previous eruptions. I was beginning to think that I wouldn't see any activity other than the soft white smoke, puffing steadily from the volcano mouth. But the volcano would not disappoint today.

Just to remind us that she could wake at any time, Merapi gave us a small demonstration of her tremendous power. At first, we could hear only a faint crackling; then it was a bit louder; and then there was a clearly audible rumble followed by a low roar as we watched lava and gas erupt and rocks hurtle down her side.

Our guide was impressed, "Oh, this is big. This is a big one."

A big one? Like, 'let's get out of here' big, or 'we can watch from here as long as it doesn't get bigger' big?

We stayed and watched. About a week later, I saw the cover of the Jakarta Times, which had a picture of Merapi. The caption mentioned a minor eruption a week earlier and the current level of alert. Did I see the eruption it was talking about? Who knows? But I know one thing: I had the privilege to stand at the bottom of one of nature's most powerful forces and watch as she flexed her muscle in warning.

Because I was in a Muslim country after the end of Ramadan (a month-long religious observance that requires fasting during daylight hours), travel options were severely limited. At the end of the fasting period, everyone travels to visit relatives and celebrate. Most people live in Jakarta, but visit with family at their original homes elsewhere in Indonesia during the week or two after Ramadan. How did that affect me? Because of the timing, a train ticket for departing Jakarta was easily obtained, but a ticket for arriving there was next to impossible to acquire.

The clearest indication of full trains and buses is the price of tickets on the black market and the unwillingness of scalpers to negotiate. I tried for four days to get the scalpers to come down on their prices without success. The ticket I wanted had a list price of 140K rupiah ($15), but its Ramadan season black-market price was 250K rupiah ($27.50).

Looking at those prices now, I think, "Big deal. What's so bad about 27 bucks for a train ticket halfway across Java?" But consider the mindset of a budget traveler. A markup like that is unacceptable, or at least not without a fight. Try as I might, however, the scalpers would not come down.

My pigheadedness forced me to take a third-class train, which departed Yogya at 6 p.m. and arrived in Jakarta at 5 a.m. I paid 120K rupiah ($13) for a 36K rupiah ($4) ticket.

A third-class train is not traveling in style. The bench seats are stiffly upright. Standing tickets are sold when the comfy seats are filled. That means the aisles are full of bodies sitting, lying or sleeping on the floor, blocking a hasty exit in case of emergency or even a trip to the bathroom (which could also be an emergency). In addition, many Indonesians put their lives in Allah's hands by clinging to the top of the train as it hurtles along rickety tracks. Deaths from the inevitable falls are not uncommon. It's a sad state of affairs. Painful state, too.

One of the last things I did in Jakarta was to tour the Navy research facility where my friend, Mark, works. I found this to be a great educational experience. I've always heard of research facilities that study infectious disease such as the Centers for Disease Control in Atlanta. I've read about such places in books like Hot Zone or seen them in movies about infectious diseases that threaten the world. So I was excited to actually tour one.

The labs, lab coats, and microscopes were all as I expected. But several things had not occurred to me before: considerations such as how do you keep the mosquitoes alive?; how do you feed mosquitoes?; how do you track field samples or other data from current and past research projects?; how do you access information from other research facilities around the world?

I found it fascinating that warm-blooded animals had to be kept on site as blood donors for feeding test mosquitoes. Or that certain mosquitoes can be fed through a thin latex membrane while others require live subjects. Some mosquitoes alight on vertical surfaces, while others tend to settle on the ground.

After spending a few more days enjoying the fine company and good cooking of the Lacys, I flew to Padang in western Sumatra. I quickly found a bus to deliver me to the quaint mountain retreat of Bukittinggi. It was a nice relaxing place to escape from the heat of the lowlands.

I didn't do a whole lot while there, passing the time writing and walking about the town. The most interesting thing about Bukittinggi was my van ride out of the town. I scheduled a trip to Singapore that involved an overnight stay in the central Sumatran town of Pekanbaru. The first leg of the trip was a nine-passenger van ride about five hours long.

The morning started unpleasantly as I was forced to listen to ear-splitting '80s dance music. I quickly found the earplugs buried deep in my bag, but that victory was short-lived. Although the music stopped 30 minutes later, the driver decided to set the land-speed record between Bukittinggi and Pekanbaru. This isn't unusual in Asia, by the way. For some reason, all van and bus drivers feel that the more erratic and high-speed the driving, the better. There is no pride in being smooth.

After passing vehicles on five or six blind corners, we hit a straightaway that allowed him to redline the Mitsubishi engine and really build up a head of steam. As he edged right to pass a truck (they drive on the left side here), I noticed another white passenger van approaching on our right.

"Whoa, this is going to be close," I thought.

Suddenly I heard a loud smack! Glass flew inside the open window and shot about the cabin. I thought the other van had thrown something at us.

I looked up at Mario Andretti in the front and noticed our driver-side mirror was missing. The only thing left was a broken stub. We had slapped mirrors with the oncoming van!

I looked at the idiot in the driver's seat with contempt. There's something about a near-death experience from recklessness that leaves a bad taste in your mouth. Fortunately, he traded out with a saner driver in the next town, and I never saw him again

Here are some impressions of Indonesia:

-- Because it is an Islamic country, several times throughout the day you can hear men singing prayers over loudspeakers from mosques. One time, in Bukittinggi, the singing stretched from 4:24 to 6:24. I can't tell you whether he was on key, but I can say that the volume was plenty loud.

-- The Indonesian language is easy to pronounce and read. I think one could become street fluent in a month or two of intense study.

-- Instead of exclusively scooters, Indonesia has a healthy percentage of motorcycles in the traffic soup. I enjoyed the sight of the big bikes after dodging swarms of scooters in Cambodia and Vietnam. They looked, well, masculine next to their petite cousin. In general, traffic in Indonesia looks similar to traffic in America. We're still talking apples and oranges, but they're both fruit.

-- Indonesian people were as quick as any to return a smile from a stranger on the street. I admit I was apprehensive going into the country, especially after the State Department warnings. I had wondered if Muslims would have an innate dislike for westerners and Christians. Although I spent very little time there and spoke at length with very few Indonesians, I left Indonesia with my fears abated. Sure there are some who hate me and want to bomb my church, but I believe the vast majority are peaceful and open to good relations with the West and other religions.

-- A number of Indonesians were under the impression that the United States had forbidden travel to Indonesia. I think they had read an article in the Jakarta Times about the State Department warnings. The written word has the power to inform or mislead.

-- After eating at the street joints in Bukittinggi for a couple of days, I decided to splurge and have lunch (less expensive than dinner I assumed) at the most luxurious hotel in town, the Novotel. I would give it four stars, best described as a lovely place to have brunch. It was quite nice.

The difference in the price between four-star and one-half star dining was $2. (I decided to eat dinner there as well.)

-- Almost every man smokes. Almost every woman does not. Actually, the gender/smoking correlation applies to all of Asia. The only women I saw smoke were either younger people in bars or elderly. In either case, the sight has been rare.

An inexpensive (not American) pack of cigarettes costs 4,000 rupiah. At a pack a day, that equals 1,460,000 rupiah a year. (American brands cost about 8,000 or 9,000 rupiah.)

A worker at an Internet café in Bukittinggi told me he makes 250,000 rupiah a month (3,000,000 rupiah a year).

A worker at a Kentucky Fried Chicken in Bukittinggi makes 150,000 rupiah a month (800,000 rupiah a year).

Let me spell it out: Some Indonesians spend half of their annual income on cigarettes.

I can't remember if I saw any male workers at KFC in Indonesia. I know I didn't see a single one in Bukittinggi. I understand why now. They wouldn't make enough money to smoke.

17

There's Something Fishy About Transport to Singapore

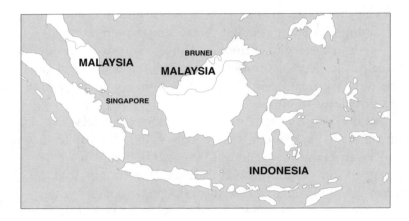

This is the story of how I got to Singapore, a daylong ordeal that began at 6 in the morning and didn't end until late in the evening. Traveling from Pekanbaru in central Sumatra to the port city of Buton on the east coast took five hours on an overcrowded bus with bench seating. Many sat on packages and luggage that filled the aisle. The road was dirt, and I could feel the bus slide as we wheeled our way through the sporadic patches of mud. At least this driver didn't try to break any records getting to our destination.

In Buton, we disembarked to find workers taking the luggage down from where it had been strapped on the roof of the vehicle. They smiled to us and pointed to the long dock leading out to where the ferry would tie up. Two Brits and I (the only foreigners on this journey) smiled back and watched as they loaded our bags along with others into wheelbarrows for the short trip to the landing.

We followed along to keep an eye on our precious cargo. Upon reaching the end of the narrow 200-foot dock, we were hit with an unexpected service charge -- 5,000 rupiah per bag. What? No one else was paying. Only the foreigners were approached for remuneration. I thought it was a classic example of tourist extortion, and it pissed me off. If this were the *first* attempt to rook me into paying a bogus fee, it might not have raised my ire. But after the hundredth time, I just wasn't going to stand for it anymore.

The ringleader was a personable young man who spoke decent English (apparently the reason for his leadership position). I sat off to the side and watched him work over the Brits (a male and female couple). They claimed to only have Thai baht. But this guy smelled money and wasn't to be deterred that easily. The couple looked over to me, bewildered with the predicament, and asked if I had paid.

I shook my head no and said loudly, "I think it's bullshit. I'm not paying."

They eventually got the guy down to 1,000 a bag. As soon as they acquiesced, their bags were placed under a tarp with the others, for it had started to rain. I went and sat on a wooden railing over my bag to keep an eye on it. A man with apparent authority came out and told everyone to leave the landing area. Although he spoke only Indonesian, I got the point from the accompanying hand motions.

I picked up my bag and placed it under the tarp with the others before leaving. The ringleader protested, saying I had to pay him a fee. After two weeks in Indonesia, I was able to say a couple of local phrases quite well, one of which was, "What's your name?" I said that and followed with "Polisi." Then in English, "Why don't we go visit the police and have a talk about this? Come on. I'll lead the way."

Suddenly the guy couldn't speak English. He clammed up and turned away. I put a finger near his chest and said sternly,

"My bag had better be right here when I come back, understand?"

Walking back to the shore, I realized the folly of my action. I anxiously wondered if my bag would be "accidentally" kicked off the dock and into the water. My victory in the bag-charge scam would have been pretty hollow—saving 50 cents but losing everything that I owned. "Man," I thought to myself, "I better cool it with these guys."

Thirty minutes later, I made the 200-foot walk out to the ferry that had docked at the end of the pier. Bags were being thrown on the top by both dock and ferry workers. The only things left to load were the bags people carried themselves and a couple of packages of vegetables -- and my backpack lying by itself off to the side.

Good thing I checked, right? I picked it up and handed it over to one of the workers on the boat. I then stood back and watched until I saw it disappear among the other bags on top. So much for that brush with disaster.

The ferry to Singapore took about five hours. Besides the traditional Indonesian dance and song videos, we were entertained with WWF "Super Summer Slam" on the television. All eyes, other than those closed in slumber, were glued to the set. This was a strange sight.

By the way, this brings up another point I've been meaning to relate. The major American sport that is popular throughout Asia is NBA basketball. Although baseball is king in Japan and Korea (primarily their own teams), from China southward the U.S. sport that is most watched is basketball. I've caught it on "Star sports" and other stations. More than once when I mentioned that I lived in Phoenix, I was met with the response, "Oh, Phoenix Suns. Very good!" Somebody in NBA marketing needs a pat on the back for bringing American basketball to Asia. I'm sure the salaries of NBA participants receive a boost from this expansion.

Back to WWF (another popular form of American showmanship that I've seen across Asia on hotel TV as well as bus trips). After about 45 minutes of initially entertaining and then repetitively mind-numbing Super Slam, the audience began to lose interest. Most went back to chatting or sleeping. I read.

The ferry landed on an Indonesian island just south of Singapore, and there would be another 45-minute ferry ride. I waited in the gaggle of passengers beside the ferry as we looked for our bags. Arms, legs, bags, and crying babies seemed to be everywhere. I spotted the deckhands struggling with the weight of my bag and pushed to the front of the crowd. There are no pleasantries exchanged in scenes like this. A judicious use of muscle and force is called for and expected. If you don't reach your bag before it hits the ground, guess what? It hits the ground and lolls about in the sludge of a harbor jetty.

Although I reached my bag before such an occurrence through a combination of yelling and elbowing, I could not prevent the treatment it had received earlier. I picked up the pack and began walking toward the terminal building. Once out of the chaos of the crowd, I noticed a foul smell. Thinking it must just be the landing area, I continued toward the shore. But the smell didn't go away. In fact, I couldn't seem to escape it.

I set my bag down on a railing and examined it closely. My fears were confirmed. The awful odor came from my own pack. I had no idea what it was, but it smelled to high heaven. There was a hint of what I've become familiar with in Asia -- something of the sea, like octopus or drying squid. Whatever it was, it was gross, and I had to wear it. To make matters worse, the substance was isolated in the one area that could most readily and unavoidably reach my nostrils as well as be pressed to my body, right on the shoulder strap. Damn!

Despite the pungency of my pack, I soon enjoyed the transformation from developing to developed world. Even the departure terminal from Indonesia to Singapore has a developed feel to it. Suddenly everything was quiet. A small Swensen's ice cream stand sold scoops and sundaes. Staff workers were polite and helpful. The ferry itself was only half-full and offered large, comfortable seats. I'm telling you, the experience of arriving in

Singapore is tantamount to a warrior's entering Elysium—the after-world paradise of Roman soldiers.

I felt a wave of purity rush over me as I stepped into the chilled confines of the Singapore arrivals terminal. It was so clean and so modern, so civilized and appealing. Outside, I made the mistake of asking three girls if they spoke English before proceeding with my question about which bus to catch. Everyone speaks English in Singapore -- yet another boon to the road-worn traveler.

I arrived at my chosen hotel only to find that it was changing management soon. Because of ongoing remodeling, all of the $10 rooms had been demolished, and only $30 rooms remained. The hour was late, and I had been traveling for an entire day. I splurged on air conditioning, and a hot shower was in order.

As I filled out the routine check-in forms, one of the two staff members asked me what I thought of Singapore so far. What I had experienced to that point told me Singapore would be a refreshing break from the hard knocks of Asian travel. I responded, "Great. I haven't been here but a couple of hours, but I like what I see so far. It's clean. Orderly. Modern. I like it."

"Yes," he replied. "But it's too plastic," he added, wrinkling his nose. He continued with a couple of other peeves about the city being "fake" and "stiff".

I wanted to reach out and slap him.

Keep in mind the conditions that had brought me to that emotion. I had been traveling in the Third World (with the obvious exceptions of Japan and Hong Kong) for more than four months on a shoestring budget. I had seen how the majority of people in this region of the world live -- in wretched squalor at the worst and in modest yet unsanitary conditions at the best. I had just spent the entire day either crammed into an overcrowded rattletrap of a bus, sharing a two-person bench seat with a man, his wife and their child, or on a ferry with more than a hundred other people wearing the same clothes for the past three days, as I was.

I had waited in the dust and grime of a tiny port village where dockhands think it's a major score to rip a tourist off for the meager sum of 50 cents. Later, I was forced to elbow through men, women and children to collect my bag safely at the end of the trip. And to top it all off, my backpack had been dragged through something that smelled like rancid fish sauce only to then be strapped to my back for the past hour.

It was 10 p.m., I was tired, and I smelled so repugnant that I couldn't even stand to be around myself. And here was a guy whining about Singapore being too "plastic" basically because it's clean and orderly.

Whiskey. Tango. Foxtrot. Over?

Although tempted to lash out, I bit my tongue. It was easy to do, given my weakened state. I wasn't in the mood for a big debate on sociology and politics. Plus, he seemed like an OK guy, and I didn't want to look for another hotel. I must say that I was surprised to be faced with the most common denunciation of Singapore so early in my visit. Many people have similar complaints about this country. It's too strict, too organized, too clean, too this, too that – all of which target good order.

OK. I'll concede that Singapore isn't dripping with charm. And the government is, indeed, very strict. But had I responded to my hotel friend on that first night, here's what I would have said:

"So what would it take to make Singapore acceptable to you? What would give it that 'real' feeling that you think is missing? Poverty? Pollution? Unsanitary living conditions? Lack of food? Children at risk? Poor medical care? An unreliable energy source? Rampant government corruption? Inequality?

"If you're tired of the clean streets, good education, low crime rate, business opportunities, and water that you can actually drink from the water fountain, it's a short boat ride to freedom, pal. You won't see any of these things in Indonesia. But you will see everything on my list of what might make a city charming. And oh yeah, I'm sorry, you will see a bit of plastic, too. Plastic bags and bottles. On the other hand, you will see very little of another type of plastic -- credit cards."

Enough of my diatribe. I found a $6 air-conditioned dorm room the next day at a hotel around the corner. So much for the notion that Singapore is overly expensive for the budget traveler.

18

A Pleasant Interlude in a Land of Order and Prosperity

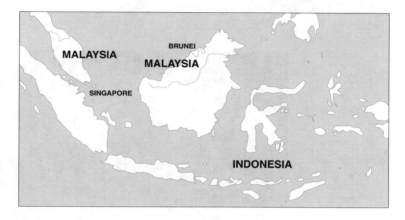

These are some of the things I saw and did in Singapore:

COLONIAL DISTRICT -- I stayed in this district, where all around is evidence of former British rule. That means colonial architecture, a giant courthouse and parliament building, and in a broader sense, British good order and discipline. (As well as driving on the wrong side of the road.) So just cruising around this area on foot made for a pleasant hour or two, as well as a noticeable change from what a similar walk would have been like in other parts of Asia.

RAFFLES HOTEL -- This hotel is a landmark associated with an earlier genre of writers. Over the years, this has been the haunt of several famous journalists and novelists. For instance, James Michener said he always kept a typewriter and a suitcase

Top:
The Merlion of Singapore.

Center:
Singapore's Botanic
Garden.

Bottom:
The Tanglin Club. Where I
learned to swim as a two-
year-old.

of clothes at the Raffles. It is also home of the original Singapore Sling served at the gorgeous wooden long bar out back. It's a ritzy place but not gauche. It will be several years before I can afford a night here.

CHINATOWN -- After walking around Singapore for about three hours, I gradually noticed a change in the architecture of surrounding buildings. I had been winding my way west from the Central Business District (like Hong Kong's, but not as big and shiny) toward Chinatown. It may seem strange to have a Chinatown in a city that is 75 percent Chinese, but after having visited Singapore, it doesn't seem odd to me at all now.

A Chinatown is a way for the local Chinese population to preserve their culture and heritage. There is also an Indian district that serves the same purpose. Growing up in Singapore is a far cry from what it's like to be raised on the mainland. A trip to Chinatown allows local Chinese the opportunity to touch base with their cultural roots. And I must say, it felt like China.

Suddenly everyone was ignoring traffic lights and jaywalking. The streets were crowded with honking cars and pedestrians. The alleys were crammed on either side with trinket hawkers and far too many people squeezed their way through. A temple decorated with the familiar dragon motif puffed incense. It was hot, noisy, crowded and sweaty -- just like China in the heat.

ORCHARD ROAD -- You can't make a trip to Singapore without strolling along Orchard Road for a spell. This is the glitzy, ultra-modern shopping district of Singapore. There is mall after mall after mall, plus movie theaters and restaurants. One wonders how so many businesses are supported. Demand must somehow keep it all afloat.

NIGHT SAFARI -- This was the most incredible zoo experience I've ever had. This has to be one of the best zoos in the world. Allow me to display some credentials, which I hope will lend credence to that statement. Here is a list of zoos and places whose zoos I have been to (as best I can recall): Atlanta; Lincoln Park in Chicago; Duke Primate Center in Durham,

N.C.; Guangzhou, China; Panda Conservatory in Chengdu, China; Pensacola, Fla.; Phoenix and Tucson, Ariz.; London; and San Diego.

The quality of the animal exhibits coupled with exceptional customer service, organization, and top-notch visitor facilities made this a world-class experience. But the thing that really made the trip to Night Safari at the Singapore Zoo so amazing was the activity level of the animals.

How many times have we been to the zoo only to find the lions sleeping? Or maybe the polar bear tucked behind a rock in the shade? Disappointing? Frustrating? Make you want to throw a stick and wake him up? But you know you're not supposed to do that, so you sigh and move on to the next display.

Maybe the monkeys will put on a show.

Not at Night Safari. No sir. Upon entering the grounds, I decided to take the tram, which carries you through the nether regions of the park. There is a walking path as well, but you don't go deep in country. I hated to spend the extra $5, but my gut told me this would be worth it, and was it ever.

The first exhibit was a rhinoceros. I wasn't sure exactly what to expect but thought that I would see the standard animal-in-the-distance sort of view. The tram rounded a corner, and there, standing perfectly still in the spotlight not 20 feet from our tram, was a giant black rhino.

The narrator (who was a little melodramatic about the grandeur of the animal kingdom and trying to set the mood in a whispery voice by saying, "Imagine yourself in the jungles of central Africa and allow the moonlight to take you awayyyy!") was saying something about rhinos, but I had stopped listening as soon as I spied the animal. Then, just as my part of the two-car tram passed by, he turned his head and wiggled one ear. Right on cue!

I looked back to see if he made any other movements. Nothing. The skeptic in me bubbled to the surface. "Oh man, that's got to be a robot," I thought. We were passing deer on the side of the road in the dark (no fence between us), and I wondered, "Are these guys fake, too?" That's how realistic it all was. More real than real.

Next came the lions, a perennial favorite and notoriously inactive. These guys were a little farther away than some of the other exhibits but still well within a good view. I noticed a male at the top of the hill pass another lounging male while holding a cub in his mouth. "How cute," I thought.

But something wasn't quite right. Then I realized, "Wait a minute. Males don't carry cubs around." He stepped a bit closer into the light and turned his head to the side, giving us a nice profile view of his cargo, a large deer carcass!

"Holy cow!" I've never seen animals fed food in its natural form. Usually it's just ground beef or steaks or whatever. But an actual deer? This was great.

The park was divided into environmental regions of the world so those animals that naturally share the same environment were clustered together. Exhibit after exhibit of quality natural settings showcased animals actively going about their day. The designers made clever use of vegetation and elevation to disguise the barrier between observers and the observed. As you sat in the tram and looked up to the display area, you could not discern where the tramway ended and the exhibit started.

Let me reiterate. My trip to Night Safari was the finest zoo experience I have ever had. If you're saying to yourself, "Jeez, he really raved about that place," then good. That's how great it was.

FAMILY HISTORY DAY -- What follows is Jones family-oriented and may be of little interest to the general public. Feel free to skip to the Yee and Janet Wang section of this letter.

From June, 1970, to April, 1972, my family lived in Singapore while my father covered the Vietnam War for NBC News. I was born in August, 1969, which means I was a toddler, and unfortunately I remember little of our stay. But I've heard stories throughout the years of our life in Singapore and have wondered about it from a very early age. "Dad, tell me again, WHERE is Singapore?"

So I wanted to see for myself the places where we walked,

shopped, swam and especially, lived. I wrote to my parents for guidance and then set out on my pilgrimage. The first stop was the Tanglin Club.

The TANGLIN CLUB is a British-oriented facility (the fine-dining area is called the Churchill Room) that accepts members of all nationalities. This is where I learned to swim, with water wings and all. I wanted a tour but knew the club was for members only. So I pleaded my case with the women at the front desk who softened up after hearing my tale. Plus, it helped that I had exact addresses and names, which gave my story credibility. Fortunately, the public relations office was willing to give me a tour, although I was not allowed to take photographs.

Nice place, the Tanglin Club. The primary thing I was interested in was the pool. Quite fittingly, a woman was teaching young children how to swim in one corner of the shallow end. I walked outside and took several clandestine pictures over the wooden fence. I felt like Fletch.

C.K. TANG'S -- This is a shopping mall that my mother used to frequent. I am told that my big sister Stephanie loved the trips to C.K. Tang's. From what I gathered, the current location is slightly different from back in the '70s. C.K. Tang's now sits where Cold Storage grocery store used to be (another landmark for our family). I, of course, don't know what it was like back then, but today the department store is similar to Saks or Neiman Marcus - upscale and modern.

THE OLD APARTMENT -- The most rewarding site of all. My mother had given me good approximate directions to the apartment building where we lived, which my father supplemented with the exact numbers. Combined, I was able to navigate on foot directly to our former residence on Orchard Court.

Remember that this building has been around since at least 1970. A lot of construction has gone up nearby since then. As I rounded the corner onto Oxley Road, which runs perpendicular to Orchard Road and acts as a feeder for Orchard Court, I knew right away which building was ours. Sitting on a hill were two matching and distinctly '60s style buildings, 12 stories high with balconies that faced Orchard Road. Everything matched the description.

But even more so, they triggered something deep in the recess of my memory. Maybe this was a confabulation, I don't know. But the building and the parking lot and the balconies all seemed faintly familiar. I took a couple of pictures and noticed the "No Trespassing" sign. Figuring this was worth the risk, I braved the warning and took a stroll around the parking lot where I rode my bike with Stephanie on training wheels.

I decided to go inside. At first, the numbering system threw me for a loop. The elevator went from 1 to 13. My mother had said we were on the twelfth, the top floor. Puzzled, I pressed 12 and rode it up. En route, I realized that the standard way for the British to number their apartments and hotels is from G (for ground) to 12 (or whatever the top floor is). The floors must have been renumbered.

I continued up to what is now called the thirteenth floor and stood in the landing area, wondering what to do next. I was almost certain this was our old apartment but needed confirmation.

I had noticed the new brass signs outside each apartment, telling of its new address. As I looked around and up above one of the doors, I noticed an old black sign with white letters nailed into the wall. "25L". And then it hit me.

I quickly pulled the address from my pocket.

"23L Orchard Court. On (or just off of) Oxley Rd."

I was excitingly close. What if that sign was a fluke and the others had been taken down? There was one way to find out.

I walked around the corner, and there she was - 23L.

On the other side of that door was the genesis of family stories, both good and bad, that have been told for years. I have a scar above my right eye from a minor altercation with my sister in there. I was notorious for throwing all kinds of items off the balcony. "Jason say bye-bye!" My two-year birthday party was here. How many times had I gone through that door as a child?

I took a picture and made my way back down to the parking lot. While sitting there, I considered going upstairs and knocking on the door. But I thought better of it when I remembered the strict Singapore government and the sign that read, "Trespassers WILL be prosecuted!" I satisfied myself with just relaxing in the shade and taking a moment to pause.

YEE AND JANET WANG -- The last two days of my stay were spent with a family of Chinese Singaporeans who are fellow members of SERVAS, the international hosting organization I belong to. Janet and Yee are in their mid–40s and have three boys, 15, 13 and 9. Janet is a general practitioner who works part–time at a clinic, and Yee is a high school English and physical education teacher. Once again, the opportunity to spend time with locals enhanced my trip significantly.

Within 30 minutes of meeting Wang Yee, he had me hiking a trail in the Bukit Timah nature preserve in the center of Singapore island. It was a beautiful place with a few colonies of long–tailed macaques zipping around and Nepalese Gurkha soldiers exercising on the park's steep hills. Hiking through the dense jungle here almost makes you forget how close you are to civilization (minus the rifle fire from the nearby firing range).

I didn't know who the Gurkhas were before seeing them training here in Singapore. For those of you in the dark, too, the Gurkhas are mercenary soldiers known around the world for their skill and bravery. The British army has enlisted these men since 1815. According to Wang, it is a great honor to be handpicked from your village in Nepal to join this elite force. I was told that formerly the Gurkhas engaged in a ceremony to mark the end of their initial training during which a goat is decapitated with one stroke of the traditional Gurkha knife.

Among other things, the Wangs took me to Victoria Concert Hall (colonial Singapore at its best) for a performance of the high school orchestra; the botanical gardens for a view of the orchids; a feast of chili crabs (local specialty) at their home; and visits to the boys' schools for general errands to include rugby practice.

Through the process of running errands and touring the

botanical gardens, I was able to ask Janet some general questions about Singapore. That discussion shed some light on the country's collective awareness that while it is an amazingly successful and multicultural nation, it is at the same time in constant jeopardy of becoming culturally bland and an overly regimented society. Here are some interesting tidbits:

- Although the population is approximately three-quarters Chinese, the country was founded on the premise that all races would be treated equally. Singapore broke from a union with Malaysia in 1967 in large part because Kuala Lumpur demanded special treatment for ethnic Malays. (That is according to the National Museum in Singapore.)

This is entirely plausible. I learned subsequently during my trip to Malaysia that in order to own a business, you must have a Malay business partner who owns 1 percent of the business. (Or you can be of any ethnicity as long as you are married to an ethnic Malay.) Ethnic Malays make up 60 percent to 70 percent of Malaysia.

- To preserve ethnic culture, Singapore has instituted compulsory mother-tongue education that begins in kindergarten. That means if you are ethnic Chinese, you are taught Mandarin. If you are ethnic Malay, you learn Bahasa Malaya. If Indian, Tamil, and so forth.

- In another effort to safeguard cultural heritage, each ethnic group maintains the celebration of various festivals and holidays. The government encourages this.

- The education of its children is of utmost importance to Singapore. The pressure on children to perform well in school and be accepted to the best high schools and universities is intense.

- There's a saying among Singaporeans. "This is a FINE country. You chew gum, you get fined. You jaywalk, you get fined. You litter, you get fined. Yes, this is a FINE country."

The point: Singaporeans are well aware of how strict their government is and are able to poke fun at it.

My gut tells me that most of the citizens of Singapore think of themselves as Singaporeans first, ethnic whatever second. Here's a quick story that helps demonstrate how I arrived at that conclusion:

I made a trip to the Nepalese embassy to apply for a visa. No one from Nepal actually works here. Instead, the office is manned entirely by Indian-Singaporeans. Unfortunately, my visa application could not be processed within the time frame that I required, so I packed my bags to leave. In the process of doing so, I chatted amiably with the staff.

> "So I'll be going to India after I visit Nepal," I said.
> "Oh, really? That will be nice," a woman replied.
> "I'm not sure exactly where I'll be going. I'm going to spend about a month there though."
> "Great."
> "Do you have any suggestions for me? Anything I can't miss? By the way, which part of India are you from?"

> I felt lightning strike the back of my head as I realized I had put my foot in my mouth. I wanted to suck the words back in. But there ain't no way to get un-pregnant.

> "I've never been to India," she said. "I am from Singapore."
> "What I meant was what part of India did your family originally come from?"
> "I have no idea," she said. "Generations and generations have been here."
> Looking now to the older gentleman sitting across the room, I asked, "When did your family arrive here?"
> "Oh, I think it was my great-grandfather that came to Singapore" he said. "But I'm not sure."

This was a lesson to me about the people of Singapore. It's really no different from the United States. Other than native people's, Americans' lineage diverts at some point to places outside of our borders.

"Hey, that's just like me! My family comes from Scotland and Ireland, but I live in America now, and that was ages ago."

They appreciated this, and I was allowed to leave with some semblance of dignity.

The final anecdote I have for my visit to Singapore came from my visit to Wang's oldest son's rugby practice.

First, I found it interesting that rugby is the sport of choice in Singapore. I don't know why, but I think it's interesting.

Second, I noticed the ethnic makeup of the boys playing on the field. Chinese, Malay and Indian children were hustling and struggling together as a team. This seemed to me like a microcosm of Singaporean society. Citizens grow up together, play together, and must certainly work together as adults.

Finally, as I stood on the sideline watching practice wrap up, Wang introduced me to a couple of the fathers who were waiting with us. He told them about my trip and where I was from and then mentioned how Singapore was a particularly interesting stop for me because my family had lived here for two years.

"Oh really? What did you say your name was again?"
"Jason Jones."
"Really? Hmmm," one of them pondered. "I used to know a Jones. Long time ago though."
"Oh?"
"Yeah. I can't remember his name though. I had a different job at the time."
"Did he have a good-looking kid running around with him, about this high," I asked, holding my hand out.
"Ha, ha, ha. No, don't remember that. But I definitely remember a guy named Jones."
"What did he do?"
"He was a journalist."
Sensing the more real possibility of a "small world" experience now, I said, "Really?"

"Yeah."

"When?"

"I guess that would have been around 1970 or so."

"Where did he live?"

"I think off of Oxley Road, or somewhere like that."

"That was my dad!"

It turns out Wee Ban Bee was the public relations representative for Jurong Town Corp., a large construction firm. Occasionally the company held news conferences that he helped organize.

I took a good look at his son before they walked away. Who knows, right?

Here are a few observations about Singapore:

– People follow the rules in Singapore. It is similar to Hong Kong as far as Asian countries go. The British influence is apparent.

– I saw Asian women in short-shorts and skirts. This was particularly noticeable after having just arrived from the Islamic country of Indonesia. (Head-to-ankle covering there.)

– The influence of Chinese and Indians is manifested in the food. And speaking of food, restaurants abound! I only wish I had more time and money. I would compare it to San Francisco in this regard.

– Pay phones are handy and only cost 10 cents. Street signs are in English script and on almost every corner; navigation is easy. The names of many roads and subway stops are of British origin. Cross Street, Temple Street and Smith Street are three examples of roads I saw in *Chinatown*. Most other types of signs are in English, although a few use Chinese characters as well.

– The Internet connection is lightning-fast.

– Singapore has the nicest subway stations in the world. They feel like the lobby of a fine hotel with ferns, polished marble floors, and classical music playing in the background.

That's a random assortment of stuff that maybe only a traveler would notice. And for that very reason, I couldn't help but wonder how the miracle that is Singapore has come to be. What forces have been at play? The prime minister who led the country from the days of its birth as a nation until the early '90s, Lee Kuan Yew, has just published his memoirs. When it comes out in paperback, you can bet that I'll pick up a copy.

The contrast between Singapore and every other nation in Southeast Asia is unmistakable. Thailand and Malaysia begin to approach Singapore's success in the comforts of good living, but everywhere else is a pale shadow compared to this jewel on the tip of the Malay peninsula.

I walked away from Singapore with a positive impression of the people and the land. Sure, lots of people criticize the stiffness or strictness or whatever other complaint arises from the zealous pursuit of good order and discipline. Or maybe they say there's no character to Singapore. I take issue with the latter. To the former, I say that the pursuit of order, fair treatment of the people, and an open business environment have created one of the most successful nations in the world. The way I see it, Singapore embodies many of the things a country should strive for: It's clean, safe, prosperous and fun. It seems this nation's reputation suffers from its own success.

But I think it's a fine place (ha, ha). I'm not saying I would want to relocate to Singapore and become a citizen. I'm too American for that. But I'd sure take a look at living there for a few years if business or otherwise called.

19

Hello, Buddha. Como esta?

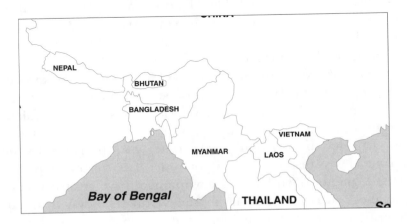

For two days, I had been touring the ancient city of Bagan, Myanmar, a fantastic place with a seemingly endless supply of pagodas and edifices. One of the most pleasant aspects of Bagan is the sparse tourist business and lack of souvenir salesmen at most of the temples. The major attractions, however, each have their own cadre of hawkers and beggars to pester tourists.

Near the end of the second day, I approached my tenth major pagoda. Although calloused and immunized against the pleas of temple mountebanks after five months of world travel, I had a breaking point like any other human.

I drew near Manuha Paya (a temple with four enormous Buddhas squeezed into matchbox-sized quarters - just looking at them induces claustrophobia) and groaned at the sight of so many tourists and locals. I don't mind the other tourists, but where there's prey, so will there be predators.

Shin Pyu Me Paya (Pagoda) in the ancient city of Mingun. (near Mandalay, Myanmar)

"Looks like another round with the hawkers," I thought. "Lace 'em up."

I parked my bicycle beside the front gate, and before I could dismount, three young beggars approached me. Ignoring the children and their incessant pleas, I sat on a dusty step to take off my boots and socks (a requirement for all Burmese temples).

It had been a while since I had called upon my fake Spanish technique of deflecting hawkers and beggars. But I was using it again in Bagan with good success.

A little background: I had humored myself while traveling through China by responding to hawkers in a gibberish form of Spanish. I can barely remember 'hello' and 'goodbye' after two years of high school Spanish and a year in college, but can, like any other American, say "tacos y enchiladas".

So when a hawker says to me, "Hello, you want statue?" I respond with, "Tacos y enchiladas?"

And when he follows with, "Where you from?" or "Where you going?" I use my second response, which is, "Los pantalones son negros y amarillos." (The pants are black and yellow.)

I successfully employed the Spanish language gig to which she responded, "I don't understand you."

"Good," I thought to myself, a little tired and ill-tempered. "Now go away."

She did – and I was pleased.

But one of the young girls was not so easily dispatched and began to trail me as I explored the grounds. I thought I had ditched her at one point as I entered the pagoda, but upon exiting through a side door I found her waiting patiently on the marble walkway.

(Looks like she knows the routine, I thought.)

I sighed and just accepted that she was going to be with me for the duration. She continued to ask for money and either point to her mouth or palm, the first in reference to food, the other regarding a ballpoint pen. "For my school," she said.

At first I thought I would just ignore her like the thousand beggars before. But for reasons unknown to me, as I reached the corner of the building near the back entrance to the fourth Buddha image, I snapped.

She had been playing with a small rock. I held out my hand with a curious look, asking to see it. I had not spoken a word of English up to this point. In fact, I had barely uttered a sound.

She reluctantly handed it over with a suspicious look. It was a small piece of the white marble walkway that we were standing on. I put it in my right hand and knocked it against my left palm.

(Puzzled look)

I tapped it against the side of my head.

(Another puzzled look)

I finally put it between my teeth and, with an exaggerated motion, bit down.

Imagine a monkey who has somehow found a flashlight in the jungle. He doesn't know what to make of it, but gives it a series of 'tests.' That's the look I was going for.

After finishing with the Curious George routine, I shrugged my shoulders and handed the rock back to her. She had watched carefully throughout my act. I hoped she would now consign me to the category of "weird guy" and leave me alone.

Not a chance. But she DID stop asking for money. Maybe she wondered what in the world I would do next. I did not disappoint.

She stuck beside me and pointed to the entrance of the temple not 10 feet away. "You can go inside."

We walked inside the tight confines of the back room to find a 90-foot reclining Buddha. That's a Buddha lying on his side with his head resting on his right hand—as if he's watching TV.

The young girl marched up to the Buddha and helpfully banged her rock on his arm - which gave me an idea.

I put my ear to his arm and also knocked on the Buddha. Startled and amazed, I flashed her a what-was-that? look.

I knocked again - louder this time and followed by my gibberish Spanish.

"Tacos y Enchiladas?" "Como esta?"

I alternated astonished glances between her and the point where I had been 'listening.'

I went back to knock again. With purpose this time.

"Como esta?" "Los pantalones son...(continued incoherent babbling)"

I parked an absolutely flabbergasted look on my face coupled with I-swear-I-hear-something and then motioned for the girl to listen for herself.

She took it hook, line and sinker—never even blinked.

When her ear was about an inch away from the Buddha I yelled, "BOO!!!"

Oh, man. You should have SEEN her jump. The construction guys outside who had witnessed the exchange were chuckling loudly. Both the girl and I were laughing together and enjoying how gullible she had been. In the flash of a moment, our relationship had unexpectedly changed. We were no longer beggar and tourist. Instead, quite pleasantly, we were friends.

Of course, I didn't mind her presence anymore as I continued to stroll the grounds of Manuha Paya. In fact, I engaged her in conversation with the help of my Burmese phrasebook.

> Me: "How old are you?"
> Her: "Eight."
> Me: "What's your name?"
> Her: (Too long and hard to pronounce/remember, but I understood her at the time.)
> Me: "Where are you from?" (This got a smile.)
> Her: (Duh) "Myanmar"
> Me: (returning the smile to say, 'I know that silly, but where in Myanmar?') "Bagan?"
> Her: "Yes, New Bagan" (One of the three or four little villages around Bagan.)

As I unlocked my bicycle, put my bag in the basket, and generally got organized for the ride back to my hotel, I turned and said to her in Burmese, "I've enjoyed talking to you."

Then the strangest thing happened. She handed me a five kyat (chat) note. Five kyat is worth about a penny, but of greater value to her, of course.

I didn't know what to make of it. I wasn't sure if she was making a last ditch effort to show me what she wanted, or if she was actually giving me the money. Trying to sort it out, I took the bill and motioned, 'for me?'

She gave a slight nod and continued to look at me. I couldn't read her face. A bit confused, I handed the bill back to her, smiled and shook my head no.

I felt as if I had crossed into some strange realm. A beggar handing money to ME? It just didn't make sense. Even if all she wanted to do was provide a visual example of her request, to put money in a foreigner's hand was HIGHLY unusual. If her intent was to give me the money, I was certainly no longer on planet Earth.

I smiled again and said in Burmese, "I'm going now, OK?"

She nodded OK.

I hopped on my bike and started to ride off. After about three pedals' worth of travel, I looked back and saw her watching me go. I dropped the charade and yelled out to her in perfect English, "Good luck!"

She probably didn't know the words, but I like to think she understood the meaning.

20

Feeling the Repressive Touch of Big Brother in Myanmar

The plane flight from Malaysia to Myanmar (formerly known as Burma) is a good place to start this account. I was under the impression that Myanmar, like the other Southeast Asian countries I had visited, would be lush and green. On final approach to the Yangon airport, I was surprised to look out the airplane window and see the color brown everywhere. Brown dirt roads and brown dirt fields. Palm trees interspersed throughout.

My two weeks in Myanmar were spent in dry, dusty locations: Yangon, Mandalay and Bagan. These three cities form a triangle that covers the central swath of the country running north to south. It's an arid region, save for the meandering rivers.

The airport in Yangon is a 30-minute drive north of downtown. I stopped at the taxi booth inside the airport lobby

Top:
A lion stands guard at Sandamuni Paya (Pagoda)
near Mandalay.

Center:
The glorious and relatively tourist-free temples
of Bagan, Myanmar.

Bottom:
The Petronas Towers of Kuala Lumpur, Malasia.
(Tallest in the world.)

and bartered a fare to the city from $5 down to $3. On my return ride two weeks later, I paid the correct "market rate" of $1.75.

Quite predictably, and against my vehement objections, the cab driver tried repeatedly to convince me that the Holiday Inn was closed and I should try another hotel. He claimed to know of several that would be good for me. On top of that, the dispatcher at the airport had given him a few curt orders in Burmese after I said the name of my hotel. That always raises my suspicion.

The modus operandi of almost every airport and bus-station taxi driver in Asia is the same. A tourist can clearly say the name of a hotel, sometimes write it down and on a few occasions even point to it on a map, only to have the taxi/rickshaw driver inform him five minutes into the drive that the named hotel is either closed or "dirty." The driver will conveniently have another hotel in mind that is, "Very clean. Western toilet. Hot water. Many Westerners. Many tourists. Good price."

On this occasion, I would not relent. I repeated "Holiday Inn, Holiday Inn, Holiday Inn, Holiday Inn" until I was blue in the face. "I don't care that it's no longer there," I told him. "I want to go to the 'closed' Holiday Inn."

The poor guy eventually gave up. In an astounding twist -- this is truly mind-boggling -- the Holiday Inn was closed. He took me to the address in my tour book, and I could see the old sign. Maybe it had moved. I don't know. But I couldn't expect him to willingly find a place that I didn't know the location of and he wouldn't get a commission from. (Isn't it awful what the Third World has done to my expectations for professionalism and honesty? They are at rock bottom.) So I gave him my criteria, "I need someplace clean, near the center of town and approximately $10 a night."

Not five minutes later, I was checking into a decent little place with air conditioning, private hot shower, and CNN for $12 a night.

One of the reasons I used the airport taxi stand as opposed

to hailing a cab was a currency issue. For good reason, I had not changed even a small amount money at the airport as I normally did. Although I had $196 of Myanmar official money in my possession, I had exactly zero currency with which to purchase items on the street such as food or a taxi.

What in the world am I talking about?

Upon arrival in the vanguard of free enterprise known as the Kingdom of Myanmar, each tourist is *required* to change 200 U.S. dollars into notes labeled "Foreign Exchange Certificate" (FEC). I kept a couple just for souvenirs. Here's what they look like:

One side has the number 1 in the middle with the words, "Equivalent to US$1," written below. The other side says, "This certificate can only be used within the Union of Myanmar and is convertible. No claim on any loss whatsoever of the certificate will be considered by the Central Bank of Myanmar."

These little babies are useful only for paying hotel bills, travel expenses (bus, train, and plane tickets), and tourist entry fees at the pagodas. I suppose they would be accepted at any other government-registered or -owned enterprise, but they are useless on the street to pay for food, souvenirs, or taxi fares.

At my hotel, I quickly discovered the exchange-rate disparity between dollars and FECs. First, there's the government's official rate of exchange: $1 equals 1 FEC, and $1 equals 6 kyat (pronounced "chat," the local currency).

The street rate of exchange is much better: 1 FEC equals 310 to 340 kyat, and $1 equals 410 to 440 kyat.

So what is the point of all of this? Basically, the $200 I was arm-twisted into exchanging at the airport for Foreign Exchange Certificates had been subjected to a 25 percent levy. My $200 should have been worth 86,000 kyat (the dollar street rate equaling 430). Instead, when I exchange the FEC, I will receive only 64,000 kyat (FEC street rate equals 320). That's 25 percent less!

So I spent time trying to figure out if I should pay my bills in kyat or FECs. Although the tourist sites will accept only FECs, the hotels will often accept kyat as well. But the hotels will always set their price based on a dollar-per-night rate. If the hotel used a dollar-to-kyat exchange rate that was less than what I was able to get on the street, I would pay in kyat and save a little money. Their poor exchange rates rewarded the customer for paying in kyat that were purchased on the street at a good exchange rate.

On the other hand, I needed to spend the FEC notes before leaving Myanmar, because it would be a losing proposition to try to exchange FECs to kyat to dollars. Obviously, FECs are non-exchangeable outside of the country, as kyat are, too.

That was a lot of complicated, boring and dry currency-exchange talk that's no fun to write about. In fact, I'm parched from the exercise. It's also no fun to deal with in practice. But I wanted to give a small taste of the effects of this ridiculous government system on the local currency exchange and a guy on a tight budget. In short, I was annoyed.

By the way, the "street" currency exchanges often took place in a clandestine manner. When I changed dollars in Yangon at a large jewelry market, the woman I traded with said, "Careful, much security here." On the other hand, when I changed a $20 bill in Mandalay, business was transacted openly. The small shop was set up for currency exchange and didn't appear to hide anything. Maybe some are registered and others are not.

If you finish reading this and say, "You know, all of that sounds like a real hassle," then I've accomplished my mission.

YANGON

I spent much of my time touring Yangon on foot. It was a good city to walk around and take in the atmosphere. Two things that struck me immediately were the way men dressed and the makeup on women's faces. Both were exotic.

The men wore a long skirt known as a lougyi. Few men wore pants. The lougyi looks like a sheet that men wrap around their waist and knot in the front. The design is usually a simple brown-checked pattern although other styles are worn, too.

Almost every woman I saw had at least a small amount of beige clay rubbed on her cheeks. Most children and some teenage boys adorned their faces with the same substance. Some women had makeup all over their arms and faces, but usually the pattern was a simple two-inch wide rectangular stroke on each cheek. According to the people I asked, the compound was formerly made naturally by mixing a special tree substance with water. They believe it protects the skin from sun damage. In the modern day, companies manufacture this skin protectant for sale in stores, and I saw it advertised on TV.

It's hard to describe how strange those things looked when I first saw them: men in long skirts and almost every woman and child with painted faces. I wondered why I had not read about this in my travel book. These two features were the most visible distinctions between Myanmar and the other countries of Asia.

As I walked around the cities in which I traveled, I sometimes was reminded of other countries and the cities therein. On this occasion, Phnom Penh, Cambodia, came to mind. Both are the capitals of poor, underdeveloped Southeast Asian countries. They share a history of past military conflict, and both have a visible presence of soldiers with rifles slung over their shoulders. But Yangon was somehow a step up on the development ladder.

For instance, most of the roads (within the city, that is) are paved. The buildings are in better condition, although occasionally appear in need of paint and new brickwork. And palpably, Yangon feels relatively safe, even to walk around at night (admittedly an easy category in which to outpace Phnom Penh).

This last observation could be due to the fact that a paranoid military dictatorship governs Myanmar. This was the most strictly state-controlled country that I had visited yet. That fact alone made the trip to Myanmar worth the effort; it's a feeling I had yet to experience. Take, for example, the billboard I saw riding from the airport to downtown upon my arrival, not one hour into my stay in Myanmar.

PEOPLE'S DESIRE
- Oppose those relying on external elements, acting as stooges, holding negative views.
- Oppose those trying to jeopardize stability of the State and progress of the nation.
- Oppose foreign nations interfering in internal affairs of the State.
- Crush all internal and external destructive elements as the common enemy.

Can you believe this horse hockey? This was a large red billboard written in white lettering that I saw in two places around Yangon and once in Mandalay. A similar sign written in Burmese accompanied the billboard in Mandalay. That's right; this sign was in English. To whom were they communicating?

To me, it sounds like Cold War rhetoric concocted in the Kremlin. All that it's missing are "Comrade" and a reference to the proletariat.

I also found out firsthand how wary the citizens are of speaking about the government. On the drive from the airport, I asked my cabby why he felt a certain area of town was dangerous. He had been pointing out some major landmarks and tourist sites and noted that one of the pagodas was "no good for him." He said something I couldn't decipher about the monks in residence there and their connection with the government. I queried further only to be blunted by sudden reticence. With a grave face, he shook his head no and said, "Government. No talk." How terrible it must be to live under such a regime.

I don't mean to judge (even though I just did), it's just that I feel sympathy for the oppressed. I try to maintain objectivity, but this is too much. I'm a free-enterprise, capitalistic, give me liberty, or give me death kind of guy. I pity the good people of Myanmar and hope that this yoke of repression is lifted one day.

BURMESE PAGODAS

Myanmar is an overwhelmingly Buddhist country. My guidebook said 90 percent of the population follows Buddhism. Monks in robes and pagodas are common sights. Generally speaking, the pagodas of Myanmar share a few elements:

- The images of Buddha often have multicolored flashing lights that either swirl around his head in a pinwheel motion or radiate outward for a starburst effect.

- Mythical snakes called "nagas" commonly decorate the grounds. They look like cobras and sometimes have multiple heads (up to 10).

This brings up an interesting point. Honestly, I don't know if these snakes are actually called nagas when used in Buddhist imagery. I learned while touring the temples of Angkor that nagas are the natural enemy of the garuda -- a half-man, half-eagle character. A garuda served as the vehicle of Vishnu, one of the three primary Hindu gods. This apparent sharing between religions is a common theme among the countries of Asia. The religious imagery becomes a part of the culture and vice versa.

In addition, I have found most people in Asia to be tolerant of other religions. In Nepal and Indonesia, for instance, all citizens, regardless of their own beliefs, revere the hallowed sites of other religions.

- A mirrored mosaic design decorates at least part of most pagodas. Imagine a mirror broken into a thousand bite-sized pieces and then glued to the wall with a half-inch space in between. Then spread this image across entire foyers or sometimes even the entire interior wall space of a small building. What you've got is a flashy show. Vegas, baby.

OK, so that's an irreverent description of what is an important religious building. Forgive me. But it's true. Sometimes the mirror explosion looked gaudy. At other times, I forced myself to appreciate the effort at embellishment and veneration. But most of the time it just looked gaudy.

While I'm reviewing Burmese pagoda presentation, I might

as well get add this one. I visited the Mal La Mu pagoda in the northern part of the city one afternoon and was amused by the garish motif. As I walked among the oversized figures of bright pink fish, giant serpents, kitsch scenes depicting events from Buddha's life, and the giant alligator that you could walk inside of, I had the nagging sense that I had seen this type of workmanship before. I just couldn't put my finger on it.

Then it hit me: Putt–Putt! The entire place looked like a giant game of Buddha goofy golf.

On a laudatory note, allow me to describe the gem of Burmese pagodas. Shwe Dagon pagoda in central Yangon sits like a bright nugget of gold in the landscape of Myanmar. This is the largest and most–visited temple in all the country. Uncharacteristically, I paid for a guide at this one, and it was worth it.

The brightly painted gold–leaf top of Shwe Dagon pagoda can be seen from a great distance on foot and supposedly (according to my guidebook) from passing airliners high above. It is enormous. Not only is the pagoda itself a monstrosity of gold, the grounds contain a plethora of what I ignorantly call mini–temples, each filled with multiple images of Buddha.

The mini–temples are simply small buildings, of maybe 400 to 500 square feet. At Shwe Dagon, each of these contained at least one, usually more, image of Buddha sleeping, resting, sitting or standing. I was impressed with the number of statues and asked my guide how many there were. "Over 1,000," he said. That may sound exaggerated, but I firmly believe it. I started counting clusters of 10 and eventually gave up. There are easily 1,000 Buddhas spread about the Shwe Dagon complex.

Shwe Dagon's gold spire towers skyward above the grounds, topped with a jewel–encrusted umbrella that is common to the pagodas of Myanmar. An umbrella is hard to describe. Basically, it looks like a hollow wedding cake that caps off the top of the temple. But of course it is made of metal, painted with gold leaf, and adorned with jewels from near and distant lands.

Of great interest to me was viewing the bright glint reflected from the giant diamond at the tip of the pagoda's spire. I sat through sunset and then viewed the pagoda illuminated by bright spotlights. My guide told me to stand in a particular spot (which I have recorded for future visits), so that I could see the reflection of the spotlights on the diamond.

Sure enough, upon following instructions, I was able to see its sparkle winking at me as I moved my head in and out of the single ray. I'm not sure why I found this remarkable. For all I know, the rock up there is just a mirror, set up to fool gullible dopes like me. But I did see pictures of an enormous diamond in an umbrella at the souvenir stands surrounding the pagoda. And it's not unreasonable to think a religion would lavishly decorate one of its most venerated places of worship. I can think of a few other religions that do the same (St. Peter's Cathedral).

Finally, and this speaks to a larger point about Myanmar, only men are allowed access to special parts of the pagoda, namely, the upper levels (it is multitiered at the base) and the sacrosanct interior—both places of spiritual importance. Inside the temple stands an image of Buddha with glowing ruby eyes. To worship under the gaze of this figure is a hallowed privilege. But outside of the inner sanctum, on closed-circuit TV, anyone walking by can view the image also. I suppose this is done so that women can be "seen" by the holy image as well as men. Peculiar.

My point is that Myanmar is a strongly male-dominant society. At the temple, my guide told me it is a "Myanmar Buddhist tradition" that only men are allowed access to certain areas of the pagoda. The split between men and women elsewhere is easily noticed. Take the "cold drink" shops around Yangon, for instance.

A cold drink shop is the Burmese version of a coffee shop. Usually it consists of a small street-side proprietor who serves tea, sugarcane juice, and other beverages to patrons who sit in tiny plastic chairs on the side of the road. Many times I noticed that every customer was male. Sometimes I saw a female or two dotting the edges of a crowd of 20 to 30 men, but this was infrequent.

It was common to walk a little farther and see small clusterings of women and children at similar establishments, sitting on the street and eating. But I never saw large groups of women lounging about and socializing as I did the men.

MANDALAY

After Yangon, I went to Mandalay, which is north but I can't remember how far. It was far enough, however, to make my neck, legs and butt hurt from the 15-hour bus ride.

In Mandalay, I had some of the best guacamole I have ever had. Honestly. And remember, I lived in the southwest for three years. Phoenix is no slouch when it comes to Mexican cuisine.

In between multiple visits to the guacamole restaurant, I visited a few pagodas and one of the ancient cities of Burma, Mingun.

BAGAN

Next came Bagan. To be concise, a visit to Bagan is worth any hassle the Myanmar government can create with its ridiculous entry fee to the country and any hardship of travel -- awful trains or slow buses.

The site is hardly touristed (or at least it felt that way when I was there in February) and amazingly rich in offerings. Thousands upon thousands of mini-temples dot the countryside around the larger pagodas. It is one of the best-maintained and renovated archaeological sites I have seen.

GENERAL OBSERVATIONS

Myanmar was interesting for its government, people and pagodas—conspicuous in their style and presence. Like most of Southeast Asia, Myanmar is cluttered with litter, and most people live in poverty. For the most part, the people were friendly and inquisitive.

I sympathize with the plight of life under a repressive regime.

Freedom of Internet access, or whatever one would call it, is not allowed in Myanmar. I was able to send e-mail through one of the hotel accounts (at a dollar per e-mail), but not allowed to access my own account or any other part of the Internet. I sincerely doubt if the government allows access to information via the Internet or any other medium to the general populace.

The whole experience made me further appreciate our own freedoms in America. There's nothing quite like being stripped of basic rights (freedom of information) and feeling the oppression of a military dictatorship, even for just a short period of time as a transient, to bring this point home.

21

At the Top of the World, Rewarded for Pain and Hardship

As I sat down to write this, I had just completed a 12-day trek into the Everest region of Nepal. The experience left me enervated yet richly rewarded. I bore the temporary scars of blisters on both feet, a scraggly beard, wind-chapped hands, and recovering knees. When I would blow my nose, blood-stained mucous filled my hands. But I am also graced with the permanent memory of the world's highest peak set amid the most stunning mountain range on the planet. That's one hell of a show, the Himalayas.

I have decided to convey my trek experience as a daily journal in a sort of here's-what-happened-today format interspersed with descriptions of the lodging, food, sights, people, and other factors that greet the trekker.

Just what the heck is a "trek" anyway? That's what I thought

Top:
My guide Dak Badhur Rai "D.B." on the trail to Mt. Everest.

Center:
A docile yak outside the hotel on the Everest trail.

Bottom:
D.B. and I standing atop Gokyo Ri with a hard-earned view of Mt. Everest.

when I visited the REI store in Phoenix as I prepared for my trip abroad. I went in for the biannual sale to stock up on all the camping/travel items that had never been part of my personal gear. Other than survival training in the Navy, I had never done anything other than car camping. I didn't own a backpack, water purifier, sleeping bag, camping pillow, or anything else that should accompany an overnight hike in the woods.

I told the salesperson at REI my plan for cruising around the world, mentioning that I intended to include Nepal on my itinerary. Her eyebrows immediately shot up as she asked, "Well, are you going to do any *trekking*?"

Not having a clue what that meant, but not wanting to sound ignorant I replied, "Yeah. I want to do some trekking. Sure."

She handed me off to the backpack guy, and I never saw her again.

For those who aren't privy to the lexicon of backpacker types, I have a simple definition for you: Trekking equals "walking."

It's a little more involved than that. A trek implies donning a backpack and staying overnight on the trail in either a hotel or a tent. So in that sense, it's really a form of hiking, now isn't it? I liken it to the way hurricanes in the western Pacific are called typhoons. Same thing, different name.

My experience on the trail and the things I write about are not meant to suggest what others have experienced or what your trek would be like. About 30,000 people enter Sagarmatha National Park (the Everest region of Nepal) each year, and I guarantee that each person comes out having seen and felt different things.

But without question, my story will provide an idea of what to expect in the way of accommodation, food, sights, sounds, and smells on the trail. But each trekker's experience will be influenced by a host of factors that are too numerous and tedious to list. Suffice it to say this is just one guy's thoughts, affected by his physical condition, time of year, spending level and pure luck (or lack thereof) among other things.

Here is a list of adjectives that describe what I saw and how I felt:

Beautiful beyond words
Freezing
Scalding
Healthy
Debilitating
Energizing
Agonizing
Uplifting
Demoralizing
Challenging
Peaceful
Annoying
Fun
Painful

And in the final analysis, *worth it.*

My trek to Everest required physical stamina and a positive mental attitude to overcome adversity. I don't want to give the wrong impression. A hike through the Khumbu region of Nepal (more precisely where Everest is located) is not incredibly difficult. At the same time, it's no walk in the park. One does need to put forth some effort. And if you combine the strain of long days of steep hiking with high altitude, failing knees, and unfortunate health problems -- well, I had a little more of a challenge than I had originally bargained for.

So here's my 10-day, no 12-day, no, make that a 14-day, now back to 12-day, trek through Nepal.

KATHMANDU (4,265 feet)
Feb 18-19, 2001

There are many ways to organize a trek in Nepal -- by oneself, with a small group organized locally, or with a professional tour group organized overseas, for example. Nepal offers a wide variety of trails in separate regions of the country. From this selection, a trekker can choose to hike the entire trail over as many days as his visa will allow, rush through a small portion of the trail over the span of a few days, or do anything in between.

My first task was to find a trekking company in order to hire a guide. I debated just going it alone, but had not spoken with anyone about that possibility and did not have enough information to feel comfortable with that option. In hindsight, I could have easily done the whole trek by myself, but am glad I spent the extra money on a guide. The next time, however, I think I'll be going solo lobo.

I spent two days schlepping around Kathmandu (a pleasantly grimy and touristy place, if there is such a thing), comparison-shopping between tour operators. After checking four outfits, I decided on Global Adventure Trekking (P.) Ltd. (The "P." is for private.) I liked the presentation the managing director made, as well as the low price. Without any prompting, he underbid one company by $100 and offered more benefits. Plus, he was the only operator to mention mountain rescue and safety.

The director, Suman Dahal, had been a guide himself for more than ten years when he and his two brothers (also guides) had decided to start their own trekking company three years earlier. Theirs is a small outfit in a fiercely competitive market in which the big companies listed in travel books have a great advantage as they swallow up the majority of tourists.

Suman employs touts to get people off the street and into his office. His tout was the only one I engaged in conversation. I wouldn't have agreed to visit the office, but I had just checked three of the big names and didn't like the prices I had heard. I was debating just grabbing a map and heading out alone and therefore figured, "What have I got to lose by checking this guy out, other than my time and patience?" Fortunately, I had a little of both at the time.

Here's the deal Suman offered (copied verbatim from the company letterhead):

10 days Everest trekking

Services:
Guide
Permit $15
Transportation (to and from the airport)
Accommodation
Meals /B/L/D
Tea drinks
Drinking water (boiled)
Hot shower
Equipment: jacket
Rescue services
First aid treatment

Because the runway at Lukla (to which trekkers usually fly) was closed for repairs, I would fly to an alternate airport in the town of Phaplu. A helicopter flight to Lukla was possible, but exorbitant. The helicopter operator was gouging passengers because there was no fixed-wing competition. My airfare would have increased by $110 had I opted for the chopper. In addition, I had to pay for my guide's airfare (he lived in Kathmandu, as I believe most other guides do).

Unfortunately, Phaplu is two days farther from Mount Everest than Lukla. That effectively added four days to my trek. Four days was significant for me, in time and money. Alas, I couldn't afford the extra cost of the helicopter flight.

The round-trip airfare for me to Phaplu was $170, plus $30 for my guide (notice the enormous disparity between "foreigner price" and "Nepali price").

The Services charge (listed above) came to $260. So my total cost would be $460 over ten days. That came to $46 a day -- over my $40 per day budget, but easily countered by the cheap living in Kathmandu and elsewhere in Nepal. Plus, how often would I have the chance to see the most famous mountain in the world?

"Jason, sometimes the great experience is just going to cost you a nickel. Deal with it."

I slept on it for a night and realized that this was something I really wanted to do. The next morning I revisited Suman's office and conveyed to him my desire to go with Global Adventure, as well as what a good presentation he had made.

(On the way to cinch the deal, I stuck my head into one more outfitter's door. Just a last check. Like the other major companies, it wanted about $600 for the same deal. Not even close.)

Suman was pleased, of course, and like a good sales rep, asked if I would like to add two more days at a cost of $25 a day. Based on my introspection of the night before, I was receptive to his offer. I knew this would allow me to extend my range and provide greater flexibility and choice. I agreed to the terms, and we closed the deal. I was to meet my guide that night at 6 o'clock.

With all the negotiating and shopping around done, I felt a burden had been lifted from my shoulders. I was excited: "All right! I'm gonna see Everest. The king daddy! The big kahuna! Top of the world and all of that stuff."

I headed out into the streets of Kathmandu, deflected the gratuitous offers from rickshaw drivers and Gurkha knife salesmen, and continued my search for trekking equipment. I was surprised that with my limited knowledge I had actually packed most of the things I would need for this frigid trek in Phoenix, way back during the heat of September (100-plus degrees).

The things I took with me on the trek that I already had in my backpack were:

Pepto-Bismol tablets, Sudafed decongestant, DayQuil (a non-drowsy form of NyQuil), antifungal cream, antibacterial cream, moleskin, a flashlight that attaches to a baseball cap to work as a headlamp, my wool watch cap from the Navy, sunscreen, lip balm, and a small patch of rip-stop nylon adhesive to repair tears in my bag.

Of course, you can add to this list warm clothing, camera, film, pen, paper, etc. I needed to buy only three things: warm gloves, thick wool socks, and long underwear pants (which I had packed in Phoenix but mailed home from Japan to lighten my load).

I would make use of everything except DayQuil and the rip-stop nylon.

On Feb. 19, I returned to the office of Global Adventure Trekking to meet my guide, Dak Bahadur Rai, or D.B. for short. I didn't realize until after a couple days on the trail that Rai was the tribe to which he belonged. In Nepal, the people use their ethnicity as a last name. For instance, the famous Sherpa who helped Sir Edmund Hillary summit Everest in 1953 was named Tenzing Norgay Sherpa (also sometimes spelled Tensing).

As D.B. told me later during our trek, the people who inhabit the Everest region of Nepal consist of basically four tribes. In ascending order of elevation, they are the Brahmins, the Rai, the Tamung, and the Sherpas. D.B.'s hometown was a two-day walk from Phaplu.

I liked D.B. the moment I laid eyes on him. He was a short, distinctively Nepali-looking man who always wore a baseball cap and had a broad smile that showed his bottom teeth. He was 31 years old, with a wife and 2-month-old baby girl he had named Salim Yuki. Salim is a twist on the name of the town where he met his wife, and Yuki is Japanese for "white." He said his daughter's color was noticeably white at birth -- the reason for the name.

D.B. spoke excellent English and had been portering (lugging heavy loads up mountains for a pittance), cooking, and guiding on treks for 13 years. The past ten years had been spent in the latter role. He had trekked all over Nepal, and this would be his first trek of the spring season. The two trekking seasons in Nepal are fall (October and November) and spring (March and April). For the previous three months, he had been "playing" in Kathmandu and taking care of a newborn.

D.B. typically would go on four to five treks per year. That's about all the trekking industry can provide for a guide, though I doubted he would go on more even if he could. From conversations with him, I got the idea that many Nepali people tend to work very hard during their seasons (be it planting and sowing, or whatever else) and then cool their heels for the rest of the year.

I sat down next to D.B., and we got acquainted. We agreed to meet the next morning at 8 to head for the airport.

THE TREK

Day 1
Kathmandu (4,265 feet) to Phaplu (about 8,000 feet) to Ringmo (8,925 feet)

I met D.B. at the appointed hour and began discussing where I wanted to go on the trek. I would like to say up front that I grossly underestimated the time required for trekking in the Himalayas. The pace I had set for myself was borderline ridiculous. Someone like D.B., who had been hiking this land for 13 years, could keep up with it, but not a gringo from sea level like me.

D.B. was polite and softly informed me of the difficulty we would have trying to satisfy my proposed itinerary. When I had originally contemplated a 10-day trek, I had concocted a different and more reasonable plan. But after adding two days, I had grossly extended the range I wanted to cover. I, of course, deferred to his judgment, but pushed him a little bit to see what the limits were, as well as to test his judgment. I appreciated that he respectfully dampened my grand plans. In effect, he gave me the throttle-back signal.

Just so you have a general overview of where the trek goes (and in case you don't have your Everest trekking map in front of you), I'll briefly describe the standard route from the mountain town of Jiri to Everest Base Camp.

Trekkers have a choice of starting the trail in a few different places. For starters, one can actually walk from Kathmandu to Jiri. Or one can take the 10-to-12-hour bus, a hellacious ride I'm told. Another option is to skip over the trailhead and fly to Phaplu, from which you hike three hours up to a point on the main trail that's about a four-day walk past Jiri. The final option, and the fastest way to the peaks, is to fly to Lukla. From there, it is a steep hike down to join the main trail. One would find himself approximately six days ahead of a fast walker from Jiri. My sense is that most people fly to Lukla, or certainly the wealthy trekkers do.

The trail from Jiri winds its way east for 30 miles and turns north for 13 miles more before digressing east and then northeast for a total of 15 miles or so to Everest Base Camp. An option besides Everest Base Camp (where viewing Everest is like reading a book one inch from your face) is to climb a nearby mountain called Kala Patthar. I am told that the view from this relative molehill is splendid.

I chose a third option for gazing upon the beauty of the Himalayas. After doing a bit of reading, looking at some posters, and overhearing a few conversations, I decided to make the effort to reach a viewpoint called Gokyo Ri. ("Ri" means peak.) At the point the trail veers east along the route to Everest Base Camp, I would instead continue due north for 12 more miles to the town of Gokyo. A stone's throw away and two grueling hours of breathless hiking later, I expected to experience one of the premier vistas in the world.

But maybe not within the number of days I had scheduled. It was such a tight timeline that any little thing could destroy my plans. D.B. and I decided to press forward as aggressively as we could and see how things went.

The flight from Kathmandu to Phaplu was uneventful. Being a good guide, D.B. directed me to the left side of the small twin-engine prop. This afforded me occasional glimpses through the clouds of the white giants guarding the border of Nepal and Tibet, and whetted my appetite for the trek that awaited me.

After horribly overshooting the approach end of the runway, our pilot dragged us low across the mountainous terrain and plopped us down on Phaplu's gravel runway at 8,000 feet above sea level. We all filed out of the aircraft, collected our bags, and headed uphill to the little town.

D.B. led us directly to a restaurant that also served as the local Skyline Airways office. After eating lunch, I went with my guide for a visit with the Skyline station manager to talk about extending our flights a day or two more, beyond the revised 12-day itinerary. It turned out to be no trouble at all. With the stroke of a pen the man simply drew a line through the 03 in '03 March' and scribbled in a 05.

My originally rushed 10-day trek easily became a two-week adventure.

"Now *that* should give us enough time for Gokyo," I thought.

I headed off to join the primary trail from Jiri with fresh legs and a bounce in my step. D.B. said the hike to Ringmo (our destination for the evening) would take about three hours. Sure enough, after three hours of up-and-down terrain, we hit the main trail from Jiri right at Ringmo.

Along the way, I noticed my heart pounding rapidly and a slight headache -- both attributable to the rapid jump in altitude. In addition, my pack, although less than half as light as it had been for the previous five months, started to feel like a lead weight.

About an hour into the hike, I stopped to put some moleskin on a blister that had quickly developed on the inside of my right heel. I looked inside the shoe to see how I could have aggravated my foot so quickly and saw a hole in the padding that I hadn't noticed before the trek. My heel was rubbing against the plastic frame of the boot.

"That's pretty annoying!" I thought. They were Columbia boots, the ones that say, "Don't even *think* of bringing those boots inside!" on the box. They should have been a lot tougher than this. I hadn't been hiking that much in them over the past several months, and they were failing me when I need them most. Thank goodness I had the moleskin.

By the time I reached our stopping point, I had the start of a good-sized blister. It wasn't hurting too much yet, but I wasn't going to take any chances. The next day I would wear double socks with the hope that my feet would toughen up.

I kicked a flat, miniature soccer ball around with a couple of kids and wrote a bit in my journal while trying to keep my hands thawed. That's one thing about the hotels on the Everest trail; they all had wood-fired stove-like heating contraptions in the main dining room. But none of them had really effective heating units for the common areas, or any type of heating in the bedrooms. Electricity was always a pleasant surprise, never a standard amenity.

Writing this, I referred often to my written journal. I just read the final line of my entry for this day and realized it exhibited uncanny foreshadowing. It said, "As long as my body holds up, this should be a really fun trek."

I guess I didn't knock on wood.

Day 2
Ringmo (8,925 feet) to Bupsa (7,745 feet) -- 6.5 miles

Again, I'll quote directly from the journal. The first sentence under the heading Day 2 is:

"Today was brutal."

I remember how depleted I felt when I wrote those words. I was void of energy and filled with consternation. This was only Day 2! I had 12 more to go. If this was how I felt at the two-day point, how was I ever going to make it? Could I really have become so weak after five and a half months on the road?

I'm sure my travels played a large part in wearing my body down to the point that I was in poor shape to begin such a trek. But as I found out shortly, my feeling of pain at the beginning of the trek was an all-too-common state among fresh trekkers. That evening I spoke with a Dutch guy and a Brit who had hiked in from Jiri. This was their fifth day, and although tired, they assured me they had gone through the same "growing pains" and felt much better after a few days on the trail.

Here's how the day went:

D.B. and I began the morning with a 40-minute climb uphill to Traksindo La. ("La" means pass.) He mentioned when we got there that 40 minutes was a fast pace. It felt like good exercise to me, but not particularly blistering. I assured him that I would be tired later in the day, but presently felt great.

From the top of the pass, it's a three-hour walk downhill to a village called Jubhing. Not 10 steps into this downhill portion, my left knee began to bother me.

In college, I had done a lot of running. I had also run quite a bit during flight school. During these years, I developed knee problems that alternated between the left and the right. There was no rhyme or reason to it; they just hurt after long runs.

In the intervening years, I had dramatically decreased my running. I hadn't had a problem with my knees for years. But I hadn't subjected them to the same punishment that I did in my early 20s. I guess adding 20 pounds to my body weight (my backpack) and pounding them thousands of times on the steep descents of the Everest trail allowed that old pain to find a way back to my knees like a long-lost enemy.

To complicate matters, although my right-heel blister didn't bother me on the downhill, I was developing a new blister on the ball of my left foot. I spent most of my time looking for flat rocks for my feet to land on as we descended. Much of the trail consisted of uneven boulders that exacerbated the blisters by inducing foot-twisting action.

D.B., meanwhile, practically bounded down the mountain in front of me in his featherweight Nepali running shoes that he purchased for $4.

We spent about an hour in Jubhing eating lunch and licking my wounds. Already I was starting to have doubts about how far I'd be able to go on this trek. The rational side of my mind still said, "Hey look, this is only the beginning, where you're expected to get a couple of blisters. They'll toughen up, and the knee will, too." But I couldn't help peering down into the dark side of my mind where lurked the threat of failure to reach Gokyo Ri -- my destination.

After two hours of hiking uphill, I really began to drag. The ever-growing blisters and pain in my knee were starting to piss me off. And I was hiking at an elevation I had rarely experienced while following the pace of a guy who had lived here his entire life and guided treks for a living.

Near the top of the hill, we ran into another guide from Global

Adventure hiking with his client, a Canadian. Each of us chatted respectively with our "caste mate." The Canadian was in great spirits. He was on a four-week vacation to hike to Everest Base Camp and wherever else he could fit in. He was covered with dirt and had a scraggly beard and rips in his clothes but a big smile on his face. I was relatively clean, no holes in my clothes, fairly clean-shaven, and in great pain.

He asked how long I had been on the trail.

"This is Day 2," I replied.

"You must still be excited," he said, with an all-knowing smile. "Another friend of mine got tired of the walking. He's taking a helicopter out of Lukla. Me, I'm still not tired of it yet. When I'm done, I have to go back to work."

He droned on for a while making pleasant conversation, but I didn't hear much. I was too busy thinking about the pain in my legs.

They finally left us, and we pressed on. About 10 minutes past our pow-wow on the hill, we crested a ridge and descended gradually for 30 minutes to the base of a new and steep hill. D.B. said he thought it should take about 45 minutes to the summit, maybe 30 if we went fast.

I regained a little bit of energy during our pause and was able to start at D.B.'s pace. It was 4 p.m. We had begun our hike at 7:50 a.m., a little over eight hours earlier. Given that we had an hour for lunch, I had now been hiking for seven hours.

It was on this hill that I died.

I had begun at the pace D.B. had set all day. But about 10 minutes into the hump, my legs began to shake, and I knew that I had to slow down if I wanted to make it. I had been doing a good job of hydrating, so I knew my problem wasn't water. But I was breathing like a horse and cursing the altitude.

Then, without explanation, I was delivered. I was granted an image that saved the day.

A common sight on the trail is the Nepali with a ridiculously heavy and oversized load in a basket strapped to his or her head. That's right, baskets are loaded with up to 110 pounds of cargo, sometimes strapped with boxes six or seven feet high, and then carefully positioned on the back of a human. The manner in which they are held is something I have seen elsewhere in Asia.

Let's role-play as a Nepali porter for a moment. Imagine a duffel bag with a long strap between the ends and place it behind you. Now bring the long strap up from behind, and place it across the top of your forehead. Your neck and spine will support the weight of the bag resting on your back and leave both hands free. One of your hands will hold a short support stick that is shaped like the letter T. When you are tired, you will carefully stop your forward travel and place the T-stick beneath your buttocks. Now you can rest in a half-standing, half-sitting position while the trekkers who ultimately buy your goods pass by.

The only images you need to change are the duffel bag to a large wicker-type basket and remove whatever shoes you were wearing to be replaced by flip-flops. No wait, that sounds too sturdy. A shower shoe more accurately describes the footwear. Some porters wear nothing at all.

As I started to wonder if my legs would give out, the Nepali porter image came to mind. Those folks take it slow and easy. I decided to slow to their rate of walking. Sure enough, as long as I focused on steadily putting one foot in front of the other, plodding along and inching my way up the hill, I felt as if I could make it. I reached the top in 42 excruciating minutes.

That was the worst portion of the entire trek.

What made the hill so bad was not the pain, in and of itself, but the dreadful thought of how poorly I was faring this early in the trek. It was not as if this were the final push to finish the two weeks, or even to make it up Gokyo Ri. This was just a random hill at the end of Day 2.

The thoughts going through my mind as I climbed up to Bupsa (the town at the top of the hill of pain) remind me of the foreboding words uttered by Goose in "Top Gun": "This is not good, Mav. We are waaayyy low on gas!"

I got to the hotel and climbed in my sleeping bag for an hour. I needed to get horizontal for a little while, like a corpse. I was encouraged by the words of my Dutch and British compadres as we commiserated that night at dinner. The Dutch guy complained of knee trouble also, making me feel better. I'm sure my pain lessened his, too.

Day 3
Bupsa (7,745 feet) to Chaurikharka (9,055 feet) -- 6 miles

Big improvement today, I was happy to report. The terrain had not been as severe as the day before, I had paced myself from the very beginning, and I was more used to it than the day before.

After a quick bowl of noodle soup, D.B. and I started the day at 8 a.m. I made sure that I did some quick stretching and filled my drinking bottle with boiled water. The heat of the hot bottle felt good on my hands in the crisp air of the early morning. I suspected the temperature was hovering just above freezing, but as soon as we got moving, I warmed up enough to shed my outer shell and hike in a fleece pullover and watch cap.

The first bit of trail in the morning was an ascent to a high pass at 9,385 feet. It took 45 minutes, which is probably too fast, but I was feeling OK. The next two hours of hiking was fairly flat, allowing me to enjoy some of the view -- the reason I had come here in the first place.

This is a good place to describe what the lowland portion of the trek to Everest looked like. The trek can be easily divided into two sections: before you get to the high altitude town of Namche Bazar and after. The first portion requires no altitude acclimatization and offers views of green hills, rhododendron forests, terraced fields, and the towns that overlook them. The second, the upper portion, is noted for a decrease in green terraced fields, but an increase in the mountain views that are the primary drawing card of Nepal.

As I hiked along this knee-friendly portion of the trail, it rewarded me with gorgeous views of the valleys stretched out below. The day before and in the days to come, I was to see the effects of the enormous glaciers to the north manifested in crystal-blue streams gushing and rumbling over boulders in the riverbed.

A smooth dirt path wound its way through pine trees that looked strikingly like northern Arizona. I passed waterfalls and crossed suspension bridges as we meandered to the higher elevation.

To be out in the mountain scenery of Nepal for several days on end blew the dust from a soul that for too long had been inundated with the poverty, pollution, and money-grubbing hawkers of Asia's cities. In both a literal and figurative sense, this was a breath of fresh air.

I felt pretty darn good at the end of today. My blisters had stabilized, as well as the pain in my left knee. Although my muscles were sore, I knew they would start to recover in a day or two, just as they had for the Brit and the Dutchy. I even caught up to those guys on this day and hiked beside them for the last one and a half hours. The only new pain I felt was from my pack. I might not have had it sitting properly on my hips because the tops of my shoulders hurt right where the straps crossed.

(Note: This trip was a major learning experience for a novice trekker like me. I became far more comfortable with my gear after five months on the road. I learned how to position my pack for the greatest comfort and discovered how to conveniently organize my equipment.)

Everyone I had met so far on the trail had told me that Gokyo Ri was the best place to go if you were after a view. This affirmed my decision to go there, instead of Everest Base Camp and Kala Patthar, so I was sticking with the original plan -- barring any unforeseen developments. My aches and pains were under control. My only remaining fear was the great crapshoot of high-altitude trekking -- acute mountain sickness (AMS).

AMS is a lurking ogre in the mind of every trekker who has paid the money and endured the strife of hiking up to the Everest region. There are no rules to why it strikes one person or another, only guidelines to minimize its effects, which, in mild cases, consist of headaches, nausea, sleeplessness, and erratic heartbeats and breathing, among other symptoms. Normal acclimatization includes all of those to a lesser degree. Severe AMS results in far worse effects. Depending on your physical condition and whether you receive treatment, you could die.

Descending is the best cure, and ascending at a slow rate (no more than 1,100 feet per day) is the recommended prevention.

So far, my only symptoms had been consistent with normal acclimatization. Each time I ascended to a higher altitude, I had great difficulty sleeping, maybe getting two hours of sleep a night. (That didn't help with the trekking, by the way.) As I lay in my sleeping bag, shivering for warmth, I could feel and hear my heart racing in my chest. My normal resting heart rate is 60 beats per minute (bpm). Since I had landed in Phaplu, my heart rate had been hovering at 80 bpm, climbing to above 100 at times while I was lying in bed.

The worst thing, however, was the breathing. As I lay in the rack and finally drifted off to dreamland, I had been shocked into consciousness by a lack of oxygen as I gasped to recover my breath. For a few minutes, I had to breathe deeply from my mouth to re-establish the proper oxygen level in the blood and the brain. I'm telling you, it was weird and unpleasant -- and it got worse later in the trek.

Day 4
Chaurikharka (9,055 feet) to Namche Bazar (11,285 feet) -- 8.5 miles

The knee took a turn for the worse on this day. It was strange because this was a portion of the trail considered by my guidebook writer to be "flat."

(Flat, that is, except for the final ascent up to Namche, a heart-pounding 1,450-foot climb over one mile. That approximates climbing Camelback Mountain, near Phoenix, Ariz., but add the factors of starting at about 10,000 feet and carrying a backpack.)

In actuality, the trail here was not flat at all. When juxtaposed with the preceding terrain, yes, it was flat (relatively speaking). But the meaning of "flat" in the Himalayas comes nowhere close to its textbook definition of "level, even, without irregularities; horizontal".

What a joke. Tell that to my knees.

As I hiked along, motoring up the ascents but wincing on the descents, I began pondering why I had come to Nepal and, specifically, why I had paid the money and put forth the effort to do a trek. Yes, I like hiking, and yes, the exercise is good. It was great to get away from the city, and it was great to see how the locals live. But time and time again, my mind kept returning to the one necessary condition that would make my trip to Nepal a complete success: a brilliant view of the Himalayas, and that view had to include Everest.

I didn't want to see a poster, a postcard, or someone else's photograph. I didn't want to see it from a plane or a helicopter. I wanted to stand before those beautiful mountains and fill my own eyes with their glory -- in person and unadulterated.

But I had developed this knee problem that might shoot the whole deal, which might efface the dream. And what was worse -- much worse -- was if I caused a completely debilitating injury, how would I continue the next six months of walking around the world?

That was my greatest fear.

As soon as I realized the potential gravity of the situation, which at the present was merely pain and not injury, my decision became much easier. Although I have a strong streak of "toughen up and finish what you started," the pragmatic side of my personality took over. I decided to forgo the aggressive hike up to Gokyo peak and its world-class view, and instead to make a much shorter and less taxing hike to the town of Tengboche (five miles east of Namche), where I would also have a nice view of the mountains and Mount Everest.

Here's what my guidebook says about Tengboche:

> "Climb steeply at first through forest and then more
> gradually to the Thyangboche saddle. At dawn the view is
> magnificent: Kwangde (6,187 metres), Tawachee (6,542

metres), Everest (8,848 metres), Nuptse (7,855 metres), Lhotse (8,616 metres), Ama Dablam (6,856 metres), Kangtega (6,779 metres) and Thamserku (6,608 metres), all arrayed in a stunning panorama."

So that didn't sound so bad. I was disappointed, to be sure. But I wasn't wringing my hands and crying in my beer. I would still achieve my goal, albeit something less than what could have been. I perked up and decided to make the best of the situation.

"Hey, I'm hiking in Nepal, right? This is a good time, and a lot of people are jealous. So what if you can't go to Gokyo Ri? There's a lot of other great stuff to see and do."

When I thought about it, in the comfort of a Kathmandu cyber café, that streak of accomplishment and finishing what you started did come through in my decision to truncate the trek. I was willing to swallow my pride and not carry out the original trekking plan in order to complete a much larger mission -- the rest of my world trip.

It reminded me of what we used to say in the Navy when discussing air-to-air combat. A pilot may find himself in a jam and not be able to gain the offensive against his enemy. His only choice is to bug out (that is, run away). There is no shame in this. The saying goes, "Run away to fight again another day."

I read *Into Thin Air: A Personal Account of the Mount Everest Disaster,* by Jon Krakauer during my trek. In 1996, several expeditions made an ascent on Mount Everest on May 11. The weather turned sour, and several people perished. Turnaround times were ignored, and several people pushed on when turning back might have saved their lives. I believe the fighter lesson can easily be applied to mountaineering and a host of other activities.

I informed D.B. of my decision, and we discussed what we could do with the extra days in the highland region that had just been created. I had also created more leeway on how far we would need to hike each day upon our return to the lowland region. This thought gave me comfort. I couldn't help but think of those steep hills and the pain they would deal on the hike back to Phaplu.

The final push up to Namche was challenging. But there's something about being near the end that allows you to push on. The hike had not been as demanding on this day as the day before (minus the joint pain), so we made it to the top in good time. I used a technique that I learned from my flight-school buddy, Jack "Hoss" Ledford.

Hoss was a Marine, and in a lot better shape than I. After flight school we took a cross-country trip that included a stop at the Grand Canyon. Hoss had never seen it and was as giddy as a schoolboy to run down to the bottom and back.

Not realizing what I was getting into, I had bounded along behind him on the South Kaibab trail (the steepest one) to the bottom with two 16-ounce bottles of water and a camera. It was late May, and the temperature was climbing. We ignored all the signs about water ("this trail is not recommended during the summer months" and "don't attempt this trail unless you are in exceptional shape, have at least a gallon of water per person," etc.) The kicker was the sentence about mule rescue, "Mule rescue is very expensive and unreliable. You will not be rescued after dark."

We even took pictures beside the signs, laughing in the face of these warnings.

The trip down took little time and filled our eyes with magnificent scenery that I photographed. However, the trip back up has two photos: one about 100 feet from the bottom of the South Kaibab trail, and one at the top -- of two depleted, stupid and lucky young men. Well, Hoss had a lot less trouble than I and could have made it up the canyon much faster if it weren't for me slowing him down.

The problem was hydration. As much as I told my legs to move, they started freezing up. That damn sign about mule rescue and all the other stuff kept springing to mind. I couldn't believe how irresponsible I had been.

But Hoss saved me with his hiking technique. We started

using our watches to hike for a set amount of time, no matter what, and then rest for a set amount of time. No more, no less. I think we started off by hiking for 10 minutes and resting for two. My legs got so weak that by the end we were hiking for one minute and lying on our backs in the middle of the trail for five minutes while people stepped around us. Whenever we started up, I would glance at my watch at the 20-second point in the hopes that a minute had passed.

At the top, Hoss bought me a grape Gatorade. I've loved that stuff ever since.

That's the technique I employed on the hike up to Namche. But this time I was feeling much better. We hiked for 15 minutes and rested for two. At a rest stop halfway up, D.B. said we had about 45 minutes left. Perfect! That's just three of those 15-minute increments. It really helped the mental attitude.

Day 5
Namche Bazar (11,285 feet)
Rest Day

As I lay larva-like in the cocoon of my sleeping bag during the wee hours of the morning, my mind began to spin ideas of how I would return to Kathmandu. I was looking for the most pain-free route that would maximize my time in the highland area of the trek.

While contemplating the adversity of the steep hikes to be found in the lowland portion, a voice came to me in the dark. It was the words of the Canadian hiker I had met on the trail two days earlier: "Another friend of mine got tired of the walking. He's taking a helicopter out of Lukla."

A helicopter out of Lukla! That sounded like a brilliant idea! I was scheduled to fly from Phaplu to Kathmandu on March 5. If I flew from Lukla instead, I would save at least two days, probably three, and be able to change my plans back to seeing Gokyo Ri. Plus, I would minimize the knee problems that would certainly plague me on the return route.

How much would this be worth to me? To minimize the

chance of injury, maximize time in the highland region, and get my view from Gokyo peak? I put a ballpark figure at $100 and went to talk with D.B. about it.

D.B. didn't bat an eye. He informed me that the direct flight from Lukla to Kathmandu would be more expensive and harder to arrange than hopping on one of the frequent supply runs to Jiri. From there, I could take a $3 bus to Kathmandu. That sounded reasonable to me.

Because he would still fly back from Phaplu, we would have to split up at some point. We worked out a deal for how much money he would leave with me for breakfast, lunch, dinner, lodging, etc., and I agreed to pay him the same daily wage that Global Adventures does for the two extra days we had added onto the trek back in Phaplu ($14 a day). The money I had paid up front was for a guided trek through only March 3. So the extra two days would have been paid to Global Adventures back in Kathmandu at $25 a day with this new plan. I saved $11 a day but wouldn't have the use of a guide or expenses.

Another way to look at it is I spent $14 a day on nothing.

But in my defense, I would have never been able to work out this deal with Global Adventures back in Kathmandu. They wouldn't make any money on the deal, and it would keep their guide in the field for two extra days, right when the season was getting busy.

After some quick analysis of days left, money spent, and time that I wanted to spend back in Kathmandu and then India, I elected to fly out of Lukla on March 3, taking my trek back to 12 days long.

D.B. got the hotel staff to dial Lukla airport and put Chungba Sherpa on the line, the local chopper-ticket guru.

> "Hello. Yes, I would like to take a helicopter from Lukla to Jiri," I said. "Is this possible on March 3?"
> "No problem," he said. "Just arrive at the Khumbu Resort the day before by 4 o'clock.
> "Great. Who should I ask for?" I asked.

"Chungba Sherpa. Everybody in Namche knows me up there."

"How much will this cost?"

"One hundred dollars."

"OK, that sounds all right," I said.

"Yeah. You come here to the Khumbu Resort between 5 and 6 o'clock. The pilots stay here. They eat here. You can get your ticket here."

"OK, so I should be there between 5 and 6?"

"Yeah, yeah. No problem. You'll also get a refund on your ticket from Phaplu. You'll have to pay 10 percent charge, but you'll get money back."

"Oh really? That sounds great. OK, I'll see you in Lukla then."

"Yeah, yeah. Just be here around 6 o'clock. You'll get your ticket and fly to Jiri at 6:45 the next morning. You can catch the bus from Jiri to Kathmandu the same day."

"OK. Thanks. What's your name again?"

"Yeah, yeah. Chungba Sherpa," he said, a bit full of himself. "Everybody knows me up there."

So it was decided. We would split ways in about five days after hiking to Gokyo Ri and back. I was pleased with my efforts. I really had to wheel and deal to make this happen, but none of it would have come to fruition if D.B. hadn't been so flexible. I was lucky to have him as my guide. As capricious as I had been, he let it all roll off his back and did his best to help with the changing plans.

One of the most welcome results of this latest change was that today would be a rest day. To acclimatize, a rest day is recommended upon arrival in Namche from the lowland region. My body was begging for it.

I spent the day sitting in the dining room of the hotel, reading and writing in my journal. There usually wasn't a whole lot to do in Namche, but I was lucky that this day was Saturday. All of the Nepalis with heavy loads we had passed on the trail were in Namche at the weekly market.

D.B. and I went outside to mill about and work some deals for a while. Most of the things sold were quite modern: Candy bars and drink mixes for "hot lemon'" water; North Face active wear, and Caterpillar-brand work boots. Some of the less Western stuff was piles of flip-flops (shower shoes), scarves, and other clothing. We stood by the meat section for a few minutes watching as Gurkha knives were used to slice portions of cow meat.

I wound up buying five Snickers bars for 62 cents apiece. That wasn't exactly cheap, but better than the $1 per bar I had paid on the trail.

Unfortunately, a thick mist obscured the day's view of the surrounding mountains. I was to later see how beautiful the view was from this small hillside town. Namche, built on a terraced hill, sits in a bowl of a mountain. Literally, imagine a flat-topped mountain made of clay; then push a bowl in to one side of it right at the top. From one side of town you can see the other.

The lodge we slept in was nicer than most but fairly typical in design. Here is a description of what is to be found among the lodges of the Everest Base Camp trail.

First, they are all made of wood. Some have cozy cabin-like interiors, while those higher up on the trail are spartan. Each has a common dining room, the majority of which are barren, save for the eight-foot-long, two-foot-wide rectangular tables placed along the perimeter. Everyone sits with his or her back to the outer wall on bench-style seating that is built into said wall. Rugs that approximate the length and width of the tables are sat upon as you vie for the attention of generally uninterested staff when you're ready to order a meal.

What is it with the customer service throughout Asia? A few of these hotels/guesthouses were really good about showing concern for their patrons. But the majority were staffed by employees who made themselves scarce, intentionally ignored your request, or were just plain clueless.

None of the establishments had any form of insulation. The dining rooms feel especially cold because they are generally lined with wonderfully large windows. These afford spectacular views during the day, but allow the accumulated heat energy to leak slowly into the dark at night.

To heat these spacious enclosures, a variation of the standard wood-fired stove is used. But it's not really a stove, just a heating unit. And the quality is generally poor. The chimney that extends through the roof is rarely air-tight. And in the high-elevations, where ironically the quality of everything but the views goes downhill, the damn things are falling apart.

To make matters worse, in the higher elevations, above the area where trees are common and wood is generally burned, the people have adapted to their environment by burning yak dung for fuel. I don't think they use it for cooking, but they sure use it for these heaters.

I can't tell you how much I hate yak-dung smoke.

The stuff burns poorly and smokes to high heaven, and if analyzed, I'm sure would be heavily carcinogenic or something else that takes years off lives. Several of the chimneys up north leaked. Here's my postulate: The hot yak-dung smoke hits the cold air outside, is condensed and mixed with the ambient humidity, attaches itself to the chimney, and then drips down on unsuspecting tourists.

I can only confirm the last part because it happened to me. Talk about gross and unsanitary. I remember the night the hotel chimney dripped on me. The hotel manager thought it was hilarious. Yeah, real funny guy.

Tied for sanitation and annoyance honors with the choking smoke that effuses from rickety heaters into unventilated dining rooms is the inevitable addition of yak dung to your food. There's nothing more unappealing than watching a cook load yak patty after yak patty into the heater and then walk back into the kitchen to prepare your meal. Believe me, he didn't wash his hands.

As I said, the use of yak dung occurs only in the northern reaches of the trail. But as I was to find out, it didn't take long to feel its effects.

The bedrooms in Everest trail lodges are basic but reasonably comfortable. Either cement or wood floors support two wooden cots that are slightly wider than the dining tables. The mattress is usually just a one-inch piece of foam. I doubled my comfort by putting two of them together.

The outhouses are fairly uniform. Of course, in this part of the world the facilities are almost exclusively "squatters." A wood floor opens in a rectangular hole where occasionally foot markers are placed on either side. There is usually a large pile of leaves and pine straw in the room. I guess that alternating layers of waste and leaves lay below. I never remember any of these "bathrooms" smelling, and only one had a, I repeat *a* fly. But they sure were cold.

Day 6
Namche Bazar (11,285 feet) to Dole (13,485 feet) -- 5 miles

I actually had a decent (relatively speaking) night's sleep last night. My legs were no longer sore, and my blisters had a day of rest. I even walked down the stairs to go to bed without any pain in my left knee. My spirits were up, and I knew I was adjusting to both the hiking and the altitude. But I still had a way to go, so I remained cautiously optimistic.

The first 30 to 45 minutes of this day's hike was up a steep grade. We then followed a contour line east that slowly curved back to the north. At some point along this walk, a beautiful valley opened up on the right. Simultaneously, the tall peaks of the Khumbu region began to show themselves. What a welcome sight!

Back in the valley below, the Brit, the Dutchy and I had met two women traveling in the opposite direction. They related to us how great the views were up there and how much more enjoyable the hiking was because of it. Finally I was there -- able to start enjoying what I had come for.

They also said how fantastic Gokyo Ri was. They said once you got to the top, you would forget everything -- all the pain, the altitude, the blisters, the poor sleep, everything. At the time, I had not changed my plan to fly out of Lukla. I was skeptical. I somehow doubted I was going to be able to forget the brutal return hike that was hanging over my head.

But now I was basking in the fresh sun that was just starting to break from the mist of the past two days. The hike was flat (much closer to textbook definition this time), and I had a full day of rest to energize me. Plus, I was starting to see more wildlife.

Two days earlier on the hill leading to Namche, we had spotted two male danphe pheasants. On this day we spotted both a male and female. Wow, are they gorgeous, with fantastic iridescent hues of green and blue on the main body and a flash of red near the head. I took far too many pictures of what will only be a speck of color in the frame, but I just couldn't help it.

Just around the corner, D.B. spied an enormous vulture. It spread its wings, displaying at least a six-foot wingspan, and took flight. Watching the enormous bird effortlessly glide into the deep valley over which I peered was mesmerizing. It sounds silly, but I wished at that moment I could take flight with him. He flew with such grace and ease; it was a pleasure to watch.

Later in the day, flurries started to fall. After about 30 minutes, a steady snow was upon us just as we stopped for lunch in Phurte Tenge. I was excited by the snowfall. I honestly couldn't remember the last time I had seen snow falling. It had to be since before I moved to Phoenix in '97. In any event, I was thankful for the waterproof shell I was wearing and the duck's-back waterproof protector for my backpack.

After lunch we emerged to find a blanket of snow covering the forest. I was thrilled. Hardly any trekkers were continuing in the snowfall so we practically had the trail to ourselves. That might have been a factor in what I saw next.

Forty-five minutes or so into the hike, D.B. stopped and looked around carefully. We were both quiet. He took a few cautious steps, squinted, and then pointed down the hill on our right.

"Musk deer."

Sure enough, about 30 yards below us stood a doe the size of a standard North American whitetail. I felt so lucky. The view was great. There were hardly any trees to block the sight of her in the snow. She slowly walked along the side of the hill, paused, and then disappeared behind some brush. I love seeing wildlife, and this was totally unexpected.

I saw a little bit more wildlife on the trek. One morning as I sat sipping tea in the dining room, I looked up to see another pheasant-like bird sitting outside in the cold. This one was gray with white speckles. D.B. said it was a Tibetan pheasant. She must have sat there for 30 minutes, only occasionally shifting in the wind.

On the last day before descending back to the lowland region, I spotted a large brown mountain goat cross the path. What a strange and foreign sight for these low-altitude eyes. He crossed up the hill and parked himself behind a rock. I stood for about 10 minutes, hoping he would come out for a photo, but he failed to cooperate. That would just have to be a memory like the musk deer.

One common Nepali animal that is no less interesting for an American is the yak. What a big ol' hairy animal that is! I took a bunch of pictures of these domesticated and quite docile fellows. They roam freely on the hillsides, providing wonderful Kodak moments for those who keep an eye out. I have some great shots of yaks staring blankly at me with white-capped mountains and clear blue skies in the background.

This was a great day for wildlife and hiking. I really enjoyed it. If only they could all be like this, I thought.

One thing that increased my speed and diminished my pain was the use of a hiking stick, eventually two. I had never used a stick for hiking. It seemed like such a Heidi/Swiss Alps kind of thing. In fact, the Dutch guy I had met on Day 2 in Bupsa was using two ski poles to move along. I couldn't resist poking fun. The sight of him marching along the dusty lowland trail as if he were cross-country skiing was hilarious.

I made a few cracks like: "Hey, look who it is. The Alpine skier! Which way to the bunny slopes, man?"

The next day I was using one stick, and two days later I was a full convert with two. Actually, it was D.B. who convinced me to try them and ultimately found just the right sized tree branch for me to use. He then whittled off any irregularities to make a beautiful hiking stick.

Those sticks made all the difference in the world. I heard a lot of different estimates in the dining halls of various guesthouses about how much weight they relieve. The Dutchy said it was eight kilos (17 pounds). Someone else said five pounds apiece. Another story going around was if you added up all the weight that you pushed with your poles over the duration of this trek, you could lift an elephant.

Whatever the official figure, they worked exceptionally well. I felt as if I could shoot up the hills (until I exhausted myself from both exertion and the paucity of oxygen), but it took me a while to get the hang of them going down.

I was still worried about my left knee. However, the views were enough to push it to the back of my mind during the hike. It was a great day.

But trouble was brewing. Tonight would be the first in a yak-dung establishment. I was having stomach trouble, and my blisters wouldn't fully heal. I tried to sit around the heater and let air get to the right heel (it was an open wound and a little sticky), but it just wouldn't stiffen up.

I applied my anti-bacterial cream and reapplied moleskin before climbing into my sleeping bag. Some nights I had taken my socks off in the sleeping bag, in the hope that the sores would clot, but I couldn't do that up here. I would never get to sleep because of the frigid temperature.

Compared to most nights, I would sleep OK tonight, for which I was thankful.

Day 7
Dole (13,485 feet) to Phang (14,929 feet) -- 6 miles

The hike from Dole to Phang took only three hours. The first entry concerning the trail in my handwritten journal is:

"Today's hike was fantastic, albeit a little tiring in parts due to the steep climbs, but more important the higher elevation."

When I wrote that entry, I was still glowing from my luck of having the freshly laid snow to cover what is normally black tundra. The scenery in these northern parts of the trek is stark. The sharp white peaks that surround the valley offset brown or black barren hills. Nepal had not received much snow this winter, so the fortune I enjoyed by having experienced one of the few and final dustings of winter was greatly appreciated.

The snow made everything glisten with purity. It also reflected a tremendous amount of sunlight that could quickly burn an unsuspecting hiker. D.B. and I smeared a coat of sun block on our faces and necks and donned sunglasses for our walks in the snow.

The sun that had previously dodged in and out of clouds or had been entirely obscured by mist for the past several days was now unveiled in bold fashion. As the days got longer and the calendar closed in on March, the weather began to behave more and more like typical Nepali spring. That means clear of clouds in the morning with a little "weather" in the afternoon. Generally speaking, my best views came at the beginning of the day. The afternoon and early evening was always a crapshoot.

On this day, the views were inspiring. The sight of these giants gave me energy and purpose. The tallest of those within line of sight was Cho Oyu (26,750 feet) -- one of the world's tallest mountains. I was puzzled as the day went by that although the rest of the sky offered unrestricted views, the patch of blue just to the east of Cho Oyu always had a long white cloud, which blocked that half of the mountain and whatever else lay behind it. I later realized that it wasn't a cloud but snow! The wind at that altitude must be vicious and was blowing the fresh snow off of the western face of the mountain. It wasn't until the next afternoon that either the wind died down or there wasn't enough snow left to make a cloud. Impressive.

We arrived at our lodge in Phang by midday and relaxed in the sunlight after lunch. I ordered a local special called parotha. Basically, it was dough wrapped around vegetables and then deep-fried -- very tasty.

The mainstay of the Sherpa diet, along with many other Nepalis, and what one can expect to see on every menu, is dhal bat.

I'm not an expert in translation, but from what I gathered, dhal means "lentil" and bat means "with rice." So what you get is a bowl of lentil soup, a huge plate of rice, some pan-fried potatoes, and maybe some pickled cabbage or radish on the side.

Dhal bat comes in a few different flavors and forms, but is always hot and salty, and always good for you. The carbohydrates from the rice and potatoes replenish the energy burned during the day, and the protein from the lentils helps to repair the muscle damage done on the trail. I ordered dhal bat frequently, along with Sherpa stew. Sherpa stew has as many variations as there are Sherpas who prepare it. You never know what you'll be getting other than hot and salty. I always liked it however it was prepared.

One other thing about the food on the Everest trek: The majority of the dhal bat, Sherpa stew, fried potatoes, and other vegetable dishes will come with an extra condiment known as dirt. Usually, the culprit was the potatoes, although I almost cracked a tooth while munching on the lentils and rice in my dhal soup one evening.

There's not much one can do about this. What's the protocol here, after all, to send the meal back to the kitchen over a little dirt? Come on. It took more than an hour to receive the first round. I was hungry and cold. I wasn't going to cause a fuss and wait around for another hour, only to be served another plate of dirt-sprinkled potatoes.

But it's an indicator of a greater problem. The Nepali standard of sanitation on this trek route isn't at the same level as back in the States. There is a different attitude and lack of awareness. Running water is sporadic, usually reserved for the hot shower. I doubt the idea of washing one's hands before food preparation carries much weight up here. Why bother, right? They're just going to get dirty again when they dump the next load of yak dung in the heater.

As we lay basking in the afternoon sun and dozing serenely, trouble struck. Somewhere along the trail I had eaten something that finally caught up to me, and I had been having some pretty horrific gas that wouldn't abate. Eventually, I had an accident in my only pair of pants.

To minimize the weight of my pack, I had brought only one pair of pants and three pair of underwear. What was I going to do? I tentatively slid my socks and shoes on, grabbed another pair of underwear, and deftly maneuvered to the outhouse for a little damage control.

I breathed a huge sigh of relief when I saw that it wasn't as bad as I had imagined. My pants were dark blue and hardly showed the spot. My underwear was black, so I couldn't tell how bad it was, but I wouldn't be wearing these again anyway.

I returned to the lodge and swallowed two Pepto-Bismol pills. I was concerned that with my new battle I wouldn't stay hydrated enough to cope with the altitude increase. D.B. had told me to stay well hydrated; it would help with acclimatization. I had only one more ascent to go, so I figured I'd be all right.

I included this gastro-intestinal portion to give a complete picture of my physical condition. My health had a major effect on the total experience of hiking in the Himalayas. It is a critical part of understanding my mind-set and what it is like to undertake a trek in Nepal.

All along the trail, I monitored my heartbeat. Back in Namche after a day of rest, it decreased to a resting 60 bpm. On this day, it was back up to 80, which I took for normal at this elevation, without sufficient time to acclimate.

That night we sat around the heater while yak dung was burned. The dining room had particularly poor ventilation, and the condensing smoke dripped on me. My eyes became irritated, my nose was stuffed up, and I began to cough. This was where I realized I'm just not made to live in a yak dung environment. D.B. often slept in the empty dining rooms where the heater was. The night before I had slept there with him, too, but this evening I elected a freezing cold room with breathable air.

Day 8
Phang (14,929 feet) to Gokyo (15,716 feet) -- 3 miles

Making a trip to the outhouse last night, I realized how many stars I could see. I'm sure you've heard people describe the nighttime view hundreds of miles from the closest major city. You forget exactly what it's like if there's been some time between these experiences. That was one of the benefits of being at sea. No lights for thousands of miles out there. What a sight.

But just as important, my stargazing meant that the weather was staying clear. Maybe I would get an afternoon view from Gokyo Ri.

My sleep last night was fitful. The temperature dropped precipitously after the sun went down, and I woke up to find the water in my squirt bottle frozen. I was sure that it got well below freezing in my room. My nose was completely stuffed up, and I spent the night breathing through my mouth. Sometimes I felt as if I was suffocating in the thin air, and I lay for minutes on end taking deep, deep breaths. I estimated that I slept for all of two hours while lying in bed for ten.

Fortunately, the Pepto-Bismol tablets seemed to be helping. I felt as if the situation was under control and decided to wait until the evening before taking another tablet.

The hike to Gokyo was short but strenuous, again because of the altitude. The terrain was for the most part flat and covered with snow. It took us only two hours to cover the distance, though D.B. had estimated three. Again, I had walked too fast.

We passed two snow-covered lakes before arriving at Gokyo town and its resident lake. I love mountain lakes. You round a corner and think, "Hello! What are you doing way up here?" During the spring, when the ice has melted, the lakes are the most blazing and deep shade of turquoise blue. I got to see one-third of the lake beside Gokyo void of ice. Only Mother Nature can create such a color.

As we approached Gokyo, I kept one eye peeled on the clouds. It was only 10:45 a.m., so I expected the sky to be clear, and it was. I started thinking of dropping my bag at the lodge and heading up Gokyo Ri, a stone's throw away, which looms over the town.

If I could squeeze in the hike today, I would have more energy tomorrow for the return hike, as well as be the beneficiary of the afternoon sun on the mountains. The next day, the morning sun would cast shadows on the entire range to the east -- the one with Everest and all the other showpieces. At the same time, I was tired and knew it would be a tough climb. I decided to eat lunch and see how the weather looked.

As we sat in the lodge, awaiting my rice and curried vegetables, an Australian woman with a bellowing voice and forward personality came blowing in, allowing the door to SLAM behind her

> "Whoa, that was great! I can't believe how great Gokyo Ri was. Oh my God, you've *got* to do it! That was worth 12 days of being dirty and smelling bad. Not a cloud in the sky.
> "Hey! Can we get two bowls of Sherpa stew out here?" she yelled, barging into the kitchen. "Is that OK? And two diet Cokes. Yeah. Thank youuuuuuuuuu!
> "Oh, the Sherpa stew is so good here. I had a bowl back in Random Town and it wasn't near as good as this stew.
> "We're going to be checking out," she reported loudly, back in the kitchen again. "My husband's not feeling well. Something with the altitude."
> "Did you just get here?" she asked me. "Gokyo Ri is incredible. We just did it. It was so fantastic!"

I vacillated among annoyance, genuine happiness for her, and excitement for my own ascent of Gokyo Ri.

A few other trekkers (more subdued than the first) arrived at the lodge over the next couple of hours. The weather was holding up nicely, I had a full belly, and my anticipation was killing me. I decide to take a hot shower (always best during the heat and light of the day -- there is rarely a light bulb) and then make a play for the summit.

The Ascent
Gokyo (15,716 feet) to Gokyo Ri (17,586 feet) 1 hour, 40 minutes.

At 2 o'clock in the afternoon, I left the lodge and set out for the culmination of my trek. I told myself, "Well this is it. We're gonna see what this whole 'Gokyo thing' is all about."

I looked forward to the view, but felt a sense of calm and relief, knowing that the summit was within reach and I was going to get there. This was a feeling unlike that of the previous several days when I had secretly worried that my knee would give out. Or I worried that I would become too sick to continue, that acute mountain sickness would strike, or that the weather wouldn't cooperate.

None of those obstacles lay before me as I began my approach to the base of the mountain. I was going to make it.

The hike up Gokyo Ri, a 1,870-foot climb, presented one final hurdle for the intrepid view seeker. The distance covered was about eight-tenths of a mile. That means it was pretty darn steep. And the altitude was a real kick in the pants. My hiking map had an altitude/oxygen rate chart on it. The chart showed the oxygen rate at sea level to be 100 percent, compared with the top of Gokyo Ri which was a meager 51 percent. So each breath felt like only half of what I was accustomed to.

I stopped several times and gasped for breath. But two things spurred me on. The first was the thought of the boisterous woman at the lodge. Most estimates of the climb up Gokyo Ri are two hours. I asked her how long it took to summit the peak, and she said about an hour and fifty minutes. I couldn't allow myself to take longer than that. But more importantly, the second impetus that kept my legs moving and my heart pumping was the anticipation of what lay above.

Gokyo Ri is a bald, ugly, brown little mountain. It offers no aesthetic value of its own to the scenery of the Himalayas. But its purpose as a vehicle to deliver you to Nirvana is unquestioned. About three-quarters of the way up, during one of my increasingly frequent breaks, I noticed how wonderful the view had become. I thought to myself, "Boy, am I getting high. Amazing how much I can see from up here. What will the top be like?"

Ten times better.

Upon cresting the last boulder and approaching the traditional Nepali prayer flags that mark the summit of Gokyo Ri, I gazed in awe from the zenith of her heights.

I now had a sense of what it must be like for a mountaineer to make his final ascent after a long and arduous struggle. I felt emotion well up inside me as I took in the unbelievable vastness of the Himalayas. I didn't feel anything but the wonder of how glorious it was and the tingling in my nose from tears. I didn't understand at the time that I was filled with joy -- the joy of having endured, of having overcome. Of being blessed with the good health and fortune to experience one of God's most spectacular creations. I relived those same feelings as I wrote these words.

I hopped up on the stone that held the prayer flags and asked D.B. to snap a photo. I happened to be wearing my college shirt underneath my jacket so I stripped down and bared the letters of my alma mater. The mountains make you nuts.

I wasn't cold in the least for the first 10 minutes. In fact, I forgot all about what those hikers we had met earlier on the trail had said -- the bit about forgetting all of the pain and strife. I think I forgot to forget. I was 100 percent bore sighted on soaking in as much of this moment as I could. And taking some good photos so I could share it with others.

About 20 minutes ahead of D.B. and me was a Brit. Two Swedes and their guide followed us by the same margin. You should have seen the ebullience among us. We were running around swapping cameras and striking poses. And stopping to fill our eyes with all that surrounded us.

The afternoon sun was slowly heading for the horizon in the west. To the east lay the behemoths that we all had come to see. So our star performers were appropriately spotlighted for us. I could see so many mountains that it's impossible to remember all the names. But I made a special mental note of what Mount Everest looked like in the light. The one I've read about and heard tales of since I can't remember when. I'm here to tell you it's a colossus, resolute in its stand against time and the elements.

The clouds cooperated by staying either above or well to the side of the great peaks, but put on a show in the valley below by thickly blocking our view of Gokyo town. Standing above the clouds, we couldn't have asked for more.

The great divider between Gokyo Ri and the mountains to the east is the Ngozumpa glacier. It is a rocky mass of miniature mountains, nothing like the flat patch of snow and ice I had imagined. But its role in the view from Gokyo is to add a sense of grandeur and height to the Himalayas. Because it has carved out a deep valley floor, one can truly appreciate how gargantuan the snow-capped peaks are.

I'll never forget standing up there. The memory of that moment makes every tribulation, down to the smallest annoyance, worth the trip.

Afterword

I was able to record only as far as the summit of Gokyo Ri before leaving Kathmandu for Varanasi, India. I never had the opportunity to sit down and finish the writing. Although the scenic view from Gokyo Ri may be the culmination of the trek, it represented only a part of the peak's significance and the reward of my efforts. The deeper meaning was the sense of victory after overcoming the obstacles of the preceding week.

The last quarter of the trek was marked by a period of growing ill health, painful joints, and then a slow recovery. The helicopter and truck-bed journey from Lukla to Jiri to Kathmandu turned out to be one of the best days on the trek. Sometimes the most enjoyable experiences are unplanned and unexpected.

22

Where East Meets West: A Modern Confluence in Istanbul

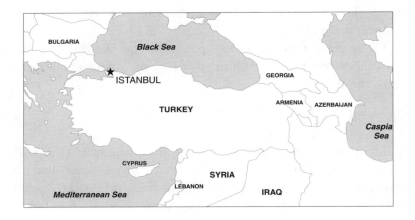

Let me tell you something: Istanbul is a great city, and Turkey is a great country.

After recovering in Kathmandu from my Everest trek, I journeyed south to India for three weeks of punishing budget travel. I came out of India distrustful of everyone and short-tempered. To say it tried my patience is an understatement. In fact, it almost broke my back.

India is well-known for its inhospitable backpacker environment. I certainly received a healthy dose of pain while battling the auto-rickshaw drivers and outright swindlers who lurk around the tourist sites. On the other hand, I was fortunate to be treated to Indian hospitality when I visited the relatives of a friend from Phoenix. Of course, I must mention the Taj Mahal

Top: Aya Sofya—built by Emperor Justinian. Istanbul, Turkey.

Bottom left: The Trojan horse at Troy, Turkey.

Bottom right: Fisherman in the village of Sariyer along the banks of the Bosphorus near Istanbul.

-- the most beautiful building I have ever seen. Those two experiences were highlights that allowed me to glimpse another side of India's complex personality. I was thankful for both.

India is a fantastically diverse country, yet the same everywhere you go. I found numerous parallels to China -- the corruption, poverty, hassle, variety of landscape, tumultuous history, and distinct culture. The nation assaults your senses. You know when you're in India.

After India, I spent ten days in a combination recovery and break-neck touring mode. My family joined me for a thorough tour of Egypt. We spent our time zipping from site to site in an air-conditioned and capacious minibus. When we weren't sightseeing, we were relaxing in high-end hotels or floating down the Nile River on a five-star cruise ship. Every meal was a feast of world-class cuisine. The nourishment was much needed on my thin frame.

In addition to the historical aspect of seeing Egypt, it was a treat to spend time together and share the experience of the trip. My love of travel began as a child, on family trips both overseas and in a station wagon traveling around the States. So it felt quite natural to tour again as a family. The whole trip came off perfectly. We didn't even have to divide the seats into "your side" and "my side."

Toward the end of the Egypt trip, I began my preparations for Turkey. I wondered what the culture and ease of travel would be like. Friends had said that Istanbul is a unique mix of Eastern and Western cultures and certainly more Western than Cairo. How Turkey came to be admitted to NATO had always puzzled me. My vision of NATO is first world, economically strong and progressive nations. How could a Third World predominately Muslim country in the Middle East fit in with the nations of the North Atlantic Treaty Organization?

So I boarded the plane with those ideas in my head. Although reports told me to expect the West, I was prepared for a more arid and underdeveloped Middle-East nation. Reality was quite the opposite.

Approaching Istanbul's international airport by air, I peered out the window for my first view of Turkey. A landscape of gently rolling hills, green, green grass, and red-roofed houses with backyard pools greeted my eyes. This wasn't what I had expected. Pools?

This account is a little heavy on the history. Maybe it's because history is one of my favorite subjects and I was impressed with what I learned in Turkey. I suppose that historical facts are important to understand why I found certain places interesting.

ISTANBUL

Istanbul felt like a European city. The town exceeded my expectations and is firmly in place as one of the favorite cities on my trip. The airport was modern and efficient. Airports are a good litmus test of what you can expect of a city, and that notion held true in Istanbul.

This may sound like nitpicking, but the little things are sometimes as important as the overarching observations. The bathrooms in the airport were clean and provided both soap and a blower for drying hands. Soap and hand-drying apparatus are exceedingly rare in Asia. Unlike in Egypt, I didn't have to tip an attendant for performing the strenuous and dexterous task of turning on the water faucet for me. My guess is that Turkey has enough of an economic base to not require menial job creation.

The cab ride to my hotel was an absolute joy. Not only was the driver courteous and silent (thus saving me from the tedious "Where you from?" conversation), but also an honest-to-goodness working meter was present and used to determine the fare. No haggling! That was the case for all the taxis in Istanbul. I loved it.

Other European-like aspects were cobblestone streets, outdoor cafes, bakeries, and the people. I hadn't thought about race when I envisioned Turkey, but this struck me as a major factor in giving the city a feel. The people of Istanbul are of East

European origin instead of Middle-Eastern. The city would have an entirely different look if everyone were Arabian. Plus, the fashion was decidedly European. Blue jeans, black leather jackets, and generally dark colors dominated the clothing. Occasionally, I'd see a splash of red or yellow, but pastels were right out. I noticed the smell of perfume and cologne on the streets for the first time on my trip. That was a pleasant change from the trash pits of many Asian cities.

The vehicles on the streets were generally mid- or large-sized without a scooter or bicycle in sight. The roads were excellent, and the buildings were either modern or quaint. I didn't see partially completed buildings or dilapidated shambles anywhere.

As I toured the city on foot, I was thinking how much it felt like Europe. Then I would remind myself that I was in Europe. Technically, the western half of Istanbul is part of the European continent. Across the waterway that splits the city in two is Asia. Although I didn't explore the Asian side, it was there that I had noticed the nice red-roofed homes with swimming pools on my flight in. Indeed, Istanbul is a modern, comfortable, Western and secular city.

Just as one reaches that conclusion, however, the Islamic calls to prayer blast from loudspeakers on the minarets of mosques throughout the city. The view from any elevated vantage point reveals a skyline dotted with these minarets that rise from the metropolis. Nothing about this scene seems out of place from a distance. But from street level, the contrast between the trappings of Europe and the unmistakable sounds of Islam is remarkable.

At one moment, you feel as if you're in the heart of Europe, and in the next you've been transported to Mecca, complete with women in full Islamic dress and a man yodeling in Arabic. Eventually you get used to the spiritual interjection, and it no longer surprises, but it reminds you that this is a predominately Muslim nation. This region hasn't always been Muslim, however, and it hasn't always been Turkey. In fact, one of the reasons that I like Turkey so much and would love to return for a deeper look is its amazing history.

Turkey was an important part of the Greek Empire, then the Roman Empire, followed by the Ottoman Empire. Istanbul was known as Byzantium under the Greeks, Constantinople under the Romans (the capital of the empire for centuries), and finally Istanbul under the sultans of the Ottoman Empire.

A vast stretch of European, Middle-Eastern and North African real estate was controlled from this great city for hundreds of years. Elsewhere across the country, Greek and Roman ruins are both numerous and widespread. Furthermore, the Hittites who fought the ancient Egyptians were from this neck of the woods. Those facts were a revelation to me. My appreciation for Turkey as an important part of world history skyrocketed after this visit.

I spent a total of 10 days in Turkey, six in Istanbul. Here are a few of the things I saw:

AYA SOFYA -- For about 1,000 years, this was the biggest church in the world. Built by the Roman emperor Justinian in 537 A.D., it became a mosque in 1453 when Constantinople was conquered by the Ottomans. Although it is now a museum, the Aya Sofya (Church of Sacred Wisdom) has an uncanny church/mosque feel. As one enters and looks up past the immense and seemingly unsupported central dome (an architectural masterpiece, so I have read), a large mosaic of Mary and the boy Jesus looks down upon the congregation. On either side and just below are billboards with sayings from the Koran written in enormous Arabic letters. Such a strange combination.

TOPKAPI SARAYI (Palace) -- This is where the sultans of the Ottoman Empire called home from the mid-1400s to 1839. For some reason, the sultan who took over in 1839 decided he liked European-style architecture and shifted his residence to a new palace up the river.

Although Topkapi Sarayi (known as the Seraglio in Europe) is a nice place with some pleasant courtyards and good views, overall I was underwhelmed. I couldn't help but compare it to the Forbidden City in Beijing and the Silver Pagoda complex in

Phnom Penh. In both opulence and artistry, I found the Topkapi Sarayi disappointing.

Why?

The primary interior decoration used during the 18th-century Ottoman Empire was tile. Turkish tile is known for its quality and artistic designs. Testimony to its popularity with the royal family is the way it is plastered over the walls of the palace. In my opinion, overkill was reached. It looks as if someone took a trip to Home Depot on an amphetamine rush.

In addition, most of the designs are bland. I suppose there are a few shining examples of decorative tile, but those are few and far between. Maybe it's just that when I see that much tile in one place, I feel as if I'm either in the kitchen or a giant swimming pool.

THE BOSPORUS—The Aegean Sea and the Greek islands are about 225 miles southwest of Istanbul. A narrow strait leads up from the Aegean Sea toward Istanbul. This waterway, called the Dardanelles, runs north for about 50 miles to the Sea of Marmara. On the northern shore of the Sea of Marmara sits Istanbul. Twenty-five miles north of Istanbul lies the Black Sea. The seas are connected by another strait called the Bosporus. Both of these straits have been enormously important to trade between the East and the West for centuries. Many a battle has been fought for control of these shipping lanes. The history here is rich.

Cruising the Bosporus in a ferryboat or simply gazing down from a rooftop cafe on the shipping and fishing boats that traverse its waters are wonderful ways to pass an afternoon. Driving along the shoreline one afternoon, I noticed scores of dolphins porpoising their way north from the Sea of Marmara and into the strait.

Each bank of the waterway is a steep hill covered with trees, houses, palaces and forts. The topography of such hills affords some excellent views from both the water to the shore and vice versa. The houses are mostly white with red roofs, surrounded by trees. Since it was spring, much of the flora was in bloom, the most common of which was a tree with lavender blossoms. The scene from my ferry looked like an impressionist painting in a Parisian art gallery.

OVERNIGHT TRIPS

I took two overnight trips from Istanbul. The first was to the famous World War I battleground of Gallipoli at the entrance of the Dardanelles to the southwest. I also stopped by the ancient city of Troy, which sits just across the Dardanelles from Gallipoli. The second was to the former Ottoman capital of Bursa and its small neighbor, Iznik.

GALLIPOLI -- ANZAC stands for Australian and New Zealand Army Corps. A nine-month battle was fought by British, Indian, French and ANZAC troops against the Turks from April, 1918, to January, 1919, on the shores of the Gallipoli peninsula. The purpose was to control the Dardanelles and conquer Istanbul and the Bosporus, ultimately establishing a warm-water supply route through the Black Sea for the Russians fighting Germany on the eastern front. In the end, the Turks held their ground and forced the invaders to retreat.

April 25, 1918, was the day ANZAC troops landed on the western shore of Gallipoli and it has come to be known as ANZAC day. Each year thousands of Aussies and Kiwis come for a dawn service to memorialize their servicemen and celebrate the ANZAC spirit.

On that morning in 1918, Turkish infantry under the command of Lt. Col. Mustafa Kemal Ataturk greeted the ANZACs. This moment, followed by another crucial battle in August, made Mustafa a legendary hero that ultimately catapulted him to the leadership of a new nation -- Turkey. Ataturk means "Father of Turkey."

The rough parallels I draw between these historical events and American history are the landings at Normandy and Teddy Roosevelt's victory at San Juan Hill in Puerto Rico. Another easy comparison is Ataturk and George Washington.

Ataturk was a brilliant and daring leader. He created modern

Turkey practically single-handedly. On the wall of a museum, I noticed a quote from Winston Churchill (who has received some historical criticism for bumbling the campaign for the Dardanelles). I will paraphrase, "Each century gives us one true genius. Unfortunately in this century, he belongs to the Turks." Like Lee Kuan Yew of Singapore, I think a little reading about this guy is in my future.

Standing on the hills of Gallipoli gives excellent geographical perspective to both modern and ancient history. The Dardanelles has been important for much longer than just the 20th century. This is the same strait that Ulysses sailed in Homer's *Odyssey*.

TROY -- Troy lies on the southeast side of the Dardanelles at what used to be the confluence of two rivers. They have since silted up and changed course, but at the time the large harbor was the focus of the city's importance and the reason for the 10-year Trojan War -- not the beautiful Helen, as Homer's *Iliad* would have one believe.

There's really not a whole lot left here. Nine cities were built on top of one another over thousands of years. The Trojan War was fought over the sixth or seventh of these cities in 1200 B.C. Which Troy it was is an archaeological debate. A large wooden Trojan horse guards the entrance to the city grounds. It is such a grossly touristy structure that it brought a smile to my face. It was well-deserving of a photo -- but only one.

BURSA and IZNIK -- These two cities are about 65 miles south and southeast of Istanbul and have interesting histories.

Iznik is known for the tile it produced in earlier centuries, although the kilns have now gone cold. The most pleasant aspect of Iznik was the absence of tourists and all that accompanies the tourist industry. I spent a most enjoyable day walking around this small town of 20,000 people.

No one hassled me to buy a rug or anything else. I was free to stroll and explore. I noticed how clean the city was. Even the poor parts of town were free from trash. This was probably due to the presence of small dumpsters spaced 150 feet apart throughout the village. When I did see a bit of flotsam lying about, it was orderly flotsam, well-organized and arranged. This was remarkably different from anywhere in Asia I had been other than Japan and Singapore. It was as if Iznik's residents valued the appearance of their neighborhood and made the effort to keep it presentable. That would be a novel concept in most places I had been so far.

BURSA -- Bursa was the first capital of the Ottoman Empire (1299). Just as notably, it was the birthplace of Iskender Kebap. Allow me to explain.

You know the Greek gyro restaurants with the mystery meat clinging to a vertical skewer? First, that's lamb. Second, it's of Turkish origin. Both those facts were news to me.

Chef Alexander (or Iskender) became a well-known culinary master when he got the bright idea to roast lamb meat on a sword placed vertically beside a stack of coals. In this way, the juices would baste the meat as it cooked, instead of dripping into the fire below. His specialty was sliced meat on a bed of Turkish bread with tomato sauce. The coup de grace was melted butter on the top. The result was a mouth-watering concoction of meat, bread, fat and more fat. Scrumptious.

I went to the famous Iskender Kebap restaurant whose owners claim to be direct descendants of Iskender himself. I expected a tourist trap, but was surprised to see only businessmen in suits. I ordered a plate of the house special (they serve only Iskender Kebap) without yogurt. I had been tipped off by a local to order without yogurt because with it they would skimp on the meat.

It was delicious, especially when the waiter in a bow tie walked up with a big pot of melted butter and drizzled that golden honey across the meat. I could feel my arteries clog while my mouth sang blissful anthems of joy.

The rest of the food in Turkey was also fantastic. I ate heartily during my stay: lots of meat (lamb, chicken and beef), mashed potatoes, tomatoes and melted cheese. Plus, it's standard practice to serve a basket of bread with every meal. I vote that all restaurants institute some variation of this theme.

Other items of interest in Bursa are a few mosques and the tombs of the first two sultans of the Ottoman Empire. It rained almost the entire time I was there, which put a damper on my touring.

GENERAL OBSERVATIONS

There wasn't a thing about Turkey that I didn't like, and there was a whole lot that I found favorable.

-- The Turks are friendly, helpful people. On several occasions, taxi drivers approached me to offer directions with no pressure to take their cab. One man even said outright that my destination was too close for a taxi. This selfless assistance from a cab driver was shocking.

-- The customer service at my budget hotel restaurant was excellent. One morning I took my cornflakes back because they tasted stale. In another instance, I returned my bowl of fruit and yogurt because the menu didn't say "yogurt" next to "fruit bowl."

I could never, I repeat, never, get away with that in Asia. But after the cornflakes incident, the young manager walked up to me, put his hand on my shoulder, and smiled, "Are we OK here, sir?"

("Sir?" Did he say, "Sir?" And was that a smile? Am I on the receiving end of polite and professional behavior?)

I almost fell out of my chair.

-- Other than the rug salesmen, the hawker hassle was scarce. Even the rug guys back off after a couple of no's or being ignored.

-- The quality of transportation and roads was excellent. I had not been so comfortable on a bus since Korea. Interestingly, the bus system in Turkey functions like the airlines in America. The bus terminal looked like an airport, and a steward offered complimentary water during the trip. The departures were on time, and we didn't stop every five miles to pick up passengers standing on the highway in the middle of nowhere.

The ferries were even nicer. Overall, travel in Turkey was quiet, comfortable, safe and dependable -- everything that travel in Asia wasn't (outside of Japan and Singapore).

-- As a Western Caucasian tourist, I was not subjected to the staring I had grown accustomed to. Although I unavoidably highlighted myself as a tourist with my day bag, tendency to frequent tourist sites, and occasional use of a camera, I didn't stick out so glaringly and racially as I did in Asia.

I don't know if the Turks would stare at a tourist of a different race as Asians had stared at me, but I somehow doubt it. It's a curious thing -- why tourists are stared at so pointedly in Asia, specifically India and China. I don't have a good answer.

-- The sense of safety and trust was high in Turkey. For instance, in Iznik I left my duffel bag securely closed but unsecured in the corner of the bus station as I toured for the day. There was another bag sitting on the floor, and I trusted the manager to keep an eye on them. I also thought there was less of a need for stealing among the people. It's not that Turkey was free from theft or unscrupulous people; it just felt safer.

Later that day I left my daypack unattended in the restaurant while I went outside to wash my hands at a public facility. I trusted the manager and waiters to watch my bag for me. I wouldn't have dreamed of doing this elsewhere. I may have been tempting fate, but it was nice to relax ever so slightly for 10 days.

Istanbul is a great city, and Turkey is a great country. I hope to return someday to explore the hinterlands east of Istanbul and down to the Mediterranean.

Maybe I'll even buy a rug.

23

Stalking the Big Five on Safari in Kenya

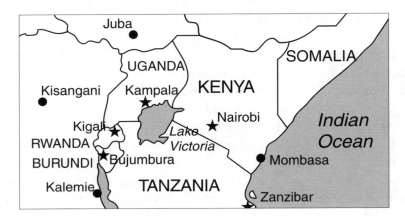

When thinking of safaris I have always imagined British safari caps, khaki jungle wear, and lots of pockets. Elephants transport the great hunter in search of white rhino or the elusive leopard. And, of course, the danger of attack by lion or hippo is of constant concern to the hunting party and its tribal guides.

That's mostly romance, of course. Commercial safaris today are far from Dr. David Livingstone or Ernest Hemingway's ventures into the hinterlands of Africa, although some aspects maintain their nostalgic lure. You still search for rhinos and leopards, tribal guards stand watch at your campsite through the night, and you can dress in multipocketed khaki if you like. But most important, the animals haven't changed. They may be fewer than in years past, but the beauty and grace, power and majesty of Africa's animal kingdom maintain their authenticity.

I thought I'd write about my seven-day safari in Kenya by

Top left: Samburu Reserve, Kenya.
Top right and bottom left: Masai Mara National Reserve, Kenya.
Bottom right: Arched tusks in Mombassa, Kenya.

combining anecdotes of animal highlights with descriptions of safari logistics (food, lodging, transportation, and costs, for instance). In this way, you'll know generally what to expect if this is something you're interested in. Or maybe this will persuade you to explore the idea of a safari in Africa. In my biased opinion, anyone would be enriched by the experience. As for me, this safari was the realization of a childhood dream.

SHOPPING AROUND

I had been told that the safari industry in Nairobi, Kenya,

(Nai-robbery, according to the locals) was much like the trekking industry in Kathmandu, Nepal. That means there are several companies to choose from, healthy competition to keep prices down and quality up, and lots of touts on the streets to *importune* you night and day. (After seven months of annoyance, I finally learned the word that best describes their behavior—importune.)

Upon checking into my half-star hotel on the edge of Thugsville, I was immediately approached by the receptionist to meet with the on-site Kenia Tours and Safaris representative. Kenia Tours had a good and longstanding reputation, according to my guidebook, so I met with its representative that afternoon.

Then I compared the price and services of four more safari operators the next day. This involved tramping around downtown Nairobi, dodging the touts, and keeping an eye out for would-be thieves.

As an aside, I was warned more times and more emphatically about the danger of walking around Nairobi than in any other city on my trip. I was told by at least four locals before I left my hotel for the first time to walk without my bag, keep little money on me, and never to take an alley for a shortcut. After the fourth warning, I figured there must be something to it, so I traversed Nairobi at a brisk pace and on guard.

I decided to take a weeklong safari instead of just a three- or four-day trip as many tourists do. I decided to split my time between two game parks and a lake known for the millions of pink flamingos it attracts. I looked at Samburu National Reserve in central Kenya, Masai Mara National Reserve in the southwest, and Lake Nakuru National Park in between. Those destinations are frequently part of package deals offered by most tour companies in Kenya.

Here's a list of my safari options. All of these deals are for "camping" safaris as opposed to "comfortable camping" or "lodge" safaris. That means I stayed in a pitched tent and slept in a sleeping bag instead of a nicer, semipermanent tent or a ritzy game lodge

Safari Camp Services -- 7 days. Samburu, Lake Nakuru, Masai Mara -- $636, plus $2 a day tip per cook (2). ($93 per day)

Safari Seekers -- 7 days. Lake Nakuru, Lake Boringo, Masai Mara -- $521, plus $8 a day tip. ($82 per day)

Game Trackers -- 4 days. Masai Mara -- $281, plus 10 percent tip. ($77 per day)

Planet Safari -- 4 days. Lake Nakuru, Masai Mara -- $55 a day, plus $10 a day tip. ($65 per day)

Because the companies' services seemed identical, I chose the one that gave me the best feeling when I visited their office (I went with my gut). I also had the chance to meet a few of their drivers and negotiated the final deal with one of the managers. Amazingly enough, the operator I decided was best also happened to be the least expensive (after quibbling over the exchange rate).

Here's the deal I took:

KENIA TOURS AND SAFARIS -- 7 day itinerary.
Mount Kenya (highest peak in Kenya) -- 1 night. (One morning hike).
Samburu National Reserve -- 2 nights. (Three game drives in the park).
Lake Nakuru National Park -- 1 night. (One game drive).
Masai Mara National Reserve -- 2 nights. (Four game drives).

The cost was $400, plus $6 a day tip ($63 per day).
Included in the price were three meals a day, tents and hot showers at the campsites, and all park-entry fees. Water and other

beverages were not included.

THE SAFARI

First, a couple of definitions:

GAME DRIVE: Riding in a safari van fitted with a pop-up roof for approximately three hours on dirt roads that snake through the parks. It is a bumpy ride for most of the way that can be spent sitting in reasonably comfortable chairs or standing in the cabin, head in the breeze, searching in earnest for wild game.

During the rainy season (when I was there), a game drive involves getting stuck in the mud or helping out another van that is stuck in the mud. I got to do a little mud wading one afternoon on just such an occasion. Another unfortunate bonus associated with the wet season is the high grass, which hides the lion and supports the grasshopper.

By midmorning, the grasshoppers are active and begin jumping to avoid the van. The result is they unwittingly wind up inside the van, usually pelting the aft passenger (yours truly) in the process. These aren't normal grasshoppers, mind you. These are African grasshoppers. I hate bugs, especially big ones with long spiny legs, huge chompers, and voracious appetites. It makes my skin crawl to even write about it.

THE BIG FIVE: At some point, it was decided that the five most important animals for a safari operator to show his clients are (in alphabetical order to avoid favoritism) Cape buffalo, elephant, leopard, lion and rhinoceros. Most tour companies proclaim their ability to find the Big Five and usually have pictures of each prominently displayed on the office wall. Of course, I was interested in seeing all five of these animals, but had never given much thought to the Cape buffalo. The lissome cheetah was far more important to me, so make it my Big Sixth.

SAMBURU NATIONAL RESERVE

There were five of us on the safari: Charles, driver and guide;

Ben, the cook; Pierre Yves and Sylvie, a French couple teaching French in Dubai, U.A.E.; and myself. We stopped at the entrance of the reserve to pay our entry fee and raise the roof on the van. Considering I was about to see the animals that I've watched on television nature shows for all my life, the anticipation was running high.

We drove inside the main gate and almost immediately began to see animals. What I was most pleased with came quickly. Charles had stopped to exchange information with a passing van from another company (information is commonly shared between drivers). He turned the van around, but wouldn't tell us what we were searching for.

We approached two other vans with passengers staring at a lone tree in the high grass. Charles stopped the van, and we waited, straining our eyes and wondering, "What on earth are we looking for?"

Then he sat up -- a large male lion. We let out a collective "Ohhhhhhhh" that I punctuated with, "There he is."

Two minutes later, another male raised his head. I was impressed. Not 15 minutes into my first game drive, we had already seen the king of the beasts. I would have been disappointed if I hadn't seen a male lion on this safari, but now there was no way to get skunked. The pressure was off.

LION ATTACK

The next day on our afternoon game drive, the most spectacular event of the safari unfolded. We were driving the van west along the Ewaso Ngiro River, which splits the park into north and south regions. It's incredibly muddy, and one can't help but wonder how an animal quenches its thirst with the reddish-brown silt. The relatively shallow river moves along at a good clip, and in spots where rocks lie near the surface, it boils. Imagine Willie Wonka's milk-chocolate river in "Charlie and the Chocolate Factory."

Charles spotted a female lion making her way toward the

river, apparently to get a drink. We maneuvered the van into position to intercept her course and waited. This was the second lion sighting of the safari and the first female. She found her way to a spot in front of us and began to walk along the road in the direction in which we were heading.

Charles fired up the van and gave chase. The lioness was beautiful to watch as she padded along, occasionally looking back as if to say, "You wanna give it a rest, pal?" The animals are accustomed to the sight of safari vans and usually don't bother to give them a second glance. Charles sped up to pass, allowing her to approach from behind, thus positioning us for a spectacular close-up shot when she walked by. I snapped a photo of her pretty face as she reached the back of the van and looked up at me. What a beautiful cat.

We kept the van at a standstill, thinking she'd head down to the river to lap up some water and mud. She was ambling along at a slow pace, but stopped abruptly about 50 feet in front of us and snapped hard right into the wind. She must've caught the scent of something we couldn't see.

Standing with her front paws on the berm of the road, she surveyed the scrub brush for whatever it was she had smelled. At first she simply scanned, but then her posture changed to that of a hunter. She extended her neck and lowered her head. Shoulders crouched and haunches tensed. She had spotted something.

"Oh please, oh please, oh please," I thought.

I was spellbound. Mesmerized. *Ensorcelled*. Now there's a 50-cent word. But it precisely describes my condition while watching the lioness stalk her prey. It means, "to be under the spell of sorcery"; my heart stopped, I ceased to breathe, and the only muscles to even twitch were my eyes as they drank in every fleeting moment of this incredible scene.

She darted forward 20 feet in a crouched position for a better view of her prey. Her head poked up above the brush and then quickly ducked behind the bushes. Slinking forward another few feet, I thought she would take a moment to size things up. Not even.

Zoom! She shot forward 100 feet in a burst of power. Things happened quickly for the next few moments, but this is what I recall:

> Black fur streaking right.
> ("Baboon!")
> Dust flying, then settling. Lion turned around, facing our position, calmly surveying the scene.
> Lion pouncing.
> Dust flying.
> Lion backpedaling as a different baboon fights for its life. Teeth flashing.
> A ball of yellow and black fur.
> Lion standing with black ball in mouth. Eyes blinking.

Wow!

I started breathing again.

The lioness, baboon in mouth, walked away from us and into the brush. Wanting to get a better look, Charles circled the van around to the other side of the field. I kept my eyes glued to the spot where we had last seen her enter the brush and was able to pick her up as we got closer.

What happened next was hauntingly familiar. It is a scene that I've witnessed numerous times with pet cats -- she started playing with her kill.

We could see her batting the poor baboon around, trying to get it to react, I suppose. Then she picked it up in her mouth and sprinted across the field. After 20 yards, she slammed on the brakes, released the baboon, and sent it tumbling head over heels in the dust. If the poor thing wasn't dead yet, it sure was taking a beating. She did the "run and drop" trick twice and then disappeared among the scrubs for good.

I marveled at how lucky I had been to witness the rawness

of nature. This was No. 1 on my wish list for the safari. Whenever I watch nature shows on TV, I find myself enthralled by the hunt and the kill. At last here I was, on a safari in Africa, and I got to see the real thing. It's beyond words.

CHEETAH HUNT

I was privy to one other hunt during my seven-day safari. It happened earlier on the day of the lion attack. Charles had spotted a cheetah in a tree alongside the road. The male stood up and slipped headfirst down the tree. He paused at the bottom to spray the trunk and then sniffed around to pick up other scents.

To our pleasant surprise, another male rose from the yellow grass nearby. They walked to a fallen tree to scratch their claws and then sauntered away. At first they strolled casually, but then perceptibly assumed a hunting air. As they walked with purpose, both necks craned high to see above the grass and through the trees toward a mixed herd of impala and oryx.

We must've watched them painstakingly stalk the herd for 30 minutes before the antelope spooked and sprinted to relative safety a couple hundred yards away. After a half-hour of moving one lithe muscle at a time, the two cheetahs relaxed on their haunches, stared at the game, and waited for the next hunt.

LAKE NAKURU NATIONAL PARK

Lake Nakuru is a much different environment from both Samburu and the Masai Mara. The vegetation is lush, and of course, the lake is the focal point. I had read about the number of pink flamingos that line the shoreline, but nothing can compare to seeing firsthand the mass of pink that circumscribes the lake. Zillions of these birds make Lake Nakuru their home.

I'm not a big pink flamingo fan. They're OK, but nothing to get excited about. There are four places where I've come across these birds before seeing them at Lake Nakuru. The first two are fancy hotels and zoos. The third is the front yard of doublewide trailers throughout America, and the fourth is the headwear of revelers at Jimmy Buffett concerts. They are always stationary, often perched on one leg, and occasionally cackle blatantly (or the bird's vehicle does, in the case of the Jimmy Buffett fan).

But the benefit of wildlife parks is to see animals behave naturally, to fly freely. The pink flamingo is fantastically beautiful in flight. The bright pink of a flamingo's body is embellished with streaks of black that can only be appreciated when its wings are spread. Watching a flight of five or six birds glide elegantly across the lake with long legs trailing in the wind above multitudes of its kind was an unexpectedly pleasant sight.

RHINO

My next animal encounter occurred beside the lake where I continued to enjoy the view of a million flamingoes. It further demonstrates the joy of watching animals in the wild as they behave naturally and sometimes unpredictably. Simply put, you get to see them *do* something.

We drove on the sand of the receding lake, past a herd of Cape buffalo munching grass placidly. Charles, our guide, was once again the first to spot another member of the Big Five -- rhino.

What made this sighting so interesting was its behavior. The water of Lake Nakuru was quite low during my visit, creating an extended beach. The distance from the edge of the lake to the tree line was approximately 100 yards. The rhino walked about in this open area by himself and must have become uncomfortable with his position for he began trotting to and fro. He seemed to be lost and confused as he trotted, stopped and then galloped.

Watching an enormous creature like the black rhino build up a head of steam is a powerful sight. Talk about a ton of bricks.

Eventually he found his way to the trees at the end of the lake where the beach was narrow and disappeared into the woods.

ANTELOPE

The most common sight on the plains of Africa is the grazers. These are wildebeest, zebra, and an assortment of antelope. Perhaps the most numerous of all antelope is the impala. It also happens to be my personal favorite, along with the sable, but I'll get to him in a minute.

The impala is a slender creature, approximately the size of the North American whitetail deer. But the antlers are of the most beautiful lyre shape, and various parts of the body are flecked with black and white streaks. My favorite quality of the impala, however, is the grace with which it moves. I don't think words can adequately describe the lightness of impala hooves on African soil. They float together in a ballet of inexpressible beauty.

The sable is my other favorite of the grazers. Known for the ferocious ability to defend itself against lion, it is a creature of stature. Long curved horns that reach back to his rump serve as rapiers when fighting a predator. He is plum-colored with streaks of white and has a massive chest. I saw only one during the safari. He was standing like a sentinel on the hill above us in the mist of a rainy afternoon. I wondered later if I had really seen him.

MASAI MARA NATIONAL RESERVE and the LEOPARD

The Masai Mara National Reserve is the most famous game park in Kenya. It is actually the northern extension of the Serengeti Park in neighboring Tanzania. Known for its abundance of wildlife and particularly for the annual migration of more than a million wildebeest, this park receives the majority of visitors who come to Kenya for game viewing.

The landscape here is primarily grassy plains and a few low mountains. I had only one more member of the Big Five to see upon entering the park, but was made whole on the first game drive we took here.

Due to some van difficulties (not uncommon, I suspect, on these safaris), we had changed vehicles and drivers between Lake Nakuru and the Masai Mara. Our new guide, Walter, took us to an elevated position that afforded a panoramic view of the grasslands and mountains in the distance, just before sunset. In a stroke of great fortune, a leopard had discovered the same spot.

I don't know why, but up to this point in my safari I had not been concerned with spotting a leopard. It was a well-decorated animal I supposed, but smaller than the lion and slower than the cheetah. I placed this animal in the nice-to-see category and didn't worry about missing him.

But as soon as the van was in position directly underneath this magnificent creature, I changed my mind. God, what a gorgeous animal.

I now understand why his coat is so highly prized. But I have never been enamored by leopard-skin clothing or rugs and still am not. In the flesh, however, on a live cat, the pattern is one of the most alluring in Africa. It is another example of the indescribable beauty that was becoming a common sight.

THE BIRDS

One last animal experience that I want to convey, which is often overshadowed by the larger species, is the bird life of Africa -- particularly the smaller species. As the safari van made its way along the dirt roads of the reserves, a variety of songbirds was flushed from their perches. I'm not sure how many species of birds there are in Kenya, but I would safely bet the number is well into the hundreds.

I saw two of the most beautifully colored songbirds I have ever seen while zipping along in search of elephant and lion. The first was an iridescent starling, and the second was a lilac-breasted roller. There are others just as interesting and beautiful, I'm sure, but these two stood out.

By the way, the names of these birds brings up a facet of game drives that I should mention. I didn't discover the name of the roller until almost two months had passed. Whenever I asked our guide the name of an animal or plant, I received an almost indecipherable answer. This was primarily due to unfamiliarity with the Kenyan accent.

Kenyans tend to pronounce their R's like L's. For instance, giraffe is pronounced, "gilaffe." However, the reverse is not true. Elephant is pronounced, "elephant," like it is spelled. This becomes troublesome when the guide quickly shouts back the name of a fleeing bird as the van rushes by.

> "Walter. What's the name of that beautiful bird that just flew in front of us?"
> Oh, that's a lilac-blested loh-lah.
> "Huh?"
> A LILAC-BLESTED LOH-LAH!
> (What the hell is a loh-lah? Oh well, forget it.)
> "What about the other one? The one we saw perched on top of the acacia a while back?"
> That was a tufted tufted-mumble-lumble.
> "Huh? What's that again?"
> A TUFTED LUFTED-MUMBLE-LUMBLE!!
> "Oh, I see. Thanks."

THE CAMP

Remember that I took the low-rent route on this safari. It's possible to stay in upscale lodges that afford opportunities to relax with a Tanqueray and tonic while watching crocodiles and other such creatures that inhabit the local surrounds. My accommodations were more of a Pabst Blue Ribbon experience.

The first three nights were spent in a small two-man tent with my trusty sleeping bag. The third night, at Lake Nakuru, where there is no camping, was in an honest-to-goodness hotel. And the final two nights were in fixed tents at the permanent Kenia Tours campsite. Tents in the Masai Mara camp were made of simple Army-green canvas but had bed frames with mattresses and were large enough to stand in.

Going to the bathroom was an interesting matter. Any aversion I may have had at the beginning of my journey to outhouses has long since vanished. However, when I am told there is even the slightest possibility of wild animals, specifically large meat-eaters, interrupting my visit to the loo, I think twice about that 4:00 a.m. nature call.

We were told that the resident Masai warrior in our camp would be alert to the presence of any wild animals that may inhibit the successful completion of a trip to the toilet. But when I roused myself out of the rack and walked 150 feet to the outhouse at O-dark thirty, I didn't see or hear the vigilant warrior anywhere. I wasn't too worried about lions, but I did have the resident troop of baboons that hangs around the campsite on my mind. Can you imagine startling one from his slumber? I'll bet they can be pretty cranky.

I wasn't taking any chances. That walk to the john was made in the same manner as I walked the streets of Nairobi -- in haste.

The food and its preparation deserve mention. Knowing that you have a good meal waiting on you at the end of a long game drive makes an enormous difference to your enjoyment. I was impressed with the quality, quantity, and speed with which our food was prepared. I left the table quite satisfied at the end of each meal. Dishes included spaghetti with meat sauce, beef stew, fried fish, and chicken curry. Our cook, Ben, was a whiz at whipping up vegetables, rice and a main dish over a campfire using only a few pots and pans. I am told these culinary skills are common among the various tour operators, which is good news for safari patrons.

WRAP UP

I hope this summary has painted a fair picture of a safari in Kenya. I saw far more animals than I have written about here. In fact, other than some antelope species, I can't think of a major animal in sub-Saharan Africa that I didn't observe over the seven days, despite its being the off-season, when much of the wildlife has migrated south into the Serengeti of Tanzania.

After I left Nairobi, I traveled east to Mombassa, where I visited the beautiful coast of Kenya. I was fortunate to meet an expat British family at a dinner theater and wound up staying with them for a few days. The husband manages the nicest hotel on the coast, Hemingway's, which I was allowed to lounge around for a while. I met the former CEO of Kenya Airways there, and between the two of them and a few Tuskers (beer), I learned a great deal about the politics and culture of the country.

I made my way south through Tanzania, Zambia and Zimbabwe over the next month and am now in South Africa, where I will stay until July 1. A great deal has happened, and I've learned much about the turmoil and changes taking place in these countries.

My next stop will be Guatemala, where I plan to spend two months. I've got it in my head that I'm going to learn Spanish. I guess I'll find out how much high school Spanish is still floating around in the grey matter of my brain.

24

It's Smooth Traveling, Even After Wine-Tasting, in South Africa

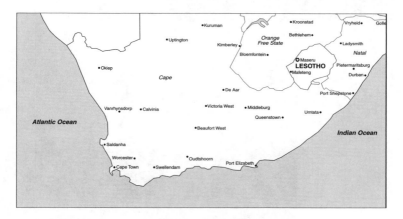

I've got a new favorite place in the world -- South Africa, specifically the Western Cape.

Why?

There's a number of reasons. First, for a budget traveler it was exceptionally easy to travel within. The buses are comfortable, professionally run, and reasonably priced. The roads are excellent. Budget lodging is both plentiful and comfortable. Hot showers, toilet paper, and seats for the toilet were always provided. (I don't take that stuff for granted anymore.) Many of the guesthouses are listed in a small brochure that's widely available. This publication complements a budget bus service that drops travelers off at the doorstep of each guesthouse. Such a well-organized system makes

Top:
Along the "Garden Route" in scenic Knysna, South Africa.

Center:
Table Mountain standing watch over Cape Town, South Africa.

Bottom:
Getting in 18 at the Paarl Country Club. Paarl, South Africa.

travel logistics a snap.

The quality of lodging and traveler services such as banking, air tickets, and Internet access are as modern as it gets. And it doesn't hurt that the U.S. dollar is incredibly strong, making an already inexpensive country wildly affordable.

But South Africa offers more than just smooth traveling. The country contains a variety of environments; from grassy plains and game parks to gorgeous coastal drives, world-class surfing beaches, and strikingly beautiful winelands.

The activities are just as varied. If you want to experience tribal life in Africa, you can. If you want to see wild animals, you can. If you want some of the world's best cuisine at bargain basement prices, you can have that too. In the morning you can tour outlying townships where for decades indigenous Africans were relegated to live in poverty and then visit the symphony that night. And you can also delve into fascinating history, politics and social interaction.

When I consider all the factors, South Africa vies with Turkey for best-all-round honors on my trip.

I spent three and a half weeks in South Africa. Approximately half of that time was in the Western Cape (the southwest province of Africa). I'll start with that area, as it was my hands-down favorite.

My travel partner for the final 10 days of my tour through South Africa was an American I met in Harare, Zimbabwe, who had been traveling through Africa for four or five months. Lira Lee, originally from Tenafly, N.J., now lives in New York. She's in the same boat as I -- early 30s, currently unemployed and fulfilling a sense of wanderlust. We traveled together for a while in Zimbabwe, and our plans coincided in South Africa, fortunately for me for a few reasons.

First, I had someone to share expenses with, namely a rental car. Second, I did things that I wouldn't have otherwise done because they're difficult to do alone (extensive wine tasting, for example). And third, it was fun to travel with someone for a change.

Although I've traveled for a day or two with other backpackers, in general I have avoided it. I suppose the most important reason is because it insulates you from meeting locals. Another reason is that I haven't met another backpacker, other than one American guy in China, whom I wanted to spend more than a few days with. But Lira had a personality and sense of humor compatible with mine, except she's far too liberal and needs to stop smoking. You hear that, Lira?

CAPE TOWN

I arrived in Cape Town under the cover of darkness, which is less preferable than daylight. I like to be able to see new places when I arrive and get a quick feel for them. So I woke up the following morning, stepped outside the hostel, and looked up to find scenic Table Mountain towering above me. It was one of those "Holy cow! There's a mountain here" kind of moments.

One of the best things about Cape Town is its beautiful location. The city center lies in a bowl cupped by mountains on two sides and the Atlantic Ocean on another. The city itself is aesthetically dull other than a few colonial structures. There are no hallmark office buildings.

But what the city lacks in style it more than makes up for in location and quality of life. Superb! Here's a few of my activities from the four days of unusually pleasant winter weather I was blessed with.

TABLE MOUNTAIN—This is a flattop mountain that hovers above the city. For those of you familiar with Phoenix, Ariz., it is the Camelback Mountain of Cape Town. But this one takes about an hour and a half to climb instead of 30 minutes. I took the path with signs that read, "This is the dangerous route." The return signs read, "This is not an easy way down."

"How dangerous could it be?", I thought. Pretty damn dangerous actually. I've never done any freestyle rock-climbing so I don't know what to compare it to, but there were several places where I found myself clinging by my fingertips and wondering where my to put my foot.

In retrospect, this activity was one of the most fun in Cape Town. And it had a stellar view at the top.

BOULDERS BEACH -- Cape Town has a few colonies of Jackass penguins. Don't you just love the name? Somebody in charge has changed it to South African penguin, but many still call them Jackasses. I know which I prefer.

The name originates from the neighing call they make. I wouldn't have believed the sound had I not heard it for myself, but they neigh just like a donkey. And when you visit the colony at Boulders Beach just outside of the city and one or two of those birds get the rest of the crowd going, you understand why the name fits.

By the way, have you ever seen a penguin climb stairs? It could bring a smile to anyone's face. Damn funny sight.

THE CAPE OF GOOD HOPE—This is the southwestern-most point on the continent of Africa. The neat things about the Cape of Good Hope are the view and the knowledge that this is the official spot where the Atlantic and Indian Oceans meet. Maybe that's not interesting -- but it worked for me. I arrived just before sunset, so I wasn't able to see the dividing line that is sometimes visible because of the two major currents that meet at this point.

But what I did see was beautiful. To the east, one looks across the bay to towering mountains in the distance. To the south and west is open ocean. And to the north, one gazes up the spine of the Cape Peninsula across the game park of the southern tip. The sun set over the water while flocks of cormorants arrived to bed down in the cliffs of the cape for the night. Waves slammed against rocks, churning up a mist of salty air. The sky went from gold to pink to purple and red. And on the drive out, I had to slow down for a herd of antelope crossing the road. All of this is only 30 minutes from the city. Location, location, location.

ROBBEN ISLAND—This is where Nelson Mandela spent the majority of his time in prison. I went on a good tour that would have been a lot better had I known more about Nelson

Mandela and his time behind bars. Like many experiences on my trip, I filed this one away for retrieval when I take the time to read his book.

I will note, however, that during my stay in South Africa I was impressed with Nelson Mandela's stature -- among people of all colors and ethnicity. He was a force for peaceful change and still wields powerful influence. After speaking with a variety of people from different backgrounds, my gut tells me that South Africa has managed the radical transformation from apartheid to a representative democracy as well as can be expected. Without question, Nelson Mandela has been of immeasurable importance in this process.

A side benefit of the 30-minute ferry to Robben Island (just northwest of downtown and in the Atlantic Ocean) was the view of Cape Town from the water. Taking a step back to view the mountains on two sides and ocean in the foreground made for a Kodak moment. I still couldn't get over the good weather I was enjoying.

THE WATERFRONT—Here is a zillion-dollar shopping complex on the northern edge of the city. Everybody winds up at the waterfront at some point during a stay in Cape Town. For one thing, the ferries to Robben Island depart from there, so it's practically unavoidable. But it does happen to be a pretty nice mall. There are great restaurants and coffee shops (both ubiquitous fixtures in the Cape Town landscape).

I took in a Chinese movie at the Waterfront one night -- "An Emperor and an Assassin." Three hours of subtitles -- whoa. I felt like an idiot though, because it wasn't until the liner notes that I realized the story was about the king who built the army of terra cotta warriors in Xi'an -- the polluted city I had visited eight months earlier. I guess the toxins in what passes for air in that cesspool affected my memory. I'll probably have three-headed children because of the two days that I languished there.

Of course there's a lot more to Cape Town than what I've mentioned here. I visited Groot Constantia -- the oldest vineyard in South Africa. It's a beautiful place, but unfortunately a peevishly arrogant woman barked at us for being a few minutes late for the vineyard tour, triggering a knee-jerk "well, kiss my grits" reaction in me. (Don't worry. I kept it to myself.) The buildings and scenery were better than the wine.

The beach suburbs on the west side of town such as Hout Bay and Camp's Bay are ritzy enclaves for the Cape Town well-to-do. Nice places for a stroll and dining. Kirstenbosch Gardens deserves mention as well. This is an enormous tract of land that was set aside by Cecil Rhodes for preservation. It now houses beautifully manicured grounds that display the flora of South Africa.

The gardens are close to the city center, just on the other side of Table Mountain. It is possible to hike from the city up Table Mountain and descend into Kirstenbosch. We spent an afternoon cruising around the various partitions of plant life. There's a lot of oxygen in a place like that, you know?

THE WINELANDS

I do not have adequate command of the English language to pay sufficient tribute to the beauty of the winelands in South Africa. I absolutely loved touring this part of the country and hope to return someday. As I told a friend, "Man, I've got to make some cash and buy a vineyard here."

The wine country of the Western Cape covers an extensive area, but three villages in particular have the highest concentration of vineyards. These little towns are filled with B & Bs, coffee shops and delicious dining. In the order that I visited them they are: Stellenbosch, Paarl and Franschhoek.

Instead of providing a rundown of each city, I'll just cover the region in general. The cities are similar in most respects anyway, but if I had to list them in order of preference I'd place Stellenbosch first, followed by Franschhoek and Paarl (though the first two are a near toss-up).

I spent four days zipping about this wine triangle, eating fine food, tasting wonderful wines, and even managing to slip in a couple rounds of golf. This may sound strange to everyone back in the real world, but it was one of the few times on my trip that I felt as if I was on vacation.

As it turns out, Lira is a bit of a wine connoisseur. I, on the other hand -- well, I like wine, I just don't know too much about it. I often bought a bottle of red on each trip to the grocery store, but on a Navy man's salary, I never had the capital to experiment with a lot of the good stuff.

So it was quite fortunate that I had a knowledgeable and experienced taster to hit the wine circuit with. Both of us hoped to ship some wine home, and at the exchange rate in effect, it would have been a sin not to (one dollar to eight South African rand—that's good). Wines that go for more than $100 at a restaurant in New York were less than $15 at the vineyard. Even with the added cost of shipping, these wines were a steal. And they were good, too.

Here's how the tour went. Twice we played golf in the morning and visited four or five vineyards in the afternoon. Once we had breakfast at a coffee shop in town and then toured six wineries through the day. And on the final, varsity day, we made it to the first location at 8:30 a.m. (they had to open early for us) and 11 vineyards by the close of business (5 p.m.). That was an all-star performance if I do say so myself. This was serious business, after all. Work, Work, Work! In all, we tasted wine at over 20 vineyards.

You may be wondering how one can drink wine all day and keep a sense of taste, not to mention operate a vehicle. Not a problem. Instead of drinking a quarter-glass of wine each for every wine that was tasted, we would share a single glass. Since we were tasting only reds, that usually meant four to five wines at each sitting, instead of eight to ten if we had also tasted whites. Often we would pour out the wine that we didn't like.

For those who've never done this sort of thing, pouring out the wine is an acceptable practice. So is spitting it out, but that wouldn't have been any fun, would it?

So, doing the quick math, five vineyards equates to about

three glasses of wine spread out over about three hours. That's well within limits. This method also left enough energy at dinner to split a bottle purchased earlier in the day.

Varsity day, however, was a slight exception. Eleven vineyards in one day could affect wine tasters of the strongest constitution, especially if they taste every red available (eight) and almost split a bottle of dessert wine at the final vineyard from which they ship their cases home. But completing four days of solid work was cause for celebration, don't you think?

One of my favorite memories of these four days is the scenery and ambience. Soaring rocky mountains partially cloaked in thick white clouds set the backdrop for the manmade buildings that offer their own sense of quaint beauty. Many of the roads that approach the warehouses and tasting rooms are beautiful tree-lined drives. The fields of grapes on either side provide a reminder of what awaits you at the end.

Inside the tasting rooms, each with its own style and appeal, we were greeted by smiling and helpful staff, occasionally the owner. Because this was winter, and therefore the off-season, we had most tasting rooms to ourselves. Although a few of the best wines were not available, we were more than compensated with the undivided attention of the staff. We became spoiled by this exclusivity. In fact, at one of the most popular vineyards, which we visited out of a sense of obligation, we left without tasting the wine. There were just too many people.

And finally, there was the food. This was another area where the powerful dollar had an important effect on my experience. Because of the exchange rate, I was able to dine in four- and five-star establishments while staying on budget. The most I spent on any dinner was $15.

How do I know the number of stars to rate the restaurants? Don't trust me, of course. I admit I'm more of a Budweiser and barbecue kind of guy. But Lira had done some first-class entertaining of high-end clients during her 10 years in investment banking. I trusted her eye.

A quick note for those of you who might disparage barbecue.

And by the word barbecue I don't mean simply slapping burgers on a grill. I mean pulled pork, ribs, or barbecue beef (preferably served Carolina style with slaw on the bun and extra sauce).

Don't be too quick to knock what you may not know. I'd suggest a trip to the hallowed halls of Dreamland Barbecue in Tuscaloosa, Ala., before you pass judgment. That some fine cookin'! Nothing is too complicated at Dreamland: ribs, white loaf bread, Coca-Cola and Budweiser. Simple is beautiful. I believe it's because of its focus that the restaurant is able to serve some of the best ribs east of the Mississippi. They're succulent and tangy. In fact, if you put a plate of Dreamland ribs on your head, your tongue would beat its way through your brain just to get a taste. They're that good.

I apologize for the digression. Both the vineyards and the villages are known for the quality of their restaurants. Lunch was usually at a vineyard outside on the patio with gorgeous views of the mountains and countryside. Dinner was either at a vineyard (many are open only for lunch unfortunately) or at one of the fine restaurants in town. We explored French, Italian, Mediterranean, and local Cape Malay cuisine among others. Delish, each and every one.

WRAP-UP

I was going to write more about the rest of South Africa, but I really need to get going on my study of Spanish. Constructing English sentences and thinking of interesting words to describe what I've seen and done is forcing any newfound knowledge of a foreign language right out of my minuscule brain.

South Africa is a fantastic place to travel. I think it would be great for any type of traveler -- from high-end to budget, from single backpacker to family with kids. The country offers a wide variety of activities, scenery and culture, as well as interesting politics, history and social structure. It's also modern and very affordable.

In a sense, traveling in South Africa felt like an inexpensive

Europe with a safari theme.

GUATEMALA

I'm in the western Guatemalan town of Quetzeltenango (Xela for short), a quiet and peaceful little place with a sense of Spanish colonial charm. Every street is either cobblestone or cement brick. About 150,000 people live here, and it has a university, so there is a slight college town feel. It's much more modern than I expected and has a few nice restaurants.

Speaking of which, even after the epicurean extravaganza of Cape Town and the wine country, I must say that I'm very happy to be back in the land of tortillas and salsa. I've really missed it.

25

At the End of the Line in Quito, Ecuador, With Thoughts of Home

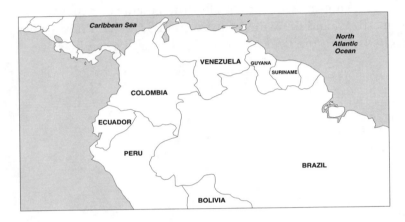

This dispatch is from Quito, Ecuador -- my last city and country. I took my final bus ride here on Dec. 14, 2001 and I can't say that any tears were shed as I disembarked. I could do for a spell without another one of those rides.

After I left South Africa, I parked myself in Quetzaltenango, Guatemala, where for two months I threw myself into learning Spanish. I wanted to dedicate all my feeble brainpower to the studies.

It worked. I now speak basic Spanish and can understand the same. But more important, I feel that I have crested an imaginary hump and entered a land of no return. By that, I mean I have permanently implanted Spanish in my head and couldn't "unremember" it if I tried. That was my goal, and I believe that I have realized it. Learning Spanish has been one of the most

Back home in the family kitchen. Atlanta, GA. USA.

rewarding achievements of my life. I have many reasons for saying that and will expound later when I summarize all that I've learned and experienced on this grand trip.

After Guatemala came two weeks in Mexico. I was in Jalapa, Mexico, on the morning of Sept. 11 (about five hours east of Mexico City) and traveled to the city of Puebla the same day (two hours east of the capital). Every TV in the city was tuned to news about the attacks. From hotel lobbies, restaurants, coffee shops and street-side electronics stores with 20 televisions all on the same channel, the city was saturated with the news. The experience was surreal.

Luckily, air travel to the United States resumed the day before my scheduled flight to Atlanta, which was on Sept. 18. I returned home for the wedding of a high school friend. Returning to the United States during the immediate post-attacks environment after a year away was another surreal experience. There were flags everywhere. I didn't watch them go up bit by bit; they were all flying by the time I came home.

The feeling in the country was so powerful; the mix of emotions and the overwhelming focus were on just one story. When I was last in the United States one year earlier, the country was in the midst of an evenly divided presidential election. But on Sept. 18, the sense of unity was beyond anything I could have imagined from abroad.

After one week in Atlanta and a small taste of what life would be like when I returned for good, I flew to Buenos Aires, Argentina. From there, my travels took me through Chile, Bolivia, Peru and Ecuador. There was a lot of ground covered and many hours in the reclined position on a bus.

I'm now entering the looking back and reflecting stage. There is so much to sift through: so many faces, places, sounds, cultures, flavors and experiences in the kaleidoscope of my memory. I think the sinking-in process will last for some time. I may need some distance from it to fully appreciate all that I've learned and the ways in which it has affected me.

How do I feel at the end of 15 months of travel? Enriched. Whole. I began this trip excited at its prospect and not entirely certain what would ensue. The world was a great unknown, and I wanted to dive in headfirst. Looking back, I feel satisfied with how I carried it out -- where I went, the things I did, how much time I spent. There's room for improvement, of course, and there are things that I would change -- but I'm not losing any sleep over them. I'm resting quite soundly, in fact.

Rest. Now there's a thought. In fact, that's stage one of the plan when I return to the States. I plan to rest, rejuvenate, and then charge forward with the next chapter in life. What I'll do in the long term is yet to be determined. The short-term involves living at home in Atlanta, working for Mom's public relations consulting firm, and maybe doing a little writing, all the while looking for an opportunity to throw my heart into.

I certainly wish I had a clearer picture of what's next, and not knowing gives me pause, to be sure. But here's the good news: When I go *home*, I'm going home to the *United States of America*. Those words never rang so sweet -- home and the United States of America. Even in a bad economy and under the threat of terrorism, my home is a land of freedom and opportunity. I know that I can make something happen in that country. I know that in that great land I can dream and achieve. What millions of repressed and marginalized people around the world desire, I have for a home. I couldn't be more grateful.

I have enjoyed each country that I visited and think we can learn from them all. It's a giant, varied, incredible world out there, and every place has something to offer. But after 15 months on the road, I'm ready to come home. I'm ready to stop traveling. That's a blessing actually. How awful would it be to feel "sentenced" to going back? Quite the opposite is true; I'm really looking forward to it.

And I'm truly going home. Back to the South, to Atlanta, to my family, and the very house that I was raised in. I'm looking forward to spending time with my parents. I want to work with my mother as we did in high school when I was in student government and she was class mom. I want to share a cigar and a scotch with my dad while we listen to old records and watch Braves baseball. And I want to spend time with my sisters and brother-in-law whom I haven't lived near for almost 15 years.

I miss America, but I didn't when I left. I was too excited about all the new things I would see and do to miss it just yet. Distant lands and foreign cultures were the apple of my eye. And I still want to see more. But I have a newfound appreciation, a newfound soft spot for America, for baseball, barbecue, country music, and a fighting spirit that cherishes our way of life. I met an Australian in an airport along the way. As we waited to check our luggage, we chatted about the Olympics in Sydney and Australia in general. At some point during our banter, he said to me, "Jason, I reckon it's the greatest place in the world to live." Well, God bless him. He loves his country, his home. And that's the way I feel about mine.

I need to take a moment and say thanks. I've met so many wonderful people along the way who have acted as guides, fed me a meal, or even allowed me to stay in their home, sometimes for weeks at a time. I also received counsel on a variety of issues from medical to travel. I'm thankful and hope that I offered something in return. If nothing else, please know that my home is always open to the traveler.

And in the same breath I want to thank all who corresponded with me along the way, even if it was a quick note just to say hello. One of the true pleasures for me this past year was to open my e-mail account in some far corner of the globe and see notes from friends. That kept me connected and was a source of comfort over long months of traveling alone.

That's a quick wrap-up of where I've been and where I am in both the geographic and figurative sense. I think I will continue to realize the benefits and lessons learned from this trip for the rest of my life. As a traveler from Finland said to me, "You've built up a lot of personal 'capital' along the way." That's true. The range of experience is deep and broad. I plan to glean from it, to pull lessons from it, for the rest of my days.

Epilogue

It's been two and a half months since I returned to America, and I'm still in appreciation mode. The list of what I appreciate is long, and includes things big and small. Some of the smaller, more personal items are sleeping in the same bed every night and Mom's home cooking. I appreciate taking showers without shower shoes, using a full-sized towel, wearing different clothes, and being able to grab a bowl of ice cream from the fridge whenever I want.

But I notice and appreciate some of the bigger things in life also. I jog through my old neighborhood in Atlanta several times a week and am always impressed with the relative opulence of middle-class America. Single-family homes with large front and backyards, two or three cars, swing sets, a dog, and room for a basketball goal: It's incredible.

This appreciation for the good life in America may subside as the years go by, but I don't think it will ever completely vanish. The awareness of how well we live compared with the majority of the world is now too deeply ingrained. This is a great place, and I'm happy to be back.

I remember walking through baggage claim at Hartsfield International Airport and being greeted by my family. Stephanie, my big sister, had made a welcome-home sign that she and Mom held. It was hung in the kitchen to remind all who entered that I had returned—and was welcome to be there.

Coming home around the holidays is always a great feeling. But this year held extra significance. The mood of the country was serious after the 9/11 attacks. People were considering their good fortune to live in America and were taking the time to think about what really matters in this life—family, friends, good health, freedom.

But in addition to the national mind-set, my homecoming held extra meaning because I had been gone for so long. It had been more than 15 months since I had left on my trip. I had spent only one rushed week at home in Atlanta over the past two years. And it had been more than 14 years since I lived in Atlanta full time.

All the intervening visits had been temporary. But this time my homecoming was for good. I planned to stay in Atlanta indefinitely and launch a new life from the cradle of my upbringing -- Atlanta, Ga. Yes sir, I was home.

The next few months were hectic. I moved my belongings from Arizona to Georgia—putting some things in my parents' house where I'm living and most things in storage. I've also become a resident of Georgia again. I registered the truck, received a new driver's license, and registered to vote.

It wasn't easy to readjust to life as I knew it. I have to budget my time, a foreign notion as I traveled the globe. I was always organized about my touring -- but I got there when I got there. Not so in the hum of American business. I've been quickly reminded that there are only so many hours in the day.

I labeled and filed more than 1,500 photographs and edited much of my writing. Although laborious, both were fun, and I know that I'll be thanking myself 30 years from now when I blow the dust off of the photo albums and take that stroll down memory lane.

I also tried to figure out what to do next. Where would I work? What type of job did I want? Did I want to start my own business, and if so, what kind? Where? Would I look outside of Atlanta and the South? What on earth would I do?

But before I got too far ahead of myself, I thought it best to sit down and reflect on the past before charging forward into the future. I thought it was important to spell out what I gained from 15 months of world travel. What were the takeaways, and were they worth it? My short answer: You bet.

GOALS

As I sat on the plane to Tokyo with the uncertainty and excitement of a great adventure lying before me, what did I think that I would gain from the experience? What were my goals?

I had been asked this question in the weeks before I left. I responded that it was tough to answer in a sound bite -- but I knew in my heart all the things I wanted to accomplish. I had not enumerated them, however. Here's what I was searching for and expected to gain from a year of independent world travel. I wanted to:

– Satisfy a basic curiosity about the world. "What is it like out there? "How do people live?"

– Find areas of the world where I would like to return for either business or pleasure.

– Build an amazing array of exotic experiences to fascinate and inform anyone who has a curiosity about life outside of the United States.

– Better myself through a greater understanding of the world, thus enhancing my ability to contribute in business, politics or philanthropy.

– Enrich my life so that I in turn may enrich others'.

ENCOUNTERS

I expected to realize these goals through a multitude of encounters. I thought it would be helpful simply to list them.

1) People and cultures
   a. Attitude
   b. Language
   c. Dress
2) Food
3) Drink
4) Animals

5) Flora
6) Environment
   a. Climate
   b. Elevation
7) Landscape/Scenery
   a. Mountains, sea, desert, plains.
8) Government (Politics)
   a. Communism
   b. Military dictatorship
   c. Democracy
   d. Corruption
9) Business environment
10) Living conditions
   a. Poverty and hygiene
   b. Contrast between wealthy and poor
11) Outdoor adventure
   a. Safari, canoeing, trekking
12) History
13) Museums
14) Art
15) Music
16) Religion
   a. Temples, mosques, cathedrals
17) Ways of life
   a. Rural, urban, jungle, river, high plains

In one way or another I successfully encountered them all. But little did I know that some of the most significant encounters would come in a different form and were not included in this original list. They were discoveries to be made slowly, over months of independent, often solo, travel. Simply listed, these are:

1) Study of religion
2) Introspection/time to think
3) Reinforcement of personal values

      a. Importance of family
      b. Independence
      c. Accountability
  4) Gratitude
        a. For being a citizen of the United States
        b. For lot in life
           i. Mental and physical health
           ii. Financial well-being
  5) Creative writing
  6) Learning a language
  7) Time to read

I know that every traveler's experience is different, but I hope that these lists will expose the reader to at least some of the potential benefits of world travel and perhaps even inspire someone to get off that couch and go see the world.

NON-REASONS FOR THE TRIP

There are two misperceptions people have about why I decided to take this trip. Allow me to discount them. They are the ideas that::

    1) I headed out into the great beyond on a quest to *find myself.*

This always makes me chuckle. Finding oneself means different things to different people, and some are in serious need of the quest. But let me assure you all—I knew myself before leaving the United States. There was no need or desire to discover any deep element of my inner self. I knew who I was and was at peace with that person.

I struck out not in search of self, but of *others*: other people, cultures and places.

Indeed, I had a few realizations along the way and reinforced much of what I consider to be core character traits, but on the whole this trip was not about *me*. It was about, about downloading as much of the world as possible, assimilating that information, and then finding a way to apply it over the rest of my life.

> 2) I headed out to all points on the globe to figure out what kind of job I wanted back in America.

If only I could have been so lucky. No, I wasn't thinking about a job in America as I haggled with the rickshaw drivers of Agra, India (although this is excellent negotiation training and a true test of anger management). Nor was I considering employment opportunities as I watched a lion kill a baboon in the scrub brush of Samburu National Park in Kenya.

I suppose if I had left the United States with employment options in mind, I would have had something to consider for the 15 months that I spent on the road. But seeing as I didn't, well, trekking in Nepal, canoeing in Zimbabwe, and hiking in the jungles of Ecuador aren't exactly goldmines for career-path decision-making.

More important, the purpose of this trip was exposure to the world and enrichment through that experience—it was not about me or a job.

QUESTIONS

I've been asked many questions about my trip. Some are philosophical; others address travel logistics; and a few are as mundane as, "Where was your worst haircut?" (Tie: India and Malaysia.)

So here are the answers:

1) How much money did it cost?

My budget was $40 a day, on average. Some countries were cheap (India, $14 a day), and others were money holes (Japan, $100 a day). But on average, I hit my target, which included everything *directly* related to my trip (transportation, food, lodging, souvenirs, entrance fees to museums, shampoo, etc.).

The exception is a batch of plane tickets that I purchased just before I left and another batch purchased later in Africa. Those tickets cost about $5,500.

So my day-to-day costs were 450 days (15 months) times $40: $18,000. With the plane tickets, that sum increased to $23,5000.

The expenses of health, renter's and auto insurance, equipment (sleeping bag, backpack, for example), inoculation shots, household-goods storage fees, and other miscellaneous costs raised the estimated total to $30,000.

2) How did you have that much money?

I have never been a big spender and was taught by the Navy to pay yourself first. That means from the very first payment I received as a fresh ensign in the Navy, I put a small portion in a mutual fund before writing checks to pay my bills. I paid myself first.

After 10 years of adding without subtracting –it added up. And when the timing was right, I had the capital to take advantage of an opportunity and make a dream come true.

3) How did you access money on the road?

Easy—ATMs. They are now in most major cities around the world. In Vietnam, however, my credit card was blocked because of attempted fraud. The account information of several cards had been stolen from an ATM. Fortunately, I had travelers' checks to use until I rendezvoused with a new card in Delhi, India. I didn't lose any money in this fiasco.

4) What were your favorite/least favorite places?

FAVORITES: Istanbul, Turkey, and the Western Cape of South Africa.

Istanbul: The city has incredible history as the capital of the Romans, the Ottomans, and now modern Turks. There is a fascinating blend of East and West where Europe meets Asia, with secular and deeply Islamic characteristics. There are the sounds of a large urban center punctuated by the call to prayer from one of the many mosques. There are great food, cobblestone streets and corner cafes and quick access to historical sites such as Troy, Gallipoli and Ephesus. The list goes on.

Western Cape: The area is amazingly beautiful, with striking mountains and green hills next to the crashing waves of the Indian Ocean. Within that ocean is the sight of the calving and migration of southern right whales. This is superb wine country with excellent and unbelievably affordable dining. The history of Afrikaners, British and indigenous tribes as well as the conversion from apartheid to democracy (societal changes, tribal versus democratic law) are interesting. Quaint seaside villages and cosmopolitan Cape Town contrast with surrounding townships. I loved it.

MOST DIFFICULT: China and India

Note that I didn't say least favorite. I don't have a least favorite.

Every country that I toured had something to offer— something to teach, if nothing else, about how people in that part of the world live, what they eat, and what the environment is like. Remember, that was my goal. But China and India presented greater challenges for me than other countries did.

China: I could not read or speak the language, and few people could speak English to assist me. Interior China is relatively undeveloped, making travel logistics hard, exacerbated by the language barrier.

India: What can I say? India gives every budget traveler fits. It's a maddening, fascinating, mind-boggling and exotic country. Unfortunately, by the time I reached my first Indian city (which happened to be at the end of a horribly uncomfortable 16-hour bus ride with Hindi movies blaring nonstop through the night) I was exhausted from five months of travel and a challenging trek near Mount Everest, high in the Himalayas. I entered India in a weakened state—which is practically suicidal.

5) Where would you return?

It depends on the situation. For work, I would gravitate toward the more developed countries and probably the Spanish-speaking ones because I enjoy the language so much. For travel, I'd go back to them all because there's tons more to see in all the countries I visited. I really only scratched the surface.

6) A year with no girlfriend? Do tell.

I don't have wild tales of women I met overseas. In fact, if you must know, this was one of the sacrifices associated with my trip. I didn't spend a lot of time hanging out in the travelers' cafes or hostels trying to meet what were invariably other Westerners, Aussies or Kiwis. I wanted to see the sights and meet the locals, not chase romance. In fact, there was very little romance over the 15 months. Very, very little.

7) What was your greatest disappointment?

Disappointment depends on expectations. I had very high expectations for the terra cotta warriors of Xi'an in central China. One of early China's leaders had built an army of terra cotta statues to accompany him into the afterlife. The army consists of two battalions of men, 4,000 to 6,000 strong, with a central command post in between.

Of course, it is always exciting and impressive to see a famous archaeological site that you've read about in National Geographic. To avoid disappointment, however, it is important to have an idea of the site's condition. I expected to see the entire army, lined up and ready for battle.

Instead, only the first 10 rows of warriors in each of the

battalions had been restored. The rest lie underground in the dirt that has covered them for centuries. That was disappointing.

8) What was your most rewarding experience?

There are two.

-- Interaction with locals: Seeing how people live, finding out what is important to them, and being welcomed and helped by the vast majority of people that I interacted with was richly rewarding.

-- Learning Spanish: This had a profound effect on my ability to meet and interact with locals and increased my appreciation for language, grammar and communication.

After months of hearing foreign tongues and scanning indecipherable print, I was amazed to finally hear a foreign language and understand what was said. It was magic. Suddenly strange sounds took shape and meaning. What was gibberish became communication.

Travel was so much easier after learning Spanish. I loved talking to the locals. They enjoyed my conversation, too—especially because I have such a gringo appearance.

With regard to language appreciation, I now recognize that the beauty and meaning of a writer's words are diminished through translation. And I see that grammar rules are critical for learning or teaching—the language itself or any other topic.

Finally, by traveling in countries where I was not able to communicate and then learning a foreign language, I realize how fragile communication is. To increase the chances of success, the rules of a language must be standardized and understood before being purposefully bent or broken for creative reasons.

9) Were you ever robbed?

The most expensive item stolen from me was a bike in Kunming, China (southwest). I did a poor job of locking it up before I checked e-mail in an Internet café. It was locked with only the hard-fixed wheel lock, not with the removable chain. I didn't want to chain it to a pole on the side of the street where the seat wouldn't be under cover from the rain. Instead, I parked it under an overhang near the building, but there were no poles nearby to chain it to. Trying to save a wet butt cost me the $25 security deposit and a walk across town to my hotel.

The most dangerous robbery experience was in Trujillo, Peru (seven hours north of Lima on the coast). As I sat down outside of an ancient ruin to fix the zipper on my day bag, a drunk and shirtless Peruvian approached and put his arm around me. I had never been touched in all my months of travel by a beggar and only a handful of times by a hawker. Immediately, I knew something was wrong.

I stood up and walked toward the street to catch a taxi back to the city. It was 4:15 on a Sunday afternoon. Fortunately, a taxi-van was driving by at that moment and waved me in. Just as I approached the door, my new chum made his move—a hit-and-run type attack to rip the watch off of my wrist.

I was stunned. Throughout my trip, I had heard tales of this tactic, but always doubted their veracity. Then, with three weeks left on my 15-month marathon, it had happened to me.

He didn't get the watch, and the taxi-van money–collector shooed him away as he urged me to hop in quickly. I decided to travel a little more carefully for the last three weeks of my trip.

The world is not an overly dangerous place. In my view, it is *rarely* more dangerous than any major U.S. city. Some places are wonderfully safe (Japan and Singapore), and others can be downright scary (Johannesburg). But though the need for caution is real, no one should forgo international travel because of its supposed danger.

A friend I met while canoeing on the Zambezi River in Zimbabwe said it best, "You have to be able to relax and enjoy the moment, but at the same time stay alert so no one takes you for a sucker."

10) <u>Did you ever get sick?</u>

Of course.

You can't expect to change your diet, sleep patterns, and daily living habits radically without some physical repercussions. That's especially so if the change involves a relentless barrage of new bacteria and the definition of "daily routine" means "constant change."

I had the standard traveler's problems—for months on end. I lost about 20 pounds and much of my strength because of (my best guess) malnutrition, incontinence, inadequate amounts of water, erratic sleep patterns, and miles upon miles of daily walking.

The nadir of my health coincided with a family reunion in Egypt. I had recently completed a punishing trek through the Himalayas to view Mount Everest and then three weeks of absolutely brutal travel through India. I was sickly and gaunt, phlegmatic even. It is an understatement to say that my mother was concerned. But I was dead-set on completing my journey and would not even think of cutting it short. I deferred to her wishes, however, and saw an internist in Istanbul. With barely a hiccup in my planning, I was able to visit the doctor and receive a clean bill of health.

Although I wasn't myself for months, I bounced back and am doing better now—although still not 100 percent. I'm back up to my pre-trip weight and am getting plenty of sleep. Although there were long periods of discomfort and pain, I'd do it all again. It wasn't *that* bad.

And speaking of food:

11) <u>What was the best food? The worst?</u>

I love good food—of all types. I love spice. And I love to experiment.

So it's tough to say what or where the best food was. For instance, I remember hopping off the bus at the first "rest stop" in India. I was traveling from Kathmandu, Nepal, to the holy city of Varanasi, India, on the Ganges River. Rest stops were made every two to three hours, but you never really knew when it would be. (So one had to monitor one's fluid intake to obviate any emergency nature calls between stops. This was painful and deleterious to one's health.)

When the bus finally stopped, everyone waddled out and had a cup of milk tea and a smidgen of whatever the roadside cooking kettle had to offer. Usually, it was either fried slices of cucumber and squash or a triangle pastry stuffed with potato and spices. All of this, and the risk of an upset stomach, cost only 20 cents.

My first bite was of a potato ball. Oh, my goodness was it good! I bit into that little ball, and a burst of India exploded in my mouth. I think Indian spices are the most exotic and distinctive in the world. So to be welcomed to the epicurean delights of that flavorful land at first opportunity really hit the spot.

Then I hopped back on the bus, and we rattled along for three more hours until the next chance to taste India came along.

But I can't declare India as the best food because that would shortchange one of my longtime favorites—Chinese. I also remember my first Japanese meal as one of the best. I couldn't understand a word anyone in the little restaurant said, and they didn't have an English menu available—so I had to resort to the "bawk, bawk, bawk" chicken call to give them an idea of what I wanted. Don't laugh—I know many a seasoned traveler has resorted to the same performance.

The staff at the restaurant had to guess what would please me most, and brother, they guessed right: chicken filets lightly battered and flavored with some soyish unbelievably delicious sauce that made me shudder. It was delicious.

And then there's all of South America, with its tongue-tingling ceviche and mouthwatering salsa. I thought we had it good in Arizona with Mexican salsa, but take a trip south of the equator, and you'll have found its match.

I could talk forever about the five-star dining to be found in the hamlets of South Africa's wine country, the spicy barbecue-style chicken in Tanzania, or even the Iskender Kebap of Bursa, Turkey (sliced lamb on a bed of Turkish bread with tomato sauce and melted butter ladled across the top, a little taste of heaven). So I'll leave it at this: There's great food to be found all over the planet. But you have to be willing to go out of your way and take a risk.

12) <u>What's the craziest thing you ate?</u>

    A partial list:
* Exotic fruits and vegetables
* Chicken and beef hearts
* Sheep kidneys
* Octopus, squid and eel
* Steamed snails in the shell
* Intestine soup
* Chunks of fat with vegetables
* Chicken cartilage
* Raw ground beef
* A cocktail of plant roots and saliva

13) <u>What did you do and think about during those long hours on the bus or train?</u>

I am the benefactor of two wonderful blessings: the knack of being able to sleep in any moving vehicle and the ability to become mentally vacant. I can sleep on command. And when not in slumber, I can go into the zone—that magical place where the mind is empty and the soul is at peace.

Of course, I occasionally tried to be productive during the monotony of an eight-hour train ride that turns into 18 because you hit two elephants leaving Victoria Falls for Bulawayo, Zimbabwe. I would read on such journeys or make an effort to chat with the locals.

Actually, a long train or bus ride is one of the best places to meet locals. You're stuck in the same small car for a day or two at a time, and for some mystical reason, it's off limits to beg or sell. Somehow, for as long as the journey lasts, you become teammates.

14) <u>Did your perception of human nature change from what you saw?</u>

No. I still think mankind has the capacity for great good and great evil, and I saw examples of both. But I think I have a better understanding of what's important to the average Joe. The needs and desires that cross all boundaries of gender, race, religion, culture and nationality.

* A job -- to make money so he or she can provide.
* A voice -- to be empowered.
* To love and be loved.

On a daily basis, the average people of the world aren't interested in economic indicators, diplomacy, grand matters of state, or what the president said today. They're worried about their jobs -- and how they can provide for their family.

When they don't have a voice, or are afraid to use it, they feel emasculated, impotent. Even if they don't use their voice, I believe they want to have one. The absence of empowerment breeds discontent and anger, resulting in violence, apathy or malaise—lack of productivity at a minimum.

As for human nature, I met both jerks and saints on my trip. By far the saints outweighed the jerks. I was taken into the homes of people who didn't know me on the faith that I was trustworthy and had something to share. I was assisted innumerable times by strangers. The vast majority of people on this planet returned my smile.

I don't mean to sound like a Pollyanna. I traveled in constant fear that someone would pilfer my belongings. There were a few hair-raising moments when I feared for my personal safety. But in my experience, the good in mankind is outpacing the bad. People want to be good. But you have to give them an environment conducive to that behavior. Give them a job, and give them a voice.

15) <u>What are the most important things you learned on your trip?</u>

    a. The needs of the average person.
    b. The importance of religion to mankind.
    c. Most people on the planet live in poverty. (A lot of people recognize this, but it's a different matter to *see and experience* than to simply be aware.)
    d. How it feels to be the object of racism (in a small sense).
    e. How it feels to be the object of sexism (in a small sense).
    f. That I enjoy creative writing/journalism.
    g. It's healthy to spend time alone.
    h. Spanish.
    i. How amazing the United States really is.

Although I'm able to list nine things here, I think much of what I've learned is yet to be discovered. So much information went into my brain over those 15 months that there's no way to pull it all out at once. Instead, the gleaning process will continue for the rest of my life. Perhaps one day I will see something and be reminded of a scene from my trip. A lesson will be realized or remembered in that moment.

16) <u>What would you change about your trip?</u>

One of my regrets is lack of historical knowledge—the background of everything I saw. I read the history section of the guidebook for every country that I visited, but that doesn't approach the level of detail and understanding that I wish I had while touring those places.

I would also have liked to spend more money. I know that sounds obvious and ridiculous, but my point is that I was exposed only to what a budget traveler can see on $40 a day. A whole other world exists that I couldn't explore as I nickeled and dimed my way around the planet.

Now I need to go make my fortune so I can do the whole trip again. Or are there any sponsors out there?

17) <u>How did it change you?</u>

In one sense it didn't. My personality and values did not change. I left the United States self-confident and at peace. I have a strong sense of self and am comfortable with the person I see in the mirror. I know who I am. There's not much in the world that could change that.

On the other hand, I don't think one could make a trip such as mine without a net change in the sum of one's being. For me, this change is additional knowledge and exposure to the world. I broadly define "world" to include all the "encounters" I listed earlier. The trip also added lessons about myself and mankind in general.

There is one other, extremely important change that took place. It was not so much a change as a return after a long period of inactivity. That something is religion.

Here's what happened:

About two weeks before departing on the trip, my little sister, Eleanor, handed me a book for the long flight from Los Angeles to Tokyo. The title was *Mere Christianity*, by C.S. Lewis.

In an unobtrusive way, she had tried for years to bring me closer to Christ. I had never given the idea much thought. I was successful and happy and therefore didn't see much need for religion. I believed in Christ, of course, and knew all of the basic stories from the Bible, but didn't think it was worth my time to delve much further.

In deference to her wishes and because I now had the time to read something other than business-school textbooks, I perused *Mere Christianity* on the flight across the Pacific. I agreed with a lot of what the author had to say, but either didn't understand or did not agree with the rest.

One thing I have learned from my trip is the importance of religion to mankind. It spans all cultures and time. It is a force that has shaped history and driven nations. As I toured Japan and Korea and spent a lot of time touring Buddhist and Shinto temples, this realization began to dawn on me. Even more pointedly, I came to realize my own ignorance on the subject of Christianity. There I was, learning all about Buddhism, but I couldn't answer elementary questions about the very religion I professed to believe in. It was an embarrassment, and something had to be done.

So when I arrived at Osan Air Force Base just south of Seoul, Korea, and was able to visit its bookstore of English-language titles, I picked up a copy of *Teach Yourself the New Testament*, by David Stone and *Siddhartha*, by Herman Hesse. I figured that I would start from the beginning -- Religion 101.

My travels continued through China with more stops at Buddhist temples, all the while reading my new books. By the time I got to Hong Kong, I was ready for the real thing. I bought a copy of the New Testament—figuring I'd concentrate on the "Christ" part of Christianity and get to the Old Testament later. To make the reading a little easier, I bought a modern-language version titled *Good News Bible*.

As I neared completion of the New Testament, I met a doctor I had recruited for the Navy. He and his family were living in Jakarta, Indonesia, where the Navy has a research facility for the study of infectious disease. Mark Lacy and his family are devoted Christians. He encouraged me to continue reading and provided me with *The Case for Christ*, by Lee Strobel. In a logically compelling way, Strobel makes a case for the historical accuracy of the four Gospels and why we should believe that Christ was the Son of God.

I had also noted a different version of the New Testament in his home that looked interesting. *The Message*, by Eugene H. Peterson, is written in plain everyday English and is easy to read. Knowing that in a few months my family would join me in Egypt, I requested that my older sister, Stephanie, bring a copy to me. She also volunteered to bring a pocket-sized version of the complete Bible as a gift for my birthday.

I read *The Case for Christ, The Message,* and a religious philosophy book, *The Universe Next Door,* by James Sire, which contrasts several religions. I then spent many hours working my way through the Old Testament, which I recently completed.

So how did all of that change me? I'm more spiritual now. I pray again. I believe I have a friend who is always here, someone who willingly faced excruciating torture and execution out of pure love for me and everyone else on Earth. I welcomed a relationship, a friendship with that man. I honor the presence of He who breathed life into my nostrils.

I feel that once in every person's lifetime he or she should ask the really big questions—Why are we here? What does it all mean? What happens next? When confronting those issues, don't equivocate. I don't profess to have all the answers, and my faith is still growing. But I'm making the effort -- and doubt that I would be had I not taken my trip.

18) <u>What's the best thing about your trip?</u>

That I actually did it. That I didn't just think about doing it and forever wonder what might have been. I motivated myself and made it happen. There's great satisfaction in that.

The following is a quote attributed to Mark Twain. I think it hits the nail on the head.

"Twenty years from now you will be more disappointed by the things that you didn't do than by the ones that you did. So throw off the bowlines. Sail away from the safe harbor. Catch the trade winds in your sails. Explore. Dream. Discover."

Index